WHALES
DOLPHINS AND PORPOISES

Francois Gohier/Auscape International

WHALES
DOLPHINS AND PORPOISES

CONSULTANT EDITOR

Mark Carwardine

Checkmark Books™
An imprint of Facts On File, Inc.

Published in the United States by
Checkmark Books
An imprint of Facts On File, Inc.
11 Penn Plaza, New York, NY 10001

Conceived and produced by Weldon Owen Pty Limited
59 Victoria Street, McMahons Point, NSW 2060, Australia
A member of the Weldon Owen Group of Companies
Sydney ❦ San Francisco

First published in 1988
Second edition 1999
Copyright © Weldon Owen Pty Limited 1999

Publisher: Sheena Coupe
Associate Publisher: Lynn Humphries
Editorial Assistant: Sarah Anderson
Index: Garry Cousins
Art Director: Sue Burk
Designer: Kylie Mulquin
Design Assistant: Veronica Hilton
Maps: Greg Campbell
Production Manager: Caroline Webber
Production Assistant: Kylie Lawson
Vice President International Sales: Stuart Laurence

All rights reserved. No part of this book may be reproduced or utilized in any form or by any means,
electronic or mechanical, including photocopying, recording, or by any information storage or
retrieval systems, without permission in writing from the publisher. For information contact:

Checkmark Books
An imprint of Facts On File, Inc., 11 Penn Plaza, New York, NY 10001

ISBN 0-8160-3991-7

A catalog record of this book is available from Facts On File.

Checkmark Books are available at special discounts when purchased in bulk quantities for busi-
nesses, associations, institutions or sales promotions. Please call our Special Sales Department
in New York at (212) 967-8800 or (800) 322-8755

You can find Facts On File on the World Wide Web at http://www.factsonfile.com

Printed by Kyodo Printing Co. (Singapore) Pte Ltd
Printed in Singapore

10 9 8 7 6 5 4 3 2 1

A WELDON OWEN PRODUCTION

The text in this second edition (with the exception of *Whale Anatomy*)
has been revised by Mark Carwardine

FRONT COVER: The long flippers of the humpback are distinctive as it breaches.
Photo by Jeff Foott/ Auscape International

PAGE 1: Right whales frequently bear whitish excrescences known as callosities. Several
can be seen on this right whale's head.

PAGE 2–3: A group of Atlantic spotted dolphins in the shallow water of the Bahamas.
Photo by Francois Gohier/ Auscape International

PAGES 4–5: Whale watchers observe as a humpback whale prepares to dive in
the icy waters of the Lemaire Channel.

PAGES 6–7: Bottlenose dolphins are the best studied of all cetaceans and the most
likely to be kept in captivity.

PAGES 10–11: A spotted dolphin plays with a photographer's bandana.

BACK COVER: Bottlenose dolphins swim in the tropical waters off Hawaii.
Photo by Flip Nicklin/ Auscape International

Colin Monteath/Hedgehog House, New Zealand

CONSULTANT EDITOR

Mark Carwardine
Zoologist, author, photographer and broadcaster, United Kingdom

CONTRIBUTORS

Dr. Lawrence G. Barnes
Curator and Head, Vertebrate Paleontology Section, Natural History Museum
of Los Angeles County, Los Angeles, California, U.S.A.

Dr. M. M. Bryden
Professor of Veterinary Anatomy, University of Sydney, New South Wales, Australia

Mark Carwardine
Zoologist, author, photographer and broadcaster, United Kingdom

Peter Corkeron
Lecturer in Environmental Studies, School of Tropical Environment Studies and Geography,
James Cook University, Townsville, Queensland, Australia

Dr. William H. Dawbin †
Honorary Research Associate, Australian Museum, Sydney, New South Wales, Australia

Hugh Edwards
Marine photographer and author, Perth, Western Australia, Australia

Dr. R. Ewan Fordyce
Associate Professor, Department of Geology, University of Otago, Dunedin, New Zealand

Peter Gill
Researcher, lecturer and writer, Sydney, New South Wales, Australia

Sir Richard Harrison
Emeritus Professor of Anatomy, University of Cambridge, Honorary Fellow, Downing College,
Cambridge, United Kingdom

Dr. Kaiya Zhou
Dean, Department of Biology, Nanjing Normal University, Nanjing,
People's Republic of China

Dr. Margaret Klinowska
Animal Welfare and Human–Animal Interactions Group, Department of Clinical Veterinary
Medicine, University of Cambridge, United Kingdom

Dr. Robert J. Morris
Principal Scientific Officer, Institute of Oceanographic Sciences, United Kingdom

Marty Snyderman
Marine photographer, cinematographer and author, San Diego, California, U.S.A.

Dr. Ruth Thompson
Author and historian, Sydney, New South Wales, Australia

P Morris/Ardea London Ltd

CONTENTS

WHALES AND PEOPLE

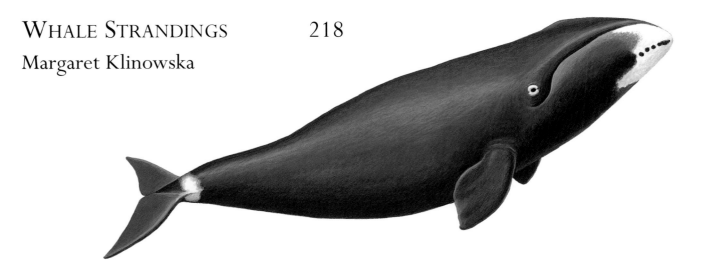

INTRODUCTION

I will never forget my first close encounter with a whale. It was in the late 1970s and I was in a small motor cruiser, rolling around in the Pacific surf near Santa Monica, California, when an enormous gray whale suddenly launched itself out of the water. Thirty tonnes of whale flew through the air just a few yards from where I was standing. My life changed as the whale hit the water because, from that moment, I was on the road to a lifetime of cetology.

Many people are deeply moved when they see whales, dolphins or porpoises for the first time. There is something very special about them, and watching such mysterious and awe-inspiring creatures in the wild is probably the ultimate wildlife experience. Whales, dolphins and porpoises really are shrouded in mystery. They spend so much of their lives hidden from view in an alien underwater world that, for centuries, the prospect of studying them wild and free must have seemed about as challenging as exploring outer space. Even today, our knowledge is so limited that we are still discovering new species.

But now we are making up for lost time with a vengeance. The number of whale researchers has increased exponentially in recent years and they are able to enlist the help of state-of-the-art equipment and space-age technology that early researchers could only dream about. Consequently, the knowledge we have amassed over the past decade is nothing short of remarkable.

This book has been written by a team of international experts who, collectively, have spent a great many decades observing and studying whales, dolphins and porpoises. They describe what they have discovered, seen and experienced, and they share their thoughts on everything from anatomy and evolution to intelligence and whaling. I hope you will enjoy reading about these wonderful animals and that the book will inspire you to support whale conservation and research efforts in any way you can. Although the worst excesses of commercial whaling are now over, there are many new threats to face and the world's whales, dolphins and porpoises still need all the help they can get.

Mark Carwardine
CONSULTANT EDITOR

Marty Snyderman

Francois Gohier/Auscape International

ABOVE: Male orcas have a much taller dorsal fin and can grow considerably larger than females.

WHALES OF THE WORLD

THE ORIGIN OF THE WHALE

R. EWAN FORDYCE

*M*ammals *are mostly terrestrial animals with lifestyles and body forms that are familiar and understandable. Cetaceans, however, are marine mammals with lifestyles and body forms that are less familiar because they are highly specialized for life in water. These specializations have, for centuries, obscured cetacean origins. However, in recent decades, and especially since 1990, many advances have been made in understanding cetacean evolutionary history. Both traditional and new approaches—using the anatomy and molecular signals of living species as well as the fossil record—have established and refined patterns of relationship which reveal that history.*

FACING PAGE: The gray whale's ungainly appearance may suggest a primitive cetacean but, in fact, the earliest gray whale fossils known are little more than 100,000 years old.

MAMMALIAN ORIGINS

In elucidating history, we must look beyond the obvious marine adaptations of cetaceans involving sensory, physiological, feeding, breeding and social systems. Other features, such as lungs, warm blood, vestigial hair, a diaphragm, three tiny auditory ossicles in the ear and gestation of young through a placenta, leave no doubt that cetaceans are related closely to land mammals. Furthermore, studies of anatomy, biochemistry and genetics point overwhelmingly to a close relationship with hoofed mammals (ungulates). Exactly which living hoofed mammals are closest to cetaceans is not clear. Both the ruminants (deer, sheep and their relatives) and the hippopotamuses have been identified as near relatives. The idea of a relationship with hoofed mammals is also supported by the fossil record, which extends back about 50 million years.

One widely discussed possible ancestral group is the Mesonychidae, a family of hoofed mammals that lived in North America, Europe and Asia. Mesonychids ranged in size from small dog-size to large bear-size animals. The skull and teeth of some mesonychids were quite similar to those of primitive cetaceans. Perhaps one lineage of mesonychids became fish-eaters in rivers, eventually giving rise to estuarine, lagoonal and shallow marine animals that dwelt in shallow waters around the edge of the Tethys—the large sea that once stretched eastward from the present Mediterranean to the Pacific, between India and Africa in the south and Eurasia in the north.

A comparison of living cetaceans and living land mammals hints at the changes that occurred in the shift to water. Initially, an otter or fur-seal habit was likely, with the limbs used to move in water. The tail also was used, with a vertical beat helping with propulsion, but it is uncertain if or how the limbs and tail worked together. At some stage, the end of the tail became flattened into flukes. It is likely that early whales were tied to the land to breed, but that otherwise they adapted rapidly to aquatic life. Other changes probably included adaptation to a salty environment (particularly adaptation of the eyes and kidneys), loss of hair, development of insulating blubber, ability to hear underwater, and development of nasal plugs to close the nostrils on diving.

RIGHT: The forebears of cetaceans were land dwellers, and may have been the dog-size animals known as *Mesonyx*.

THE EARLIEST WHALES

The earliest cetaceans were the archaeocetes—primitive archaic whales which in many ways were intermediate between land mammals and living cetaceans. For many years, such animals were known only from *Protocetus*, which lived in Egypt some 48–49 million years ago. The skull of *Protocetus* has a long slender upper jaw and a blowhole behind the tip, simple cheek teeth, widely separated eyes and a long braincase. An inflated bulla (earbone), like those of living whales, points to an ability to hear underwater. Apparently *Protocetus* had a small pelvis and flexible posterior part of the trunk; probably it could not support itself on land. *Protocetus* gives its name to a family, Protocetidae, into which many of the most primitive cetaceans have been placed.

Since 1980, new fossils from India and Pakistan have greatly expanded our knowledge of protocetids and other archaeocetes. Most localities are associated with the ancient Tethys Sea, but there are a few records from the Atlantic margin of North America. One of the oldest cetaceans, *Pakicetus*, occurs in 52-million-year-old strata in

Pakistan. It had a small high skull, small, simple and laterally compressed teeth, and a distinctively cetacean-like bulla. Another primitive whale, *Indocetus*, had a long neck, robust pelvis, and well-developed hindlimbs. In the unusual *Ambulocetus*, the fore- and hindlimbs and hindfoot were prominent, and the tail was perhaps long and without flukes. Perhaps *Ambulocetus* swam by dorsoventral oscillations of the spine, and walked on land like a fur-seal. Finally, *Rodhocetus* was a roughly 3-meter-long animal which had a large pelvis and small hindlimbs, yet probably swam by dorsoventral oscillations of a strong tail as in living cetaceans. Study of oxygen isotopes from teeth of some of these early whales points to a shift from fresh water early in cetacean history (perhaps *Pakicetus*) to fully marine habits by the Middle Eocene (*Indocetus*). Whether rates of cetacean evolution were fast or slow during the early river-to-sea phase is uncertain.

THE ADVANCED ARCHAEOCETES

Basilosaurus and related archaeocetes lived from at least 34–40 million years ago. They formed an

BELOW: A speculative reconstruction of *Protocetus*, a 2.5-meter archaeocete from the Mediterranean of 50 million years ago. *Protocetus* may have had external hindlimbs, but they were probably non-functional vestigial projections. The illustrations of the skulls of *Mesonynx* and *Protocetus* indicate the lengthening of the "beak" or rostrum as an adaptation to marine life.

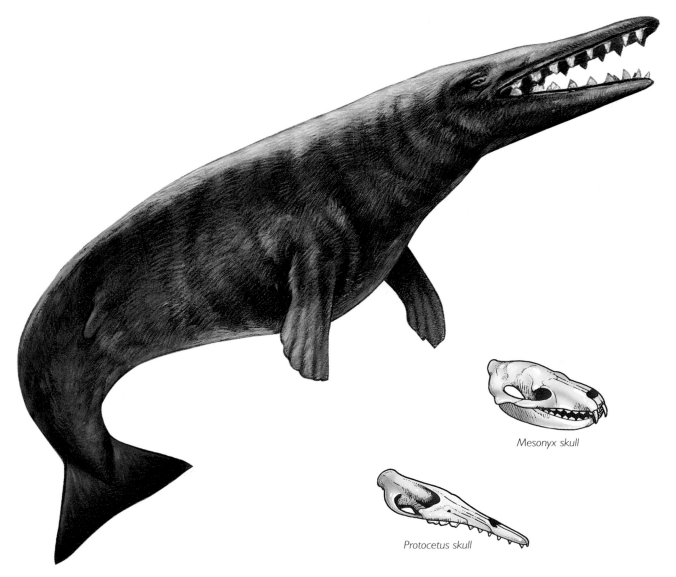

Mesonyx skull

Protocetus skull

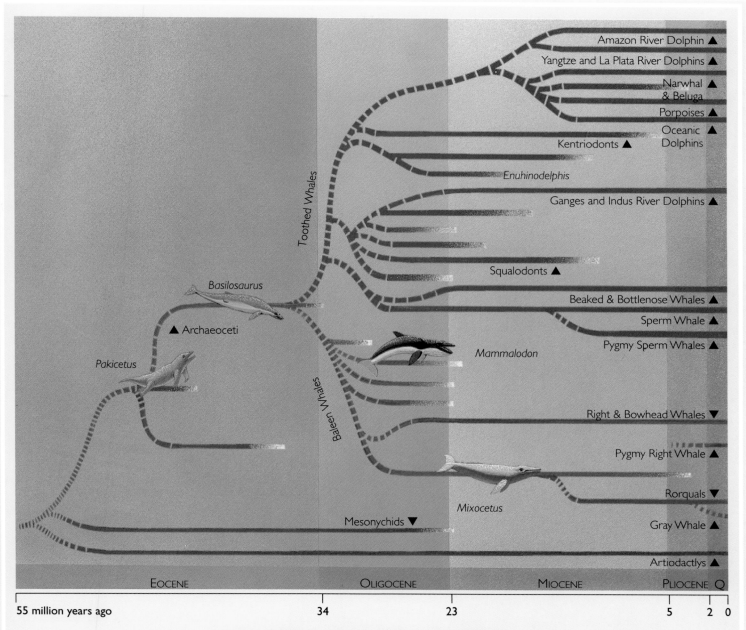

Amazon River Dolphin ▲
Yangtze and La Plata River Dolphins ▲
Narwhal & Beluga ▲
Porpoises ▲
Oceanic Dolphins ▲
Kentriodonts ▲
Enuhinodelphis
Ganges and Indus River Dolphins ▲
Squalodonts ▲
Beaked & Bottlenose Whales ▲
Sperm Whale ▲
Pygmy Sperm Whales ▲
Right & Bowhead Whales ▼
Pygmy Right Whale ▲
Rorquals ▼
Gray Whale ▲
Artiodactlys ▲

Toothed Whales

Baleen Whales

Basilosaurus

▲ Archaeoceti

Pakicetus

Mammalodon

Mixocetus

Mesonychids ▼

| EOCENE | OLIGOCENE | MIOCENE | PLIOCENE Q |

55 million years ago   34   23   5   2 0

THE WHALE'S FAMILY TREE

The ancestors of whales and dolphins are known from 50-million-year-old fossils found in India and Pakistan. These fossils represent small, perhaps dolphin-size, amphibious mammals that lived in a shallow subtropical sea—the Tethys Sea, between the Indian subcontinent and Asia. Later, continental drift pushed India into Asia, closed the Tethys Sea, and upthrust the Himalayas. Ancient marine rocks containing whale bones are now exposed on land. Among the archaic whales, called archaeocetes, is *Pakicetus*, found in sediments deposited in river or shallow marine settings. Skull bones, teeth and a lower jaw point to a small cetacean, perhaps less than 2 meters long, which had a limited ability to hear underwater. Other early archaeocetes retain a pelvis and hindlimbs, but probably swam by up-and-down movements of a strong tail, as

do living cetaceans. Overall, these animals mark an early transitional amphibious stage in the shift from land to sea.

The land-dwelling relatives of early cetaceans were even-toed hoofed mammals, the cud-chewing artiodactyls. Supporting evidence for this comes from studies on living species, particularly on DNA, chromosomes, blood composition and soft-tissue anatomy. So, sheep and cattle are among the closest living relatives of whales and dolphins.

To identify the exact ancestors, we must turn to the fossil record. One extinct group, the mesonychids, appears to include the ancestors of archaic whales. These comprise a range of animals that lived in ancient Asia, Europe and North America. Perhaps cetaceans evolved when one line of mesonychids took to feeding on fish in rivers or estuaries, rather like otters.

ABOVE: The 5-meter *Dorudon* of
25 million years ago was already
taking on the streamlined
appearance of modern dolphins.
By this stage of cetacean evolution,
the nostrils had migrated back a little
toward the top of the skull.

advanced archaeocete family, Basilosauridae, characterized by cheek teeth with multiple pointed cusps, and large air sinuses in the skull base. These features are also seen in early toothed whales (odontocetes) and baleen whales (mysticetes), pointing to a close relationship between living cetaceans and basilosaurids. *Basilosaurus* itself was rather specialized, with a large body and strangely elongated vertebrae, and possibly was on a side branch rather than directly ancestral to living forms.

More plausible ancestors lie among those more generalized dolphinlike basilosaurids known as the dorudontines—*Dorudon* and its relatives. Many species are known from North America, Europe, Africa and New Zealand, from ancient shallow-water marine sediments originally deposited around continental margins and now exposed on land. Such records only hint at the

original distribution of these animals, and it is likely that much of cetacean history took place in the open ocean from which there are few fossils. Dorudontines reached 5 meters long and had vertebrae of more normal proportions than *Basilosaurus*. They lacked the broad upper jaw, which might have allowed filter-feeding, but some species had long, narrow jaws perhaps used rather like forceps in catching prey.

THE RISE OF MODERN CETACEANS

By the start of the Oligocene, 34 million years ago, dorudontines and basilosaurines disappeared from the global rock record. (The few reports of geologically younger archaeocetes are wrong.) But they left descendants—odontocetes and mysticetes—which had an explosive evolutionary radiation later in the Oligocene Epoch. The origins of these two modern groups marked major adaptive changes.

Living odontocetes use echolocation to hunt their single prey and to navigate, and the same is inferred for the earliest odontocetes, although there is no firm evidence that archaeocetes could echolocate. Odontocetes may have been wholly aquatic even in the birth of young, while basilosaurid archaeocetes, like seals, perhaps returned to land for birth. Mysticetes differ from both archaeocetes and odontocetes in using baleen to filter-feed on large shoals of prey. Thus, divergent feeding strategies arose when the two modern groups evolved from *Basilosaurus*-like or *Dorudon*-like ancestors which neither echolocated nor filter-fed.

The evolution of modern cetacean lineages is linked with major geological changes in the Southern Hemisphere. The former huge southern supercontinent of Gondwana finally fragmented at about this time, when Australia and South America moved northward away from Antarctica. Until then the climate of Antarctica was rather moderate—despite the polar position of the continent—probably because Antarctica was linked to the north with the more temperate landmasses of Australia and South America (and, of course, there was no cold circumpolar ocean).

RIGHT: This fossilized whale ancestor,
found in Antarctica, is thought to be
about 35 million years old.

R. Ewan Fordyce

The polar climate cooled as Australia and South America drifted away to leave Antarctica insulated by the extensive circumpolar Southern Ocean. Certain oceanic features—temperature gradients and currents—today govern overall availability of food resources in the Southern Ocean, and probably did so in the past. Perhaps the development of the new oceanic and climate patterns triggered the evolution of the two groups of cetaceans, with their new feeding strategies of filter-feeding and echolocation-assisted predation.

PRIMITIVE MYSTICETES

Modern mysticetes are huge toothless animals in which baleen plates hang from the upper jaw in a distinctively shaped skull. Tiny vestigial teeth in mysticete embryos point, however, to a toothed ancestry. In recent decades, fossils have revealed much about the change from archaeocete to toothed filter-feeder and finally to baleen whale. Key fossils are from around the Pacific Ocean and the margins of the Southern Ocean around Antarctica. For example, several species of *Aetiocetus* occur in Oligocene strata (around 23–30 million years) around the North Pacific. These were small animals—perhaps 5 or 6 meters long—with elongate flat upper jaws and prominent but widely spaced teeth. In the south, the tiny *Mammalodon*, from Victoria in Australia, was a late-surviving form around 23 million years old. Its skull had a short, broad, flat, toothed upper jaw which joined loosely with the long braincase. The bones on either side of the upper

jaw could flex against each other—adaptations associated with filter-feeding in living mysticetes. The lower jaw looked rather like that of an archaeocete, with conspicuous teeth. But, as in living mysticetes, the lower jaws lacked a bony junction—again probably an adaptation for filter-feeding. High-crowned teeth with small projecting cusps probably intermeshed when the mouth was closed, and formed a sieving mechanism.

A much less well known toothed mysticete is the 28-million-year-old large-toothed *Kekenodon* from New Zealand. It is possible, indeed likely, that some of these animals had short protobaleen, which helped the teeth in filter-feeding. By about 30 million years ago, in about the middle of the Oligocene Epoch, the first truly toothless baleen whales appeared. For a short while, they were around at the same time as primitive toothed mysticetes.

Apart from having baleen in the upper jaw, these early baleen whales were quite primitive in structure. For example, many had a blowhole nearer the skull tip than in modern whales, a long braincase, and long and unfused neck vertebrae. Perhaps some had a pelvis and vestigial hind legs.

Most of these archaic baleen whales are placed in the family Cetotheriidae (cetotheres), which is an artificial group of primitive baleen whales spanning a range of small to medium-size animals that do not belong with either the rorquals, family Balaenopteridae, or the right

200 million years ago

90 million years ago

Present

ABOVE: The breakup of of Gondwana created opportunities for cetaceans to radiate.

ABOVE: *Mammalodon*, a cetacean 23 million years old from southern Australia, may have possessed "protobaleen" fringes between its large, cusped teeth. Its body was probably streamlined, with well-developed pectoral fins and no sign of hindlimbs.

whales, family Balaenidae. The cetotheres were structurally diverse, and included many genera especially from the Miocene Epoch (5–23 million years ago). The earliest cetotheres were little more advanced than *Mammalodon*, while the most recent were very similar to living rorquals. Like the rorquals, the cetotheres may have been gulp-feeders, but they seem not to have reached the size of living rorquals.

LIVING MYSTICETES

Living rorquals, family Balaenopteridae, range in size from the diminutive minke whale to the large

RIGHT: Whales had diverged into toothed hunters and toothless filter-feeders by 30 million years ago, and the many adaptations that characterize rorquals such as this minke whale were in evidence more than 15 million years ago.

BELOW: A filter-feeding strategy makes best use of large numbers of very small organisms. One of the most efficient filter-feeders is the blue whale (center), the largest animal on the planet.

Robert Pitman/Earthviews

blue whale. The ancestors of these species probably evolved from among the cetotheres around 15 million years ago. Living rorquals have pronounced external throat grooves, to allow the mouth to expand during gulp-feeding, and have a distinctively depressed frontal bone above the eyes. The depressed frontal is seen in fossil balaenopterids, which suggests that they, too, were gulp-feeders. By 5 million years ago, the balaenopterids had reached large sizes, comparable with living species. And by this stage humpback whales *Megaptera* had evolved, although it is not clear why these diverged from the other rorquals. The living gray whale *Eschrichtius* is usually placed alone in the family Eschrichtiidae, although it may be related very closely to species of *Balaenoptera*. Its short fossil record includes only a few specimens from the margins of the North Pacific and North Atlantic. They are probably the same as the living gray whale, and are little older than 100,000 years.

Right whale origins are uncertain. The small and ancient *Morenocetus* indicates that right whales, with their high-arched upper jaw and "skim-feeding" habit, evolved more than 20 million years ago. But there is no likely ancestor described among earlier mysticete fossils. Fossils of right whales, like those of rorquals, are

Francois Gohier/Ardea London Ltd

relatively common in rocks about 2–10 million years old—indeed, isolated earbones, which are erosion-resistant, are sometimes abundant. The 10-million-year gap between *Morenocetus* and these later right whales is also puzzling. The poorly known pygmy right whale *Caperea* has no fossil record. For long it has been allied with right whales, but some molecular analyses place it closer to the rorquals. Anatomically, it is distinct enough to have its own family, Neobalaenidae.

THE RISE OF ODONTOCETES

Odontocetes, both fossil and living, are more diverse than mysticetes in both numbers of species and in structure. The wide range of odontocete skull forms suggests diverse methods of feeding and probably varied use of high-frequency echolocation. There is also great variation in structure of the earbones and in acoustic air sinuses in the skull base, further pointing to complex use of sound. In the jaws, the teeth may be serrated, smooth, delicate, robust, reduced in size or naturally absent, and the upper jaw may be long and blunt, short and wide or downturned. Such structures, when viewed among fossils, indicate a significant diversity of species by the end of the Oligocene, 23 million years ago. The most archaic Oligocene odontocetes, such as *Archaeodelphis* and *Agorophius*, seem to be near the base of the odontocete radiation, but it is not clear how they relate to later-evolved groups.

Living river dolphins are often treated as a single unified group because they all have long jaws, many small conical teeth and small bodies. Yet a closer examination of their skulls and earbones reveals separate origins and, indeed, the river dolphins represent several families. The

similarities between them seem to be a case of convergent evolution—adaptations to similar environments among animals of separate origins. The South American franciscana or La Plata dolphin *Pontoporia* has fossil relatives in both South and North America. Its closest living relative is believed to be the baiji or Yangtze river dolphin *Lipotes*, which evolved from *Prolipotes*, a fossil dolphin from China. The living Amazon river dolphin or boto *Inia* has been allied, sometimes doubtfully, with varied small fossil odontocetes in the geologically young family Iniidae.

Recently, the widespread shark-toothed dolphins—belonging to the extinct family Squalodontidae—were reliably classified for the first time. They are believed to be close to the endangered living Ganges and Indus river dolphins. Typically, squalodontids have sharp triangular teeth with serrated edges and a wrinkled surface, held in a medium-size skull. Notably, the teeth are differentiated into incisors, canine teeth and cheek teeth, like those of archaeocetes. This tooth design suggests an active carnivorous lifestyle, with narrow jaws used for quick snapping. The geological range is long—about 10–25 million years ago or even longer.

Sperm whales, families Physeteridae and Kogiidae, first appeared in the Oligocene at least 23 million years ago. The fossils are fragmentary, and well-preserved specimens with the basined, high-backed, asymmetrical skull typical of the living sperm whale *Physeter* do not occur until early in the Miocene, 20 million years ago or earlier. Early sperm whales were rather small and had a tapered upper jaw with well-developed teeth; the gradual evolutionary loss of their teeth may be associated with a squid-eating diet.

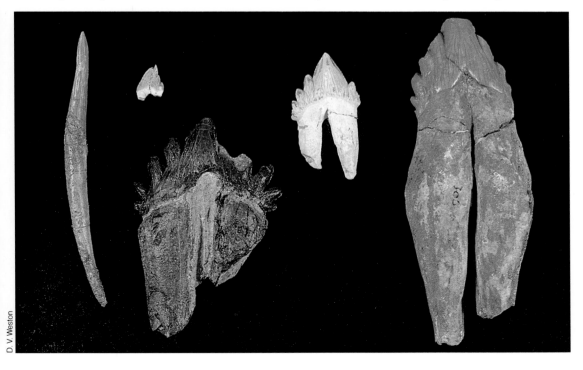

D. V. Weston

LEFT: Fossil teeth from New Zealand and Antarctica indicate the range of size, shape and complexity of primitive cetacean dentition. From left, an anterior tooth and a cheek tooth (top) of a primitive odontocete; a cheek tooth of an archaeocete; the tooth of a primitive mysticete; and the tooth of a large archaeocete.

R. E. Fordyce

RIGHT: The skulls of primitive dolphins were strikingly similar in appearance to those of living species, though their skulls lacked the unusual asymmetry, or "left-handedness" that is characteristic of the skulls of most modern toothed whales.

BELOW: A beluga glides through the water off British Columbia, Canada. While today's belugas inhabit north polar waters, their ancestors lived in warmer Californian waters.

Recently, some molecular studies have suggested that the living sperm whale is related more closely to rorquals (mysticetes) than to other odontocetes. Molecular patterns hint at a geologically recent split between sperm whales and rorquals. Such a relationship would require a reclassification of odontocetes, and a reassessment of how echolocation (as seen in sperm whales) and filter-feeding (as seen in rorquals) evolved. Also, the predicted timing does not match the fossil record. A sperm whale–rorqual relationship is not accepted by all cetologists, for there is strong anatomical and fossil evidence against it, and even some molecular studies do not support it. Pygmy and dwarf sperm whales *Kogia* spp. have a poor fossil record; they are small whales, resembling sharks in body profile, and have a peculiarly specialized skull basin and earbones.

Beaked whales, family Ziphiidae, have a patchy record before the Late Miocene (about 10 million years ago), but they are common fossils worldwide in geologically younger strata, including those from the deep sea. Many ziphiid remains include specimens belonging to the nearly toothless living genus *Mesoplodon*. Ancestral ziphiids had many functional teeth in the upper and lower jaws, as in the living Shepherd's beaked whale *Tasmacetus*; again, evolutionary tooth loss probably reflects the early adoption of a squid-eating diet. Whether beaked whales are more closely related to sperm whales, or to dolphins, is not clear. A better fossil record would help us to understand when the beaked whales radiated to become the second most diverse family of odontocetes after the dolphins.

Archaic dolphins—the kentriodontids, family Kentriodontidae—first appeared 25 million years ago. *Kentriodon*, which gives its name to the family, is known from Early to Middle Miocene strata (16–20 million years) in both the Pacific and Atlantic oceans. This small dolphin—

Corel Corporation

Fred Bruemmer

2–3-meters long—had many small conical teeth, a symmetrical face and elaborate air sinuses in the skull base. Other kentriodontids show a wide range of skeletal form. Indeed, the family is an artificial group which includes dolphins related to, but more primitive than, living dolphins, porpoises and white whales. Dolphins, family Delphinidae, porpoises, family Phocoenidae, and white whales, family Monodontidae, probably arose from early kentriodontids.

Dolphins appeared by 12 million years ago and have radiated to become the most diverse and successful group of odontocetes. They differ from kentriodontids in that the skull is asymmetrical and the air sinuses in the skull base are more complex. The fossil record still gives only moderate insight into the origins of living dolphins, with their greatly varying habits, sizes and structure.

Porpoises are small odontocetes that have been distinct from other dolphin groups since 10–12 million years ago. Early fossils from the Pacific coast of the Americas illustrate typical skull features of modern porpoises. The geographic distribution of fossils suggests porpoises originated in the North Pacific. If so, they must have spread later to the Atlantic and southern waters.

Living belugas *Delphinapterus* and narwhals *Monodon* occupy north polar waters, but early members of this family—Monodontidae—lived in warmer climates around California 10–12 million years ago. Thus, the arctic habit of belugas and narwhals is probably geologically recent.

Molecular studies help us to understand relationships between living species and so give valuable clues to the past. Fossils are also critical in establishing the time of origin for many living groups and thus for calibrating "molecular clocks." They elucidate rates and patterns of evolution, geographic patterns and ecological strategies. The picture of cetacean evolution derived from fossils and living species continues to expand. Patterns of evolutionary history are more complex than formerly suspected, but to recognize this complexity is to understand it better.

ABOVE: "Anomalous" toothed whales, such as the narwhal and the beluga, may have evolved from kentriodontid dolphins. They have many features that are far removed from those of superficially similar small cetaceans.

BELOW: A recently discovered fossil dolphin (center) from Antarctica has a skull that resembles a beaked whale's (left), but it is more closely related to modern dolphins (right).

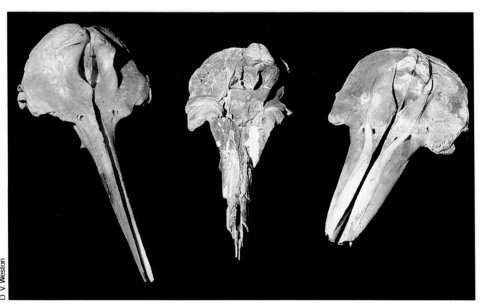

D. V. Weston

A DIVERSITY OF FORM AND SIZE

There are approximately 80 species of cetaceans—whales, dolphins and porpoises—exhibiting a surprising diversity of sizes, shapes, colors and habits, and occupying a wide range of habitats. The blue whale is the largest animal that has ever lived on earth, yet many dolphins and porpoises are no longer than humans. While some species, such as the orca, are easily recognizable, others differ from each other only in subtle ways. Some species are so rare that they are infrequently sighted. A representative selection of cetaceans is featured on these pages, drawn to size. The human diver is dwarfed by comparison to most of them.

BOTTLENOSE DOLPHIN
This familiar dolphin is robust, with a distinctive melon.

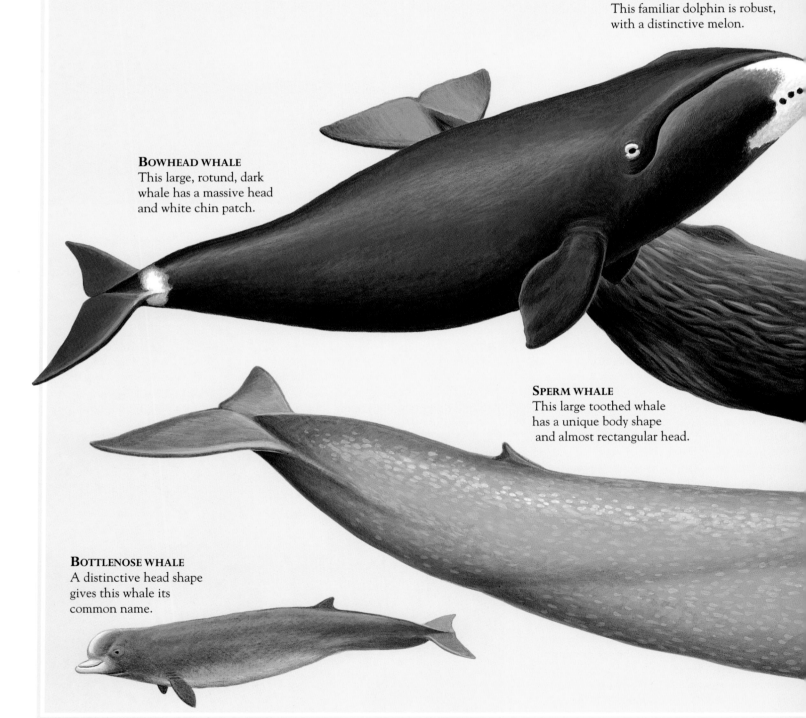

BOWHEAD WHALE
This large, rotund, dark whale has a massive head and white chin patch.

SPERM WHALE
This large toothed whale has a unique body shape and almost rectangular head.

BOTTLENOSE WHALE
A distinctive head shape gives this whale its common name.

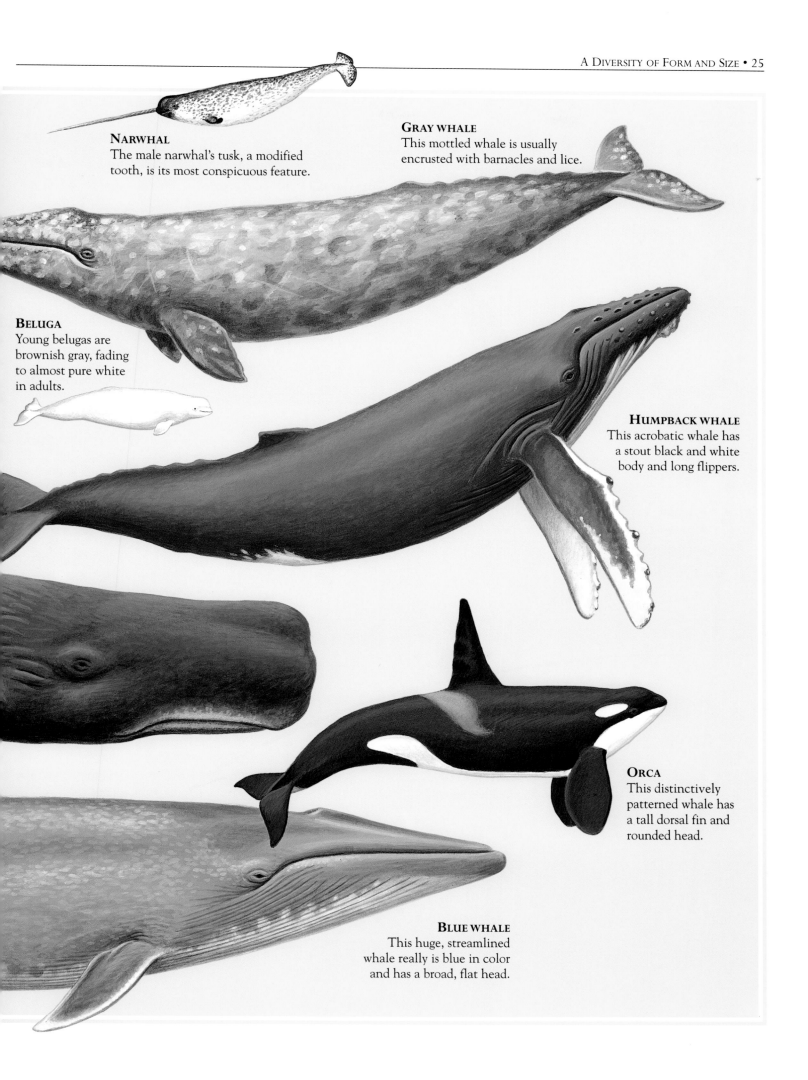

NARWHAL
The male narwhal's tusk, a modified tooth, is its most conspicuous feature.

GRAY WHALE
This mottled whale is usually encrusted with barnacles and lice.

BELUGA
Young belugas are brownish gray, fading to almost pure white in adults.

HUMPBACK WHALE
This acrobatic whale has a stout black and white body and long flippers.

ORCA
This distinctively patterned whale has a tall dorsal fin and rounded head.

BLUE WHALE
This huge, streamlined whale really is blue in color and has a broad, flat head.

KINDS OF WHALES

LAWRENCE G. BARNES

L iving cetaceans are divided into two major groups or suborders, each containing several smaller groups or families. There are 13 families of cetaceans and they contain 81 or so different species of whales. The living whales are reviewed below by suborder and family in roughly phylogenetic (evolutionary) order.

ORDER CETACEA

SUBORDER MYSTICETI
Baleen whales

SUBORDER ODONTOCETI
Toothed whales

BALAENIDAE
Right whales and bowhead whale

NEOBALAENIDAE
Pygmy right whale

ESCHRICHTIIDAE
Gray whale

BALAENOPTERIDAE
Rorquals

PHYSETERIDAE
Sperm whale

KOGIIDAE
Pygmy and dwarf sperm whales

MONODONTIDAE
White whales

ZIPHIIDAE
Beaked whales

DELPHINIDAE
Dolphins and other small toothed whales

PHOCOENIDAE
Porpoises

PLATANISTIDAE
Ganges and Indus river dolphins

INIIDAE
Amazon river dolphin

PONTOPORIIDAE
Baiji and franciscana

FAMILY BALAENIDAE
RIGHT WHALES AND BOWHEAD WHALE

Three Species

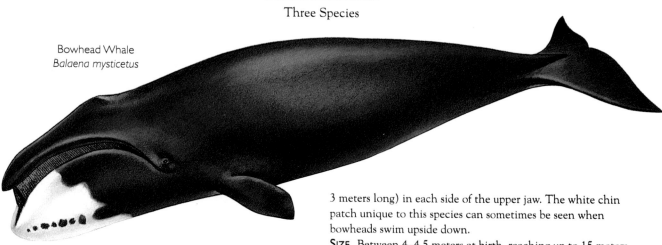

Bowhead Whale
Balaena mysticetus

APPEARANCE The bowhead whale (also known as the Greenland right whale) is the stockiest of the baleen whales, with a barrel-shaped body and a huge head (about a third of the total body size). The mouth is bowed sharply upward, and the pectoral fins are small and paddle-shaped. There is no dorsal fin and the flukes are pointed. Color is generally blue-black (young) to blue-gray (older animals) overall, with a whitish chin patch on the underside, and mottling caused by sloughing skin. There are 230–360 baleen plates (many over 3 meters long) in each side of the upper jaw. The white chin patch unique to this species can sometimes be seen when bowheads swim upside down.

SIZE Between 4–4.5 meters at birth, reaching up to 15 meters at maturity.

HABITAT AND DISTRIBUTION Confined to arctic waters, where they follow the seasonal advance and retreat of the ice. Populations are found from Spitzbergen to eastern Greenland, from Davis Strait to Hudson Bay to the Sea of Okhotsk and the Bering, Chukchi, Beaufort and Siberian seas.

REPRODUCTION Mating takes place in late summer, and calves are born in spring, after 10 months' gestation. They are weaned after six months and calving takes place at two-year intervals.

DIET Various small crustaceans.

Southern Right Whale
Eubalaena australis

APPEARANCE Originally considered a subspecies of the northern right whale, the slow-swimming southern or black right whale looks identical to its northern congener. The body is stocky and fat, and is marked with skin thickenings or callosities (home to specialized whale lice and barnacles) on the upper and lower jaws, and above the eye. The callosity on the upper jaw is often called the bonnet. The pectoral fins are paddle-shaped, there is no dorsal fin, and the flukes are extremely long, narrow and pointed. The body is pale in the young, darkening in adults to black with white patches where skin has sloughed off. There are 205–270 baleen plates up to 2.2 meters long in each side of the upper jaw.

SIZE Calves are 5–6 meters long at birth. Fully grown adults up to 18 meters have been recorded.

HABITAT AND DISTRIBUTION The main breeding populations are in southern South America, southern Africa and southern Australasia. Winters in colder feeding grounds in waters further south. The right whale was so named because it is easy to approach, lives close to shore for much of the year, floats when dead, and provides large quantities of oil, meat and whalebone; therefore, it was considered by whalers the "right" whale to hunt. It has been protected since the 1930s and is at last showing signs of recovery in its range.

REPRODUCTION Calves are born in winter after a 12-month gestation period and are suckled until they reach about 8.5 meters in length. Sexual maturity is reached at 15 meters in males and 16 meters in females. There seems to be a three- to four-year calving interval.

DIET A selective feeder on small crustaceans (copepods and krill).

FAMILY NEOBALAENIDAE
PYGMY RIGHT WHALE

One Species

Pygmy Right Whale
Caperea marginata

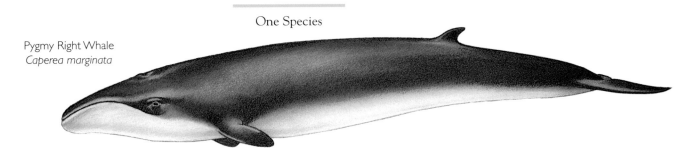

APPEARANCE The pygmy right whale is so called for its bowed mouth; it is only very distantly related to the right whales and the shape of the mouth appears to be an example of convergent evolution. The body shape is similar to the minke whale or Bryde's whale, and this species has a prominent, sickle-shaped dorsal fin. The pectoral fins are small and rounded and the flukes are broad. There is no ridge on the rostrum or the back. Color is dark gray above, becoming darker with age, fading to light gray below. There are 213–230 yellowish-white baleen plates up to 70 centimeters long in each side of the upper jaw.
SIZE From about 1.6 to 2.2 meters at birth to 5.6 to 6.5 meters and 3.5 tonnes at maturity. Female pygmy right whales are slightly larger than males.
HABITAT AND DISTRIBUTION Known only in the Southern Hemisphere, from Australia and New Zealand to South Africa, as well as southern South America and oceanic islands, such as the Falkland Islands and the Crozet Islands north of Antarctica.
REPRODUCTION Nothing known.
DIET Stomach samples of two stranded pygmy right whales contained small crustaceans (copepods), but little more is known of their dietary preferences.

FAMILY ESCHRICHTIIDAE
GRAY WHALE

One Species

Gray Whale
Eschrichtius robustus

APPEARANCE A primitive-looking species, with a long, slender head, a slightly bowed mouth, and small visible hairs in pits and on the rostrum. The body is moderately slender, with well-developed, paddle-shaped pectoral fins, almost triangular flukes, and instead of a dorsal fin, small bumps along the dorsal ridge. Coloration is mottled gray overall, but marked on the head and back by white and yellowish patches of whale lice and barnacles. There are no throat grooves. In each side of the upper jaw are 140–180 thick, yellowish-white baleen plates up to 40 centimeters long.
SIZE Calves are 5 meters and 500 kilograms at birth, reaching 12–14 meters and as much as 35 tonnes at maturity. Females are slightly larger than males, with larger heads.
HABITAT AND DISTRIBUTION At one time found also in the North Atlantic, where it is now extinct, the gray whale survives today only in the North Pacific. It is found mainly in coastal waters in the east, feeding in the Arctic and then migrating down the western coasts of Canada and the USA to its breeding grounds in Baja California, Mexico. A small population still survives in the west, off the coasts of Asia, but the population is dangerously small and therefore vulnerable.
REPRODUCTION Mating occurs in winter during the gray whale's southward migration or, more commonly, in the breeding lagoons. Calves are born in the sheltered lagoons and calm coastal areas after a 13-month gestation period and are weaned at 6–9 months. Calving occurs every couple of years and sexual maturity is reached at between 5–11 years, when males are about 11 meters and females are 11.5 meters in length.
DIET Bottom-dwelling crustaceans (amphipods).

FAMILY BALAENOPTERIDAE
RORQUALS

Six Species

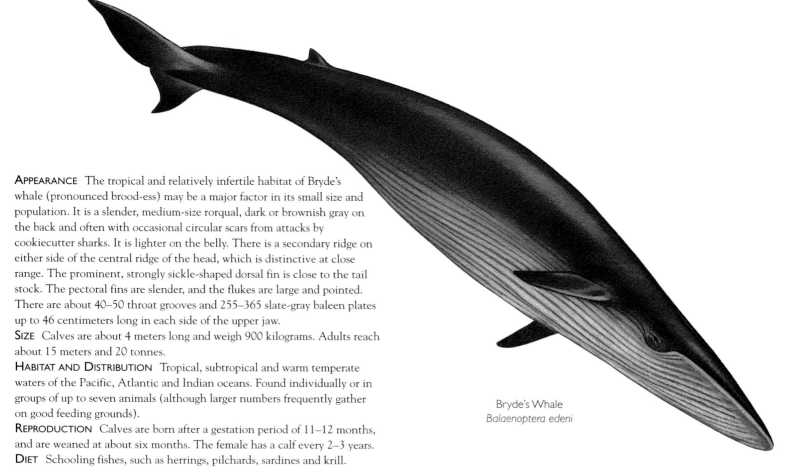

Fin Whale
Balaenoptera physalus

APPEARANCE Second largest of the whales, the fin whale or finback has a long, slender and relative narrow body, with an unusual asymmetrical coloration. It is generally dark gray to brown on the back and white below. The right side of the jaw and the right baleen plates are white, while those on the left are dark. Most animals have a gray-white "chevron" pattern just behind the head. The relatively small pectoral fins are narrow and pointed, and the flukes are large, thin and pointed. There are 262–473 baleen plates, 70–90 centimeters long, in each side of the upper jaw and 56–100 throat grooves.
SIZE Fin whales are 6.5 meters at birth and grow to an average of 20 meters as adults. Females are slightly larger than males, and the largest recorded fin whale was 27 meters.
HABITAT AND DISTRIBUTION These enormous animals are found alone or in groups of more than a dozen in all oceans,

although they tend to avoid shallow waters.
REPRODUCTION Calves are born at 2–3 year intervals after an 11–12-month gestation period and are suckled for 6–7 months.
DIET Small crustaceans and pelagic schooling fishes, such as mackerel and herring, and squid.

APPEARANCE The tropical and relatively infertile habitat of Bryde's whale (pronounced brood-ess) may be a major factor in its small size and population. It is a slender, medium-size rorqual, dark or brownish gray on the back and often with occasional circular scars from attacks by cookiecutter sharks. It is lighter on the belly. There is a secondary ridge on either side of the central ridge of the head, which is distinctive at close range. The prominent, strongly sickle-shaped dorsal fin is close to the tail stock. The pectoral fins are slender, and the flukes are large and pointed. There are about 40–50 throat grooves and 255–365 slate-gray baleen plates up to 46 centimeters long in each side of the upper jaw.
SIZE Calves are about 4 meters long and weigh 900 kilograms. Adults reach about 15 meters and 20 tonnes.
HABITAT AND DISTRIBUTION Tropical, subtropical and warm temperate waters of the Pacific, Atlantic and Indian oceans. Found individually or in groups of up to seven animals (although larger numbers frequently gather on good feeding grounds).
REPRODUCTION Calves are born after a gestation period of 11–12 months, and are weaned at about six months. The female has a calf every 2–3 years.
DIET Schooling fishes, such as herrings, pilchards, sardines and krill.

Bryde's Whale
Balaenoptera edeni

APPEARANCE The sei is the fastest of all the great whales, reaching speeds in excess of 38 kilometers per hour. The body is long, slender and muscular, with a pointed rostrum. The dorsal fin is tall and sickle-shaped. The pectoral fins are large and slender, and the flukes are small. The single central ridge from the tip of the beak to the blowhole distinguishes the sei from the somewhat smaller Bryde's whale. The color overall is dark gray, with a white chin, throat and belly. There are 219–402 baleen plates up to 80 centimeters long in each side of the upper jaw and 30–60 throat grooves.
SIZE From about 4–5 meters at birth to 16 meters or more in the adult.
HABITAT AND DISTRIBUTION In all oceans, from tropical waters to the Arctic and Southern oceans, though they avoid pack ice.
REPRODUCTION Calves are born after a gestation period of 12 months and are suckled for about nine months. Sexual maturity is reached at 6–12 years and there is a 2–3 year calving interval.
DIET The sei whale uses its extraordinary speed to pursue near-surface fishes, such as cod, anchovies, herring and sardines. It also feeds on krill, copepods and sometimes squid.

Sei Whale
Balaenoptera borealis

APPEARANCE The blue whale is the largest organism on this planet—its heart alone is the size of a small car and pumps nearly 10 tonnes of blood through the huge body. Its mouth can be 6 meters long and the flukes 4.5 meters from tip to tip. The body is slender, especially in the head and chest region. The head (like a broad, pointed arch when viewed from above) has a single central ridge from the tip to the blowhole. The extremely small, sickle-shaped dorsal fin is located well down the back and marks the end of a ridge. The pectoral fins are long, slender and curved on the leading edge, and the flukes are relatively small. There are more than 300 baleen plates in each side of the upper jaw and the highly distensible throat has 55–88 grooves. Overall color is blue-gray, mottled with light gray spots, but cold-water algae living on the belly may give this a yellowish tinge.
SIZE Calves are up to 8 meters long and weigh 2–3 tonnes at birth. Adults typically reach 23 meters (male) to 24.5 meters (females), although blue whales were larger before intensive mechanized whaling brought the species to the brink of extinction. The largest blue whale ever captured was 33.5 meters. Adults are known to reach a maximum weight of 190 tonnes, although 100–120 tonnes is more typical.
HABITAT AND DISTRIBUTION Formerly widespread, blue whales are today found in small populations with a patchy distribution worldwide, mainly in cold waters and open seas.
REPRODUCTION Calves are born after a gestation period of 11 months, suckle an estimated 380 liters of milk per day and gain 90 kilograms per day over a seven-month period. Sexual maturity is reached at five or six years, and a single calf is born every two or three years.
DIET Almost exclusively krill; some of the largest females may eat 6–10 tonnes of krill per day on the feeding grounds.

Blue Whale
Balaenoptera musculus

Minke Whale
Balaenoptera acutorostrata

APPEARANCE The minke whale is the smallest of the rorquals. It is streamlined and graceful, has a pointed head, and a single prominent ridge from the tip of the upper jaw to the blowholes. The back is black, dark gray or brown on the upperside, and the underside is white. The pectoral fins are long and slender, with a distinctive white band in many populations (particularly in the Northern Hemisphere), and there is a sickle-shaped dorsal fin. The flukes are relatively large and thin. There are 50–70 throat grooves, and 230–360 creamy baleen plates up to about 20 centimeters long in each side of the upper jaw.

SIZE Calves are nearly 3 meters long and grow up to 10 meters in length and as much as 10 tonnes in weight at maturity.
HABITAT AND DISTRIBUTION Minke whales are found inshore and offshore worldwide, although they are less common in the tropics than in cooler waters.
REPRODUCTION There is a gestation period of 10–11 months and young are suckled for less than 5–6 months. Sexual maturity is at 7–8 years.
DIET Small schooling fishes, such as herring and cod, as well as squid and crustaceans.

Humpback Whale
Megaptera novaeangliae

APPEARANCE The humpback is a stocky animal with a rounded body narrowing to a relatively slender tail stock. The head is massive and marked with protuberances, known as tubercles, which contain hair follicles. The pectoral fins are huge (*Megaptera* means "great wing") and may be as much as a third of the total body length. They are broadly serrated on the leading edge, in contrast with the flukes, which are serrated on their trailing edges. The body is black except for patches on the chin, throat, belly and flukes, and on one or both surfaces of the pectoral fins. Southern Hemisphere humpbacks tend to have more extensive white pigmentation than those in the Northern Hemisphere. Scars, barnacles and cookiecutter shark bites are common on the body. There are 12–36 deep throat grooves and 270–400 blackish brown baleen plates up to 80 centimeters long in each side of the upper jaw.
SIZE From 4–5 meters at birth, reaching a maximum of 19 meters and 48 tonnes at maturity.
HABITAT AND DISTRIBUTION Found in all oceans to the edge of ice packs, but highly migratory between polar and cool temperate waters in summer and tropical and subtropical waters in winter. Groups of one to three animals are common.
REPRODUCTION Calves are born in winter every two or three years and sexual maturity is reached at about five years.
DIET Humpbacks apparently feed only in cool or cold water, on krill and small schooling fishes such as sardines, mackerel, and anchovies.

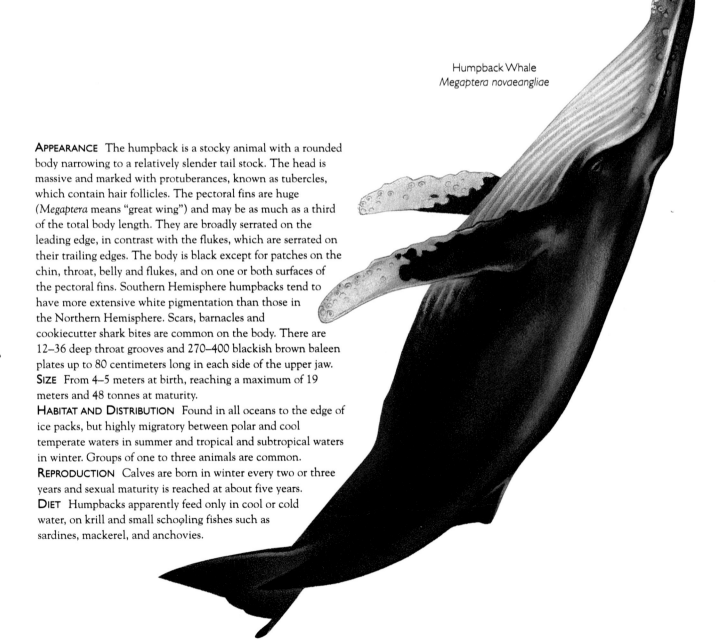

FAMILIES PHYSETERIDAE AND KOGIIDAE
SPERM WHALES

Three Species

HABITAT AND DISTRIBUTION All oceans, except polar ice fields, although distribution is dependent upon season and sexual and social status. The sperm whale has evolved to live in deep water, so it is in real danger of stranding if it moves into shallow water.

REPRODUCTION The gestation period is 16–17 months (the longest of any cetacean) and calves may feed on solid food within their first two years (although animals as old as 12 years have been observed nursing). Males reach sexual maturity when they are older than 10 years, females at 8–12 years. Sperm whales can probably live for 60 years or more.

DIET Squid, especially giant squid, as well as fishes and octopus in some areas.

APPEARANCE
Perhaps the most widely known of all cetaceans, the sperm whale is unmistakable. Its body shape is unique, with a squared, blunt head taking up almost a third of the total body length. There is a single, S-shaped blowhole on the left side of the forehead and the long, narrow lower jaw fits neatly into the underside of the head. The pectoral fins are relatively small and broad, with rounded tips. There is no distinct dorsal fin, but there is a triangular or rounded hump followed by a series of bumps along the tail stock. The light brown to blue-gray skin is rippled on the back and sides. There are 18–25 large conical teeth in each side of the lower jaw only and these fit into sockets in the upper jaw.

SIZE Calves are 3.5–4.5 meters at birth. Female adults grow to 13 meters in length and 20 tonnes in weight, while males reach 19 meters and can weigh up to 50 tonnes.

Sperm Whale
Physeter macrocephalus

Pygmy Sperm Whale
Kogia breviceps

APPEARANCE Superficially similar to its much larger namesake, the pygmy sperm whale is stocky with a square head and the upper jaw longer than the lower jaw. The back is blue-gray or brown-black, fading gradually to a light belly. There is a dark patch, then a thin light line behind the eye, giving the impression of a fish's gill cover. It has a small, sickle-shaped dorsal fin, relatively large and slightly rounded pectoral fins, and large, tapered flukes. There are 10–16 long, curved, sharp teeth in each side of the lower jaw only.

SIZE From 1.2 meters at birth to approximately 3.4 meters and 400 kilograms when fully grown.

HABITAT AND DISTRIBUTION Worldwide in deep tropical, subtropical and temperate waters, but very little is known about the distribution or numbers of this inconspicuous animal.

REPRODUCTION 11-month gestation period. Males are sexually mature at 2.7–3 meters and females at 2.7–2.8 meters.

DIET Mainly squid and octopus, but small fishes, crabs and other invertebrates are also taken.

FAMILY MONODONTIDAE
WHITE WHALES

Two Species

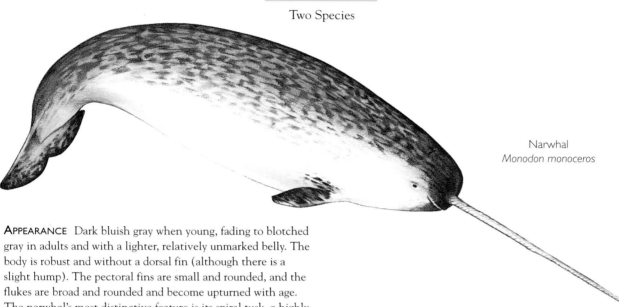

Narwhal
Monodon monoceros

APPEARANCE Dark bluish gray when young, fading to blotched gray in adults and with a lighter, relatively unmarked belly. The body is robust and without a dorsal fin (although there is a slight hump). The pectoral fins are small and rounded, and the flukes are broad and rounded and become upturned with age. The narwhal's most distinctive feature is its spiral tusk, a highly modified tooth (usually the left) that erupts from the upper jaw in males and may grow to 3 meters long. On extremely rare occasions, two tusks may erupt in males or a single tusk may erupt in females.

SIZE From about 1.5–1.7 meters at birth to about 3.8–5 meters at maturity.

HABITAT AND DISTRIBUTION Circumpolar distribution in the high Arctic—occupying one of the most northerly distributions of any cetacean. Migrations are dictated by advancing and retreating ice. Narwhals and belugas have fairly complementary distributions, since belugas prefer shallow water and narwhals are usually found in deeper water.

REPRODUCTION Mating probably takes place in the arctic spring and calves are born after a gestation period of about 15 months. Females give birth approximately every three years and the tusks begin to erupt in young males when they are about one year old.

DIET Fishes, squid and crustaceans.

APPEARANCE Dark brown or blue-gray with fine dark spots at birth, fading rapidly to gray then to ivory or white at maturity. The body is robust, with a small dorsal ridge instead of a fin, and small, short pectoral fins. The flukes are large and rounded, with convex trailing edges, which become more pronounced with age. There are 8–11 teeth in each side of the upper jaw and 8–9 teeth in each side of the lower jaw.

SIZE About 1.5–1.6 meters at birth, growing to a maximum of 5 meters when adult.

HABITAT AND DISTRIBUTION Circumpolar distribution in seasonally ice-covered waters of the arctic and subarctic, mainly in shallow bays and estuaries during summer. May swim hundreds of kilometers up river during summer.

REPRODUCTION Females reach sexual maturity at about five years, males at eight or nine years. Belugas reproduce every three years or so, with a gestation period of about 14 months and a lactation period of some 20 months. They are believed to live for as long as 25 years.

DIET A broad range of fishes (especially salmon), but also some crustaceans and octopus.

Beluga
Delphinapterus leucas

FAMILY ZIPHIIDAE
BEAKED WHALES

Twenty-one Species

Northern Bottlenose Whale
Hyperoodon ampullatus

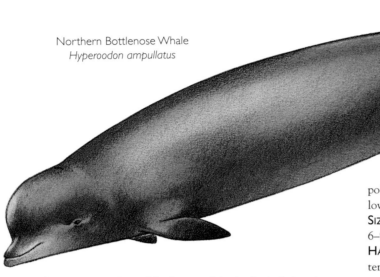

APPEARANCE One of the largest of the beaked whales, the northern bottlenose whale is brownish or charcoal gray in color and may lighten with age. Lighter on the head and underside. Males are often badly scarred from fighting with other males. The body is long and rounded, with a bulbous forehead, prominent beak, small dorsal fin, small pectoral fins and small, pointed flukes. Males have one or two pairs of teeth in the lower jaw.

SIZE About 3–3.5 meters at birth, adults reach a length of 6–9 meters (males are normally larger than females).

HABITAT AND DISTRIBUTION Deep pelagic waters of the cool temperate North Atlantic, as far north as Svalbard, with specific pockets of abundance in some areas.

REPRODUCTION Females give birth every two or three years. Young are born in spring after a gestation period of about 12 months and are suckled for a year.

DIET Principally squid, but also deepwater fishes and invertebrates

Cuvier's Beaked Whale
Ziphius cavirostris

APPEARANCE Also known as the goose-beaked whale, this is one of the most commonly sighted members of a rare family. Coloration ranges from brown to gray or purplish black, with a lighter belly and very often paler in the region of the face. White or cream-colored blotches are common, mainly on the underside or sides. Overall color fades with age. Scars are common in males, which have a single pair of teeth in the lower jaw only. Cuvier's beaked whale has small, rounded pectoral fins and large, tapered flukes.

SIZE Between 2–3 meters at birth, reaching seven meters (males) and 6.6 meters (females).

HABITAT AND DISTRIBUTION Temperate, subtropical and tropical waters around the world, mainly in deep water.

REPRODUCTION Young are born in late summer to early fall after a gestation period of about 12 months. Males are sexually mature at 5.5 meters and females at 6 meters.

DIET Deepwater cephalopods (squid, octopus), as well as some fishes and crustaceans.

APPEARANCE Also known as the giant bottlenose whale, this species is probably the largest of the beaked whales and is several times longer than some other members of the family. Coloration is slate gray, with irregular whitish spots and blotches on the belly, and fighting scars are common. The dorsal fin is small, the pectoral fins are small and slightly rounded, and the flukes are also relatively small. Males have two pairs of teeth in the lower jaw, with the front pair exposed when the mouth is closed.
SIZE About 4.5 meters at birth (more than the adult length of some other beaked whales). Males grow to nearly 12 meters and females to nearly

13 meters in length.
HABITAT AND DISTRIBUTION Deep temperate and subarctic waters in the North Pacific, from Japan to the Bering Sea and northern Mexico. It is usually seen in open ocean waters, and may be able to dive to more than 1,000 meters.
REPRODUCTION Young are born after a relatively long gestation period of 16–17 months and reach sexual maturity at about 8–10 years.
DIET Deep-sea squid, fishes and crustaceans.

Baird's Beaked Whale
Berardius bairdii

Strap-toothed Whale
Mesoplodon layardii

APPEARANCE The strap-toothed whale has a long, muscular body that tapers sharply behind the small dorsal fin. The pectoral fins are small and narrow, and the flukes are broad and sharply pointed at the tips. Coloration is predominantly bluish black, but may be dark purplish brown, with substantial white or gray areas on the beak, throat, back, shoulders and genital area. Males can be identified by the two extraordinary teeth that grow from the lower jaw, curl upward and backward and over the top of the upper jaw; in older animals, these teeth may grow so long that their tips touch and prevent the mouth from opening fully.
SIZE Calves are 2–3 meters at birth. Adults reach about 6 meters in length
HABITAT AND DISTRIBUTION Known primarily from strandings

in the Southern Hemisphere, from New Zealand and Australia to southern Africa and southern South America, between about 30°S and the Antarctic Convergence.
REPRODUCTION Very little is known, although the markings on the newborn calf appear to form the same light and dark pattern as on the adult, but in reverse.
DIET Almost exclusively squid. It is believed that males use their tongues in a piston-like action to suck squid into the mouth and the teeth may act as "guard-rails" to direct the food to the throat.

Sowerby's Beaked Whale
Mesoplodon bidens

APPEARANCE Only occasionally seen and sometimes probably confused with other beaked whales, Sowerby's beaked whale is fairly undistinguished in appearance, with an elongated body, a variable bulge in front of the blowhole, and a long beak. The dorsal fin is quite small, the pectoral fins are relatively long (for a *Mesoplodon*) and pointed, and the flukes are slender and pointed. Color is usually mottled charcoal or bluish gray, with a lighter underside and some gray or white spots. Males have a single tooth halfway along each side of the lower jaw, which are visible when the mouth is closed.

SIZE From about 2.4–2.7 meters at birth to 5 meters when fully grown.
HABITAT AND DISTRIBUTION Despite its alternative name of North Sea beaked whale, this species is by no means confined to the North Sea and is apparently widespread (although nowhere common) in cool pelagic waters of the North Atlantic, from Newfoundland to southern Norway and the Bay of Biscay.
REPRODUCTION Young are apparently born in late winter and early spring after a one-year gestation period, and are suckled for about a year.
DIET Squid and small deepwater fishes.

FAMILY DELPHINIDAE
DOLPHINS AND OTHER SMALL TOOTHED WHALES

Thirty-three Species

APPEARANCE Unmistakable, the orca (also known as the killer whale) is the largest member of the dolphin family, with a robust body boldly marked in glossy black and white. The back and sides are black, except for a teardrop-shaped patch of white behind and above the eye and a variably shaped "saddle-patch" behind the distinctive tall dorsal fin (which is much taller and more upright in males than females). The underside is entirely white. The head is rounded with no distinct beak, the pectoral fins are large, rounded and paddlelike, and the flukes are broad with a deep central notch. There are 10–13 large, conical teeth in each side of the upper and lower jaws.

SIZE Orcas are about 2–2.5 meters long at birth; females grow to about 4.6–7.7 meters and males to 5.1–9.8 meters when fully grown.

HABITAT AND DISTRIBUTION Orcas are found in all oceans of the world, from the poles to the tropics, although they appear to prefer cooler coastal areas, where their selected prey species are abundant.

REPRODUCTION Calves are born after a gestation period of 12–17 months and are suckled for at least a year. In the Atlantic, females reach sexual maturity at about 6–10 years and males at 12–16 years, while in the Pacific both sexes reach sexual maturity at 14–15 years. The calving interval is very variable and can be anything from 2–12 years.

DIET The orca eats an enormous variety of food—including seabirds, turtles, fishes, seals, dolphins and whales as large as the blue—although individual pods tend to specialize. One orca was recently observed catching and killing an adult great white shark. Pods, or family groups, will often cooperate during a hunt.

Orca
Orcinus orca

False Killer Whale
Pseudorca crassidens

APPEARANCE Also known as the pseudorca, the false killer whale is noticeably long and slender in shape, and is a glossy black to dark gray in color (paler in calves). The head is long and slender and tapers to a rounded beak. The short, narrow pectoral fins are S-shaped and have a distinctive "elbow" on their leading edge, the flukes are slender and pointed, and the dorsal fin is relatively large. There are 8–11 large, conical teeth in each side of both upper and lower jaws.

SIZE About 1.6–1.9 meters at birth, reaching 5 meters (females) or 6 meters (males) at maturity.

HABITAT AND DISTRIBUTION Highly social and sometimes forming herds of several hundred animals, the false killer whale is found in all deep tropical, subtropical and warm temperate seas. The species is typically oceanic and is rarely found in shallow waters close to shore.

REPRODUCTION Relatively little is known about the reproductive biology of the false killer whale. Calves seem to be born at all times of the year and may not be weaned until they are about 18 months old.

DIET False killer whales feed mainly on fishes and squid, but they have been observed attacking dolphins and even, on one occasion, a humpback whale calf.

APPEARANCE Over the years, more than 20 species of common dolphins have been proposed and discarded and until quite recently, only one was officially recognized. In 1994, a new species was created by splitting the original common dolphin into long-beaked and short-beaked species.

Long-beaked and Short-beaked
Common Dolphins
Delphinus capensis and *Delphinus delphis*

They are both very similar in appearance, with a distinctive hourglass pattern on their sides, where the dark-colored back, white or creamy white underside, pale gray tail stock and tan or yellowish side meet at a point below the dorsal fin. The subtle differences between the two species include a more muted color pattern in the long-beaked common dolphin and a shorter beak in the short-beaked common dolphin. There are 40–60 small, pointed teeth in each side of the upper and lower jaws in both species.
SIZE Calves range in length from 70–90 centimeters in both species. Adult short-beaked common dolphins grow to a length of 1.7–2.2 meters (male) and 1.5–2 meters (female); adult long-beaked common dolphins grow to a length of 2–2.6 meters (male) and 1.9–2.3 meters (female).
HABITAT AND DISTRIBUTION Both species live in warm temperate, subtropical and tropical seas worldwide. Occurs both offshore and inshore.
REPRODUCTION The gestation period is 10–11 months and the calves are nursed for 14–19 months. Sexual maturity is reached at an average age of 6–7 years in females and 5–12 years in males.
DIET Common dolphins feed on a variety of small schooling fishes, including sardines, anchovies, herrings and pilchards, as well as squid.

APPEARANCE Superficially similar to the bottlenose dolphin, the Indo-Pacific humpback dolphin is brownish gray, pale gray or pinkish white on the upperside and lighter on the underside. There may be some speckling on the body. The pectoral fins are broad, and the flukes rounded and triangular. The small, sickle-shaped dorsal fin sits on a fatty hump that is obvious only in animals in the west of the range (west of Sumatra, Indonesia); animals in the east and south of the range have a more prominent dorsal fin, but no distinctive hump. It can often be identified purely by its distinctive surfacing behavior (the long beak appears first and then it appears to pause at the surface before completing the dive).
SIZE From about 1 meter at birth to 2–2.4 meters (female) and 3–3.2 meters (male) when fully grown.
HABITAT AND DISTRIBUTION Widely distributed in warm temperate, subtropical and tropical

waters in shallow coastal areas of the Indian Ocean and western Pacific Ocean.
REPRODUCTION Very little is known about reproduction in this species, although calves have been observed throughout the year with a peak in summer.
DIET A wide variety of schooling fishes, as well as crustaceans and mollusks.

Indo-Pacific
Humpback Dolphin
Sousa chinensis

APPEARANCE Similar in shape and behavior to the pygmy killer whale, the melon-headed whale is bluish black, dark gray or dark brown over most of the body, with a thin white strip on the "lips," an indistinct pale anchor patch on the chest, and a gray or off-white patch on the underside. The prominent dorsal fin is large and sickle-shaped, the pectoral fins are long and pointed, and the flukes are well developed. There are between 21–25 small, pointed teeth on each side of the upper and lower jaws.
SIZE Up to 1 meter at birth and 2.1–2.7 meters (male) and 2.3–2.7 meters (female) when fully grown.
HABITAT AND DISTRIBUTION Found in tropical and some subtropical waters in the Atlantic, Indian and Pacific oceans. Most commonly seen offshore and around oceanic islands.
REPRODUCTION Little is known about

reproduction in this species, although the gestation period is estimated to be about one year.
DIET This species is known to feed on various small fishes and squid.

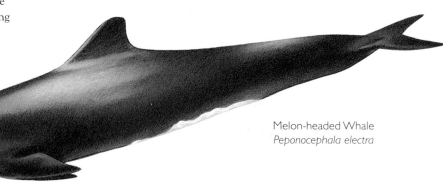

Melon-headed Whale
Peponocephala electra

White-beaked Dolphin
Lagenorhynchus albirostris

APPEARANCE Despite its scientific and common names, this species can have a white, gray or dark beak. Toward the east of the range, animals tend to have white beaks and live in smaller schools, while western animals generally have darker beaks and live in larger schools. The body is a mixture of white, gray and black, with a distinctive white or pale stripe on each side and a white or pale gray patch on either side behind the dorsal fin. The fin itself is sickle-shaped and prominent, the pectoral fins are broad-based and pointed, and the flukes are pointed with a distinct central notch. There are 22–28 small, conical teeth in each side of the upper and lower jaws.

SIZE From 1.2–1.6 meters at birth to 2.5–2.8 meters (both sexes) when fully grown.

HABITAT AND DISTRIBUTION Cool temperate to subarctic waters of the North Atlantic, over the continental shelf and particularly along the shelf edge. This dolphin is found close to shore in some areas.

REPRODUCTION Little is known about the reproduction of this species, although most births tend to take place during summer and early fall.

DIET A variety of schooling fishes, including cod and herring, as well as squid, octopus and bottom-dwelling crustaceans.

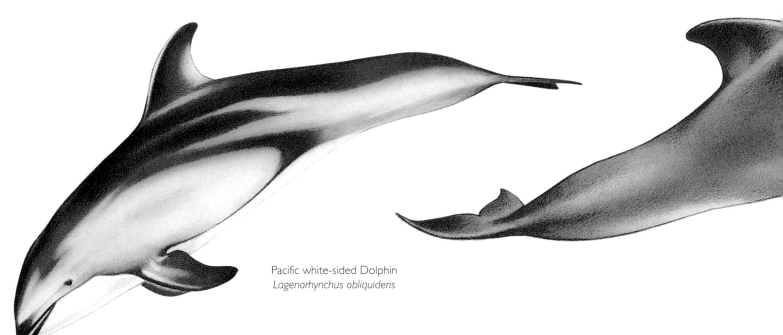

Pacific white-sided Dolphin
Lagenorhynchus obliquidens

APPEARANCE An avid rider of ships' bow waves, the Pacific white-sided dolphin is characterized by a relatively stocky body, poorly demarcated beak, small pectoral fins, and a tall, sickle-shaped dorsal fin. The coloration is distinctive, with a dark gray or black back, a pale gray streak along each side from just above the eye to the tail stock, a pale gray patch on each side, and a white belly. There are 21–32 teeth on each side of the upper and lower jaws.

SIZE From about 0.8–1.2 meters at birth to 1.7–2.4 meters (both sexes) when fully grown.

HABITAT AND DISTRIBUTION The Pacific white-sided dolphin is normally found in the open ocean in deep temperate waters of the North Pacific, from Baja California to southern Alaska and from the Kamchatka to Japan.

REPRODUCTION The gestation period is about 10–12 months and sexual maturity is reached at a body length of about 1.7–2.2 meters.

DIET A fast, active hunter of hake, herring, sardines, anchovies and squid.

Fraser's Dolphin
Lagenodelphis hosei

APPEARANCE Also known as the shortsnout dolphin or white-bellied dolphin, Fraser's dolphin has a short snout or beak and a creamy white or pinkish white belly. It is blue-gray or gray-brown on the upperside, has complex face markings, and a dark line joining the beak to the small, pointed pectoral fins. A gray or creamy white line runs from the front of the melon to the underside of the tail stock. The dark gray dorsal fin is small. There are 36–44 teeth on each side of the upper and lower jaws.
SIZE About 1 meter at birth and reaching 2–2.6 meters (both sexes) when fully grown.
HABITAT AND DISTRIBUTION Tropical, subtropical and warm temperate waters of the Indian, Atlantic and Pacific oceans. Fraser's dolphin is an open-ocean species and was not seen alive until the early 1970s. They are now commonly seen on whale-watch trips in the Caribbean, Japan, the Philippines and elsewhere.
REPRODUCTION Little is known about the reproductive biology of this species, although females may reach sexual maturity at a body length of 2.25–2.35 meters.
DIET Deep-sea fishes, squid and shrimps.

APPEARANCE Well known because of its ready adaptability to captivity, the bottlenose is the largest of the true oceanic dolphins, with a long, robust body, moderately long, slender pectoral fins and flukes, and a short, stout beak marked by a sharp crease where it meets the forehead. Coloration is usually dark bluish gray or brownish gray above, with paler sides and an off-white, light gray or pinkish belly. There are 20–26 small, sharp conical teeth on each side of the upper jaw and 18–26 on each side of the lower jaw.
SIZE Calves range in length from 0.85–1.3 meters at birth and grow to 1.9–3.9 meters (both sexes) when fully grown.
HABITAT AND DISTRIBUTION Widely distributed worldwide in cold temperate to tropical waters, including many enclosed seas such as the Black, Red and Mediterranean seas. There are distinctive offshore and inshore forms.
REPRODUCTION Gestation period is about 12 months and the calves suckle for about 18 months (although they begin to take solid food after about 6 months). Sexual maturity is reached at 9–10 years (females) and 10–13 years (males). The reproductive cycle for most females is 2–3 years and they can live for more than 30 years.
DIET Small fishes, such as eels, catfish and mullet, as well as squid and shrimps. Bottlenose dolphins have been observed chasing fish onto mudflats, then sliding out of the water to seize their prey.

Bottlenose Dolphin
Tursiops truncatus

Hourglass Dolphin
Lagenorhynchus cruciger

APPEARANCE This fast-swimming dolphin has a stout body with a high, curved dorsal fin, long, curved pectoral fins, striking black flukes and a very short beak. Its dramatic black and white coloration is unmistakable—especially with the distinctive hourglass pattern created by the white blaze stretching from the eye to below the dorsal fin, meeting a second blaze that stretches from the end of the tail stock to below the dorsal fin. There are 28 teeth on each side of the upper and lower jaws.
SIZE Little is known about newborn calves, but they are believed to be about 1.1 meters in length; adults range from 1.6–1.8 meters (males are smaller than females).
HABITAT AND DISTRIBUTION Cold subantarctic and antarctic waters on both sides of the Antarctic Convergence. Found mainly offshore.
REPRODUCTION Nothing known.
DIET Small deepwater fishes and squid.

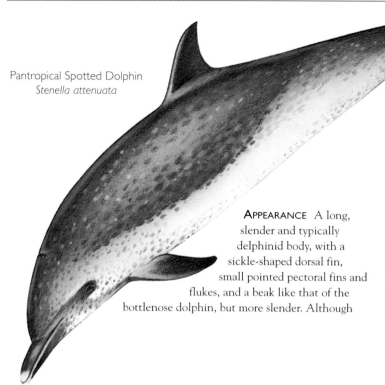

Pantropical Spotted Dolphin
Stenella attenuata

coloration is variable, it is generally dark gray on the upper side, mid-gray along the sides, and pale gray underneath. The body is covered in light (above) and dark (below) spots, which give it its name. There are 35–48 small, conical teeth on each side of the upper jaw and 34–47 on each side of the lower jaw.

SIZE Calves are 80–90 centimeters long at birth and grow to 1.7–2.4 meters (female) and 2–2.6 meters (male) when fully grown.

HABITAT AND DISTRIBUTION Mainly in tropical waters, but also in some subtropical and warm temperate waters, around the world. There are two distinct forms: the coastal and the pelagic.

REPRODUCTION The gestation period is 11–12 months and calves suckle for about 20 months. Sexual maturity is reached at an average age of 12 years (males) and 9 years (females).

DIET Mainly surface-dwelling squid and fishes, such as frigate mackerel; lactating females seem to prefer flying fish, possibly because of their high calorific content.

APPEARANCE A long, slender and typically delphinid body, with a sickle-shaped dorsal fin, small pointed pectoral fins and flukes, and a beak like that of the bottlenose dolphin, but more slender. Although

APPEARANCE The gray grampus or Risso's dolphin is a stout-bodied species, with a deep chest and a bulbous head without a beak. The dorsal fin is high and sickle-shaped, the pectoral fins are long, and the flukes are wide and pointed. The body is generally mid to dark gray, and lighter on the belly, although all the appendages tend to be darker. The body becomes lighter as animals age (older animals can be almost white) and the number of scratches and blotches increases. There are no teeth in the upper jaw and two to seven conical teeth on each side of the lower jaw.

SIZE About 1.3–1.7 meters at birth, growing to 2.6–3.8 meters when fully grown. Larger than any other cetacean with the name "dolphin."

HABITAT AND DISTRIBUTION Tropical, subtropical and temperate seas worldwide, mainly in deep offshore waters, but close to shore around oceanic islands or wherever there is sufficient depth.

REPRODUCTION The gestation period is 13–14 months and the age at sexual maturity is probably about 10–13 years.

DIET Principally squid, but also octopus and fishes.

Hector's Dolphin
Cephalorhynchus hectori

Risso's Dolphin
Grampus griseus

APPEARANCE Hector's dolphin is small and beautifully patterned. The tip of the lower jaw and the sides of the head are black, the back and sides are light gray to light brown, and the throat, chest and belly are white. There is a hooked expansion of the white belly color on the tail stock and a somewhat darker stripe along the sides from the eye to below the dorsal fin. The beak is barely discernible, the dorsal fin is distinctively rounded, and the pectoral fins are relatively large and dark. There are 26–32 conical teeth on each side of the upper and lower jaws.

SIZE From about 60–75 centimeters at birth to 1.2–1.4 meters (male) and 1.4–1.5 meters (female) when fully grown.

HABITAT AND DISTRIBUTION Found only in the coastal waters of New Zealand, especially around South Island and along the western coast of North Island.

REPRODUCTION The gestation period is not known and the lactation period is believed to be at least six months. Sexual maturity is reached at 7–9 years for females and 6–9 years for males.

DIET Mainly small fishes (under 35 centimeters), but also feeds on squid.

APPEARANCE This acrobatic species is an agile and fast swimmer. It has a slender, muscular body with a long, narrow beak, a tall triangular dorsal fin (which leans forward in some older males), and long, pointed pectoral fins and flukes. There are many varieties, differing greatly in body shape, size and color. Most have a distinctive three-tone pattern (dark gray above, lighter gray on the sides and white underneath), but eastern Pacific animals are mainly gray. There are 44–64 small, conical teeth on each side of the upper jaw and 42–62 on each side of the lower jaw.

SIZE Newborn calves are 70–85 centimeters, reaching 1.3–2.4 meters (males) and 1.3–2.2 meters (females) when fully grown.

HABITAT AND DISTRIBUTION Tropical, subtropical and, less commonly, warm temperate waters in the Atlantic, Pacific and Indian oceans. Some populations live close to shore, but most are exclusively pelagic.

REPRODUCTION The gestation period is estimated at 10–11 months and the average age at weaning varies from 11–34 months, depending on the population. Sexual maturity is reached at 4–6 years (female) and 6–9 years (male).

DIET Fishes and squid—normally species living well below the water surface.

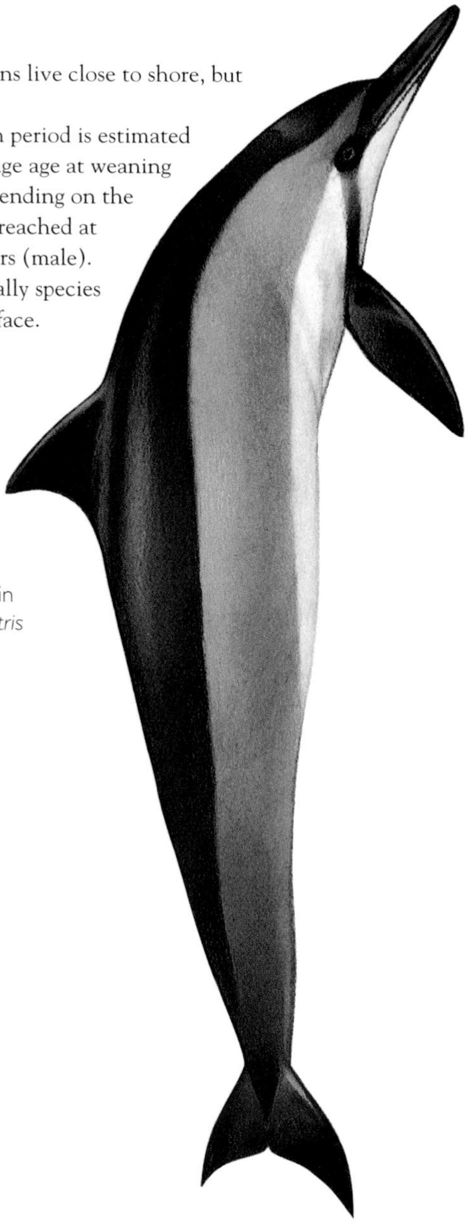

Long-snouted
Spinner Dolphin
Stenella longirostris

Commerson's Dolphin
Cephalorhynchus commersonii

APPEARANCE A striking, small dolphin with a stocky body, conical head and no visible beak. The pectoral fins are rounded and black, the flukes are also black, and there is a prominent dorsal fin of variable shape. The coloration is very distinctive. The main body color is white, but the appendages, the head, the back area around the dorsal fin, and rear half of the tail stock are all black. There are 28–34 small, conical teeth on each side of the upper jaw and 26–35 on each side of the lower jaw.

SIZE Newborn calves are 55–75 centimeters and grow to 1.4–1.5 meters (both sexes) when fully grown.

HABITAT AND DISTRIBUTION Unusual distribution, with the main population in the cold temperate waters of southeastern South America and the Falkland Islands, and with an apparently isolated population around Kerguelen Island in the Indian Ocean.

REPRODUCTION The gestation period is 11–12 months and sexual maturity is reached at about 5–6 years (both sexes).

DIET Small fishes, squid, krill and shrimps.

FAMILY PHOCOENIDAE
PORPOISES

Six Species

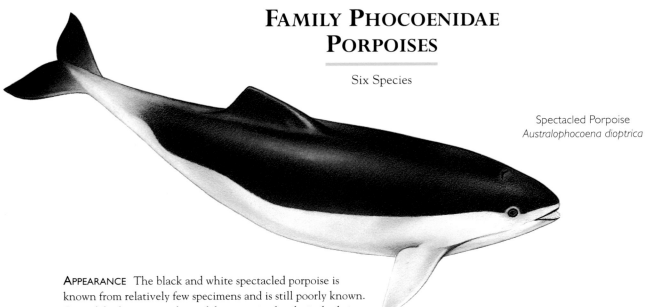

Spectacled Porpoise
Australophocoena dioptrica

APPEARANCE The black and white spectacled porpoise is known from relatively few specimens and is still poorly known. One of the largest members of the porpoise family, its body is stocky in shape, and it has short, brilliant white pectoral fins, a large rounded (male) or triangular (female) dorsal fin and small flukes. There is no trace of a beak, but there are distinctive black "lips." Coloration is distinctive, glossy blue-black above and brilliant white on the underside. There is also a black patch around the eye, surrounded by a fine white line, which gives this species its common name. There are 18–23 small, spade-shaped teeth on each side of the upper jaw and 16–20 on each side of the lower jaw.

SIZE Newborn calves are believed to be about 70–80 centimeters and when fully grown they have a length of 1.3–2.2 meters (males are slightly larger than females).

HABITAT AND DISTRIBUTION Although most reports are from the southern Atlantic coast of South America, there are also records from a number of oceanic islands from Kerguelen to subantarctic New Zealand. Mostly known from coastal areas, but the range may also include large areas of open sea.

REPRODUCTION Poorly known.

DIET Fishes and squid.

Dall's Porpoise
Phocoenoides dalli

APPEARANCE Dall's porpoise is perhaps best known for its astonishing bursts of speed and the distinctive "rooster spray"— a spray of water coming off its head as it rises to breathe. This striking black and white porpoise has an extremely stocky body, a small head with a steeply sloping forehead, small pectoral fins, flukes with a white trailing edge, and a prominent two-tone dorsal fin (gray-white above and black below). The main body color is jet-black, but there is a large white patch on the belly and sides (widely variable in extent). There are 19–29 small, spade-shaped teeth on each side of the upper and lower jaws.

SIZE Calves are about 0.85–1 meter at birth and reach about 1.7–2.2 meters when fully grown (males are slightly larger).

HABITAT AND DISTRIBUTION Cold waters of the northern North Pacific, from Japan and northern Mexico to the Bering Sea. Mainly found in inshore waters, but also in the open sea.

REPRODUCTION The gestation period is 11–12 months and sexual maturity is reached at 6–8 years for males and 3–7 years for females.

DIET This species eats mainly surface and midwater squid and lanternfishes.

Finless Porpoise
Neophocaena phocaenoides

APPEARANCE Superficially similar to the beluga, the finless porpoise is also known as the black finless porpoise. However, the body color only becomes black after death and the natural color is pale blue-gray on the back and paler below. The body is rather long and narrow, and it has a distinctive bulbous forehead with the suggestion of a beak, and long, pointed pectoral fins. There is no dorsal fin, but a small ridge covered in circular, wartlike tubercles runs along the center of the back. There are 13–22 short, compressed, spadelike teeth on each side of the upper and lower jaws.

SIZE Young are 60–90 centimeters at birth and grow to 1.5–1.9 meters (males) and 1.2–1.7 meters (females) when fully grown.
HABITAT AND DISTRIBUTION Tropical, subtropical and warm temperate coastal waters (rarely more than 5 kilometers from land) and major rivers in the Indian Ocean and the western Pacific Ocean.
REPRODUCTION The gestation period is about 11 months and the calves nurse for 6–15 months. Their age at sexual maturity is unknown.
DIET Small fishes, prawns, squid and cuttlefish.

APPEARANCE The harbor, or common porpoise as it is frequently called, is a familiar animal in many parts of the Northern Hemisphere, although it shows little of itself at the surface. It is robust in shape, with no beak, small and slightly rounded pectoral fins, small flukes and a low, blunt dorsal fin. The coloration is dark gray or black on the back and white underneath, with the body color merging from dark to light through an area of flecking. There are 22–28 small, spade-shaped teeth on each side of the upper jaw and 21–26 on each side of the lower jaw.

SIZE From 67–85 centimeters at birth to 1.4–1.9 meters (both sexes) when fully grown.
HABITAT AND DISTRIBUTION Coastal waters of the temperate to subarctic waters in the Northern Hemisphere, including some enclosed areas, such as the Black Sea.
REPRODUCTION The gestation period is 11 months and the calves are nursed for less than a year. Sexual maturity is reached at about three years in females and a little older in males. Females normally have a calf every year, with no "rest" period in between.
DIET Herring, cod, mackerel, anchovy and a variety of other fishes; in some areas, calves eat euphausiid crustaceans.

Harbor Porpoise
Phocoena phocoena

FAMILY PLATANISTIDAE
GANGES AND INDUS RIVER DOLPHINS

Two Species

Ganges River Dolphin
Platanista gangetica

APPEARANCE The Ganges river dolphin, or Ganges susu as it is often called, is almost identical to its close relative, the Indus river dolphin. There are some differences in the structure of their skulls and they are considered to be separate species. The eyes, which are capable only of distinguishing light from dark, are tiny and effectively non-functional. This species moves and feeds in a murky riverine environment using echolocation. The body is predominantly gray-brown, sometimes with a pinkish belly. There is no true dorsal fin, but there is a low, triangular hump on the back. The distinctive pectoral fins are broad and paddle-shaped, and the flukes are pointed and swept back. The beak is exceptionally long and contains 26–39 thin teeth on each side of the upper jaw and 26–35 on each side of the lower jaw.

SIZE Calves are about 70–90 centimeters at birth, attaining 1.5–2.5 meters when fully grown.

HABITAT AND DISTRIBUTION The Ganges river dolphin is found in the Ganges, Brahmaputra and Meghna rivers of India, Bangladesh, Nepal and Bhutan. The Indus river dolphin lives only in the Indus river of Pakistan.

REPRODUCTION The gestation period appears to vary from 8–12 months and the calves are probably weaned before the end of their first year (although they begin to take solid food when they are much younger).

DIET A variety of fishes, crustaceans and mollusks.

FAMILY INIIDAE
AMAZON RIVER DOLPHIN

One Species

APPEARANCE Largest of the freshwater dolphins, the Amazon river dolphin, or boto, has many unusual features. Its plump body is variable in color, from bluish gray to off-white to vivid pink. It has a small hump on its back instead of a dorsal fin. Its broad, paddle-shaped pectoral fins are relatively large and the flukes (often ragged on the trailing edge) are wide and pointed. The eyes are small, yet functional, although its slightly bulging cheeks may hamper downward vision. The beak is very long and contains 23–35 chunky teeth on each side of the upper and lower jaws.

SIZE From 75–80 centimeters at birth to 1.8–2.3 meters (female) and 2–2.7 meters (male) when fully grown.

HABITAT AND DISTRIBUTION Found throughout the main rivers and tributaries of the Amazon and Orinoco river systems of tropical South America. There are three geographically distinct populations, but these are not sufficiently different to be classified as separate species.

REPRODUCTION The gestation period is 10–11 months and it is not unusual for females to be pregnant and lactating at the same time.

DIET Huge variety of fishes and crustaceans.

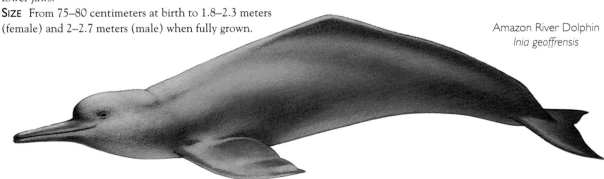

Amazon River Dolphin
Inia geoffrensis

FAMILY PONTOPORIIDAE
BAIJI AND FRANCISCANA

Two Species

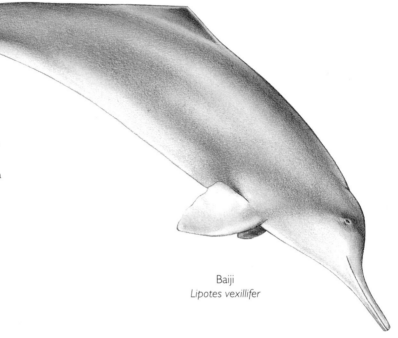

APPEARANCE The seriously endangered baiji has many different names, including Chinese or Yangtze river dolphin, beiji, whiteflag dolphin and whitefin dolphin. It has a stocky body, with a low, triangular dorsal fin and broad, rounded pectoral fins. The beak is long, thin and tilted slightly upward. The body is light to dark bluish gray on the back, fading to grayish white or white on the belly. There are 31–34 small teeth on each side of the upper jaw and 32–36 on each side of the lower jaw.

SIZE Newborn calves are 80–90 centimeters at birth and reach 1.4–2.5 meters (both sexes) when fully grown (females are slightly larger than males).

HABITAT AND DISTRIBUTION Restricted to the middle and lower reaches of the Yangtze River, in China, occurring only within small pockets of its 1,700-kilometer range. Now on the verge of extinction, there could be fewer than 50 survivors.

REPRODUCTION Poorly known.

DIET Variety of freshwater fishes, including eel-like catfish.

Baiji
Lipotes vexillifer

Franciscana
Pontoporia blainvillei

APPEARANCE Also known as the La Plata dolphin, the franciscana has an exceptionally long beak (the longest—relative to body size—of any cetacean). Its small body is fairly stocky, with a small head, a distinctive dorsal fin with a broad base, and a ridge running along the top of the tail stock. The pectoral fins are very large and almost triangular, and the flukes are pointed at the tips. Coloration is grayish brown above, fading to lighter brown on the sides and grayish brown on the underside. There are 53–58 small, sharp teeth on each side of the upper jaw and 51–56 on each side of the lower jaw.

SIZE Calves are about 70–80 centimeters long at birth and reach 1.3–1.7 meters when fully grown.

HABITAT AND DISTRIBUTION Although it is treated as a river dolphin, the franciscana is found only in the sea. It occurs in the temperate coastal waters of eastern South America.

REPRODUCTION Calves are born after a gestation period of 10–11 months and suckle for about nine months (although they begin to take solid food after only three months). Both sexes reach sexual maturity at two or three years and calving usually occurs every two years.

DIET A variety of fishes, squid, octopus and crustaceans. Franciscana are primarily bottom feeders.

BALEEN WHALES

WILLIAM H. DAWBIN

*B*aleen whales are filter-feeders, using baleen (often referred to as whalebone) to sieve out small planktonic organisms from the sea. They are sometimes referred to as the "great whales"—an appropriate name for all the larger members of the group, but somewhat less appropriate for the smallest species, which are actually smaller than some of the toothed whales, such as the orca Orcinus orca, the bottlenose whales and, above all, the sperm whale Physeter macrocephalus. However, the largest of the baleen whales, the blue whale Balaenoptera musculus, is not only the largest of all living animals but the largest ever known to have existed; it even exceeds the size of the biggest dinosaurs. Incredibly, it is the largest animal on earth but feeds on some of the smallest.

Paul Ensor

ABOVE: The feature that separates baleen whales from their toothed cousins is "whalebone": bristly plates that range in length from less than 30 centimeters in the minke whale to more than 4.5 meters in the bowhead. Straining some of the sea's smallest prey through their baleen, these whales have grown to enormous size.

A UNIQUE ADAPTATION

The baleen whales have a special adaptation for filter-feeding: a series of horny plates arranged along either side of the upper jaw. These are rather like the leaves of a book, with the inner portion of each plate facing inside the mouth and frayed out to form fine bristles. These bristles may be coarse or quite silky depending on the favored prey. Despite the name "whalebone," baleen is made of the protein keratin, which is an organic material similar to hair and fingernail.

All the baleen whales depend on searching out massive concentrations of the very small organisms on which they feed, and the method of filtration used by each species differs according to their diet. Since dense swarms of suitable plankton occur predominantly in the upper layers of the sea, baleen whales tend to travel mainly

near the surface in the top 100 meters, and to be more shallow in both their cruising and feeding movements than the deep-diving sperm or bottlenose whales. They therefore do not need to spend as much time on each dive, so there is a shorter interval between "blows"—the visible condensations of moisture in the breath expelled when the whales surface.

The shape and height of a blow are often distinctive enough to identify the species of whale. The dive interval usually varies from four or five minutes to 20 minutes, although longer intervals and deeper dives can occur in special circumstances, for example, after harpooning. However, the dives of more than two hours to depths of 3,000 meters recorded for sperm whales are unknown for baleen whales.

The families within the baleen whale group, suborder Mysticeti, are the right whales and bowhead (Balaenidae), the pygmy right whale (Neobalaenidae), the gray whale (Eschrichtiidae) and the rorquals (Balaenopteridae). There are 11 recognized species.

THE RIGHT WHALES

Right whales are distinguished from the other baleen whales mainly by their very long baleen, with an almost silky texture to the bristles. They feed on small planktonic crustaceans, mainly copepods. They are large, heavy-bodied animals with thick blubber. It was the combination of the high oil yield obtained from the blubber layer, the great value placed on their silky baleen, and the fact that they were easy to approach and lived close to shore that gave them the name of right whales, meaning the "right" whales to catch.

Because of the nature of their feeding—a skimming motion that involves ploughing through the water with the mouth partly open, the water streaming out from the inside through the baleen plates with the tiny organisms being

Francois Gohier/Auscape International

trapped on the silky bristles—there is no need for expansion of the throat, and ventral grooves or large pleats in the throat region are absent in this family. They have no dorsal fin and the mouth is greatly arched to contain the long baleen.

There are three species in the right whale family: the northern right whale *Eubalaena glacialis*, the southern right whale *Eubalaena australis* and the bowhead *Balaena mysticetus*.

The first species to become generally known was the northern right whale, which was first hunted in the Bay of Biscay by the Basques in the twelfth century. Basque whalers eventually extended their activities further into the North Atlantic and right across to Newfoundland. They were joined by whalers from Holland and Britain and so many right whales were killed that their numbers declined to a dangerously low level. Hunting in the North Pacific has also taken a heavy toll. Today, there are approximately 300 surviving northern right whales—most of them in the western North Atlantic, although there are probably a handful in the eastern North Atlantic and the North Pacific. They are showing no sign of recovery and their future is uncertain.

Northern right whales reach a maximum length of 17–18 meters. Their major feeding grounds are in the lower Bay of Fundy and Brown's Bank (off the southern tip of Nova Scotia) in Canada, and Cape Cod Bay in the United States. Their breeding grounds were recently found along the United States coast, off Florida and Georgia.

Southern right whales are so similar to northern right whales in appearance that some whale biologists maintain they belong to the same species. They would certainly be very difficult to tell apart in the field. However, on average, the northern is probably slightly larger than the southern (which is unusual because, in most baleen whales, the southern animals are generally larger than their northern counterparts) and there are minor cranial differences. There may also be slight differences in the number of callosities, or skin growths, on their heads. Perhaps most important of all, they are separated geographically and, certainly in modern times, they do not appear to mix. Some whale biologists maintain that there is a third species—the animals living in the North Pacific—but this has yet to be proven or widely accepted.

ABOVE: The first of the great whales to be commercially hunted, the northern right whale earned its name because it swims slowly, floats when dead and yields an unusual amount of baleen and oil, and was therefore considered the "right" whale to hunt.

BALEEN AND TOOTHED WHALES: WHAT'S THE DIFFERENCE?

M.M. BRYDEN

The key characteristics that separate the cetaceans into two suborders—baleen whales (Mysticeti) and toothed whales (Odontoceti)—are the presence or absence of baleen plates and teeth. However, there are many other differences between the two suborders, including the shape of the skull, the appearance of the blowhole and the form of the ribs and the sternum.

When viewed from above, the skull of toothed whales is markedly asymmetrical, perhaps because of the presence of a single blowhole (the left nostril has developed at the expense of the right nostril). Baleen whales, however, have a symmetrical skull and a double blowhole (although the apertures of the nostrils are unequal in size—the one on the left is usually slightly larger than the one on the right).

The ribs of whales show great variation in their numbers and structure, as well as in their attachment to the vertebral column and sternum. In most baleen whales (except the gray) the ribs have lost the head and articulate with their corresponding vertebra by means of the tubercle. The sternum is segmented in most toothed whales, but in baleen whales it always consists of a single bone.

The main distinguishing features of the two cetacean suborders are as follows:

MYSTICETI	ODONTOCETI
Teeth lacking (except as embryonic vestiges)	Teeth present (although in some species they do not emerge through the gum)
Baleen plates present	No baleen plates
Skull symmetrical	Skull asymmetrical
External paired nasal opening	Single external nasal opening
One to three ribs have heads	Four to eight ribs have heads
Sternal ribs absent	Sternal ribs present
Sternum composed of a single bone, which articulates with the first pair of ribs	Sternum composed of three or more bones, which articulate with three or more pairs of the ribs

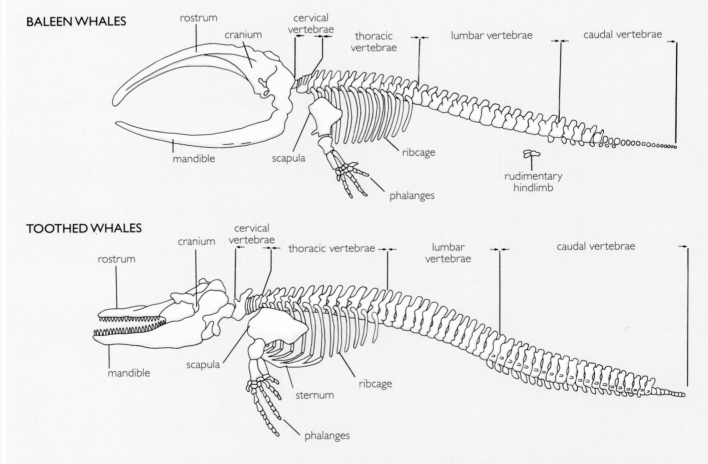

ABOVE: There are a number of differences between baleen and toothed whales apart from the presence or absence of teeth, as these illustrations of their skeletons show. The most obvious external difference, in most species, is size.

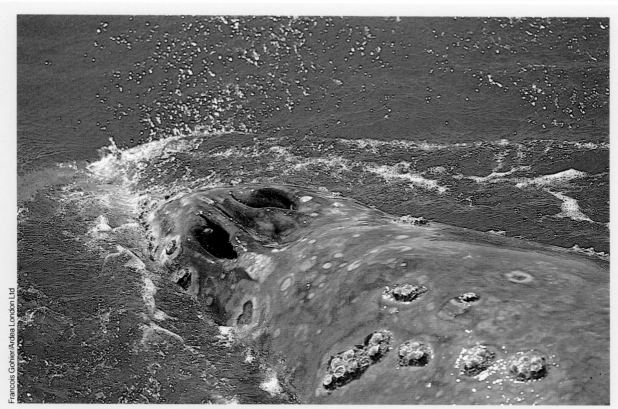

Francois Gohier/Ardea London Ltd

ABOVE: Apart from significant internal differences that suggest the two suborders of whales evolved independently, there are obvious external differences. Great size is one: few species of toothed whales approach the length of the smallest baleen whales. While toothed whales have a single nasal opening or blowhole, baleen whales have two of roughly equal size.

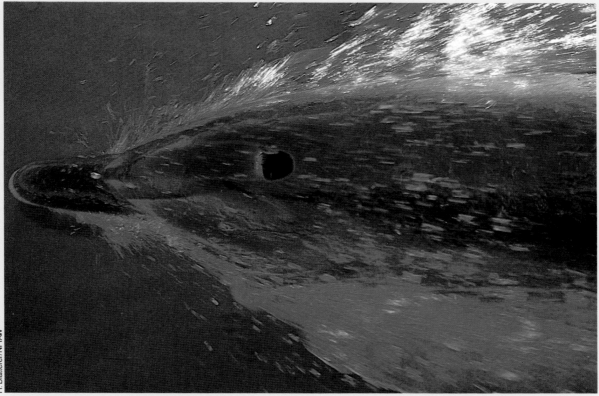

H. Blatterer/NPIAW

ABOVE: Toothed whales range in length from less than 1.5 meters to 18 meters. They are generally faster swimmers than baleen whales, since they must actively hunt their prey. Feeding is not simply a matter of swimming through a "soup" of food. As well as having only one blowhole, toothed whales have skeletal structures that differ in detail from those of baleen whales.

ABOVE: Classified as a distinct species largely because of its geographical separation from the northern right whale, the southern right whale was hunted pitilessly in the nineteenth and early twentieth centuries.

Southern right whales were hunted later than their northern counterparts but, by the nineteenth century, they were being taken in large numbers. They were originally found by American and French whalers searching for new sperm whale grounds. Since southern right whales come close to shore to breed, a great many shore stations were established on different landmasses, such as South Africa, Australia (particularly Tasmania) and around the coast of New Zealand.

One estimate gives the total number of southern right whales killed at more than 200,000, while other estimates suggest figures of 55,000–75,000. But there is little doubt that the population had reached an all-time low of only a few hundred survivors by the early 1920s. Incredibly, the numbers are recovering strongly in all their main breeding grounds: Chile, Argentina, Brazil, South Africa, southern Australia and some Southern Hemisphere islands. All three major populations (South America,

Africa and Australasia) are increasing annually by an estimated 7.1–8.3 percent—which means that they double roughly once every 10 years. The total population today is approximately 6,000–7,000 individuals.

Despite such a long history of whaling, surprisingly little was known about right whale biology until studies were carried out this century. A great deal of information has come from work by Roger Payne off Peninsula Valdes, in Patagonia, Argentina. He has been studying Patagonia's breeding southern right whales since the early 1970s and developed a photo-identification technique, using the callosities to recognize individual whales. One of his earlier discoveries was that nearly all the animals coming in close to shore—actually into the surf in some cases—were pregnant females. Calving can occur very close to the surf, and Payne was able to watch the whales' activities from the beach or from a nearby clifftop. It soon became apparent that animals that calved in one year were not seen for the next two years. New individuals appeared in these successive years, showing that the great majority of right whales calved at an interval of three years, and this has been confirmed repeatedly by known animals that have returned. The males, and immature animals, seem to remain consistently further away from the shoreline.

Most southern right whales migrate to remote southern waters to feed during the austral summer. It is not clear exactly where they go to feed, but they do not seem to migrate as far south as the rorquals. They probably do not go beyond the Antarctic Convergence—the invisible area where the cold, barely saline waters flowing north from Antarctica are pushed downward by warmer and more saline waters flowing south from temperate regions—but feed in areas that have not been surveyed in as much detail. One reason is that, unlike the rorquals, southern right whales do not feed on rich swarms of krill. Instead, they feed on much smaller crustaceans, known as copepods, each of which is roughly the size of a grain of rice.

Characteristically, both northern and southern right whales are slow swimmers. But they are very active at the surface and frequently lift their flukes or pectoral fins out of the water and will often breach many times in a row. Some individuals indulge in a form of behavior known as "sailing." They literally raise their flukes into the wind and use them as sails. This is a particularly popular activity among southern right whales in the strong, steady winds off Argentina, but has never been observed in northern right whales.

The largest, least known and, in its day, most commercially valuable of the right whale family is the bowhead. Confined entirely to arctic and subarctic waters, this animal reaches about 18 meters in length and has an enormous head that can be up to 40 percent of total body length. The upper jaw is arched, giving a mouth capacity that allows the baleen plates to reach such extraordinary lengths as 4.5 meters—more than double the length of the baleen of northern or southern right whales. This made their baleen by far the most valuable of any whale's, and the bowheads, like their cousins, were also massive producers of oil.

The bowhead whale is fairly similar to the two right whales in size, shape and general appearance. It is stocky and rotund, with a barrel-shaped body and a huge head, about a third of its body size. This head contains the longest baleen of any whale. It spends its life following the advance and retreat of the arctic ice and has the most northerly range of any baleen whale. During the long northern winter, it lives in total darkness and in freezing cold water. There are four distinct populations: in the region between northeast

Bruce Krogman/National Marine Fisheries Service

Don Croll

LEFT: Confined to far northern waters, the bowhead readily swims beneath broad sheets of ice from one "lead" of ice-free water to another. Like the northern right whale, the bowhead sometimes swims upside down. It can then be identified from the air by its white chin and belly markings.

Canada and Greenland; in the Bering, Chukchi and Beaufort seas; in the Sea of Okhotsk; and in the North Atlantic (where it appears to be virtually extinct).

Bowheads were the next species—after right whales—to be hunted by the commercial whaling industry. They were first taken around Spitzbergen in the 1600s and, by about 1700, were already scarce in the area. The whalers turned their attentions to other populations elsewhere in the Arctic and had hunted bowheads to near extinction by 1900. The population in the western Arctic is probably recovering slowly, and the world population is currently estimated at more than 8,000 individuals. However, bowheads are still hunted in Alaska by the Inuit and about 60–70 animals are taken each year. While many biologists accept that this particular hunt is not a major threat to the growing western arctic population of bowheads, it remains controversial.

ABOVE: Yielding even more oil and baleen than the other members of the Balaenidae family, the bowhead has a huge head and an arched upper jaw, with baleen plates up to 4.5 meters or more in length. It is a strong, if slow, swimmer: a harpooned bowhead once towed a fully rigged whaling ship for more than 30 hours at a steady 2 knots.

RIGHT: Just as the industrial revolution created a host of new uses for whale oil, from wool processing to machine lubrication, new uses were found for baleen. It was employed in the making of corsets, umbrella staves, venetian blinds, window gratings and riding crops—even furniture springing and portable sheep pens.

THE PYGMY RIGHT WHALE

The pygmy right whale *Caperea marginata* is the smallest of the baleen whales and grows to a maximum length of about 6.5 meters. Like its larger relatives it has long baleen inside its mouth, but it is different in so many other ways (from anatomical differences in the ribcage to the presence of a dorsal fin) that it is classified in a distinct family of its own. It is found only in the Southern Hemisphere and, until quite recently, had been known almost entirely from strandings. Most records are from southern Australia (particularly Tasmania), New Zealand and South Africa. It seems that these coastlines are somewhere near the northern extreme of the range and it is possible that, like the larger right whales, the pygmy right whale migrates into subantarctic waters during the southern summer. Like its relatives, it also feeds on small crustaceans such as copepods.

When swimming, the fin of the pygmy right whale projects in much the same position and appears similar to that of the minke whale *Balaenoptera acutorostrata*. In fact, unless the distinctive head of the pygmy right is fully exposed, which is rare, the dorsal fin and back are easily mistaken for those of a minke whale. For this reason it may well be that this species is not as rare as has been believed.

Until recently, pygmy right whale sounds were unknown, but hydrophones adjacent to a solitary animal in Victoria, Australia, picked up on several occasions double thumps like the bang of a large drum. No other sound was recorded.

THE GRAY WHALE

The 12–14-meter-long gray whale *Eschrichtius robustus* has a number of features that are sufficiently distinctive to justify separation of the single species into a family of its own. Like right whales, the gray whale has no dorsal fin, but there is a low hump instead and a series of 6–12 "knuckles" along the upperside of the tailstock. The head has a curved upper jaw, but the mouth is not as markedly arched as in right whales and, consequently, the baleen plates suspended from it are considerably shorter. The baleen also has coarser bristles and the animal follows a different feeding regime. There are usually two (but sometimes up to seven) V-shaped or parallel throat grooves—compared with none in the right whales and as many as 100 in some of the rorquals. The coloration is basically gray, as the name suggests, but this is usually broken by white, yellow or even orange mottling to give a somewhat blotched effect.

Gray whales have a more rugged, less streamlined appearance than the rorquals and their moderate swimming speeds are closer to those of the more robust right whales. However, they are capable of short, high-speed bursts in

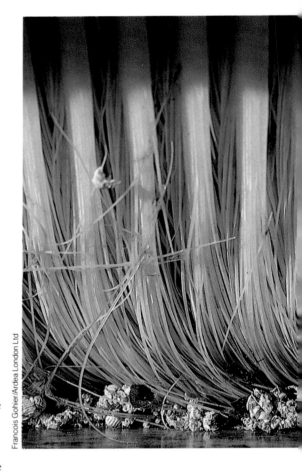

Francois Gohier/Ardea London Ltd

aggressive displays. They undertake long-distance seasonal migrations—possibly the longest migrations of all mammals—from low-latitude, warm water calving grounds in the winter to high-latitude, cold water feeding grounds in the summer.

The gray whale is the only baleen whale known to feed regularly in the sand and mud on the seabed. It literally sucks up the sediment, uses its baleen plates to filter out the benthic amphipods on which it feeds, and then discards the rest. For some reason unknown to scientists, most gray whales feed by rolling onto their right side—and the baleen on that side is often worn down—but a few "left-handed" individuals have been seen with their left-hand baleen plates worn away in a similar fashion.

Gray whales in the North Atlantic were extinct by the seventeenth or eighteenth century, possibly as a result of some unknown natural processes and merely speeded up by commercial whaling. They certainly occurred in the North Atlantic, but it is curious that they do not feature in many of the old whaling records, and we may never know for sure why they disappeared. In the North Pacific, however, they were hunted heavily. The western population has never really recovered and is poorly known: the estimated population of around 250 animals spends the summer in the Sea of Okhotsk and migrates down to the mainland coast of Asia for the winter.

G. L. Kooyman

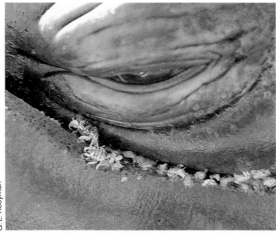

LEFT: The gray whale's eye, a little larger than that of an ox, is almost lost in its huge head. Nevertheless, it is functional both in water and in air, and can distinguish objects at some distance as well as at close range. Whale "lice" inhabit skin folds around the eye and throat grooves.

These animals are now among the world's most critically endangered large whales. In contrast, the eastern population has made an impressive recovery and the current population of around 21,000 may even be higher than pre-whaling levels; it has become one of the great success stories of conservation.

The majority of the eastern animals feed in the northern Bering, southern Chukchi and southwestern Beaufort seas during the summer, and breed along the Pacific coast of Baja California, Mexico, during the winter. They

BELOW: Gray whales feed primarily by stirring up bottom sediments, searching the seabed for small organisms and fish, but they also take mouthfuls of kelp from which they strain small creatures. Most grays are "right-sided" feeders, swimming on their sides to feed and wearing down the baleen plates on the right side of the mouth.

Gerard Wellington/Earthviews

RIGHT: Celebrated by Herman Melville as the most "gamesome and lighthearted" of the great whales, the humpback breaches more often than most other baleen whales and can leap almost clear of the water. This behavior is particularly common on the breeding grounds, but solitary humpbacks have been observed breaching by themselves, perhaps for sheer pleasure.

BELOW: The humpback's large head, enormous flippers and stocky body are in sharp contrast to the sleek, streamlined appearance of other rorquals. Like them, however, it has throat grooves that allow it to take in extraordinary amounts of water and to engulf schools of fish or shrimps by surfacing with its mouth agape.

are among the best studied and most watched whales anywhere in the world. In recent years, approximately 140 gray whales have been taken by the native people of the Chukotka Peninsula, in arctic Russia. But it is unlikely that this limited catch has a great impact on what is clearly a thriving population.

THE RORQUALS

This family of six species contains several of the largest of all whales, but also includes the minke, which is considerably smaller than some cetaceans in other families. All, however, share a number of features in common. Their overall shape is streamlined and they have a broad, flat head, a pointed snout, a distinctive dorsal fin, and relatively small pectoral fins. Above all, they have a series of longitudinal throat grooves, or pleats, extending from immediately under the chin to well behind the pectoral fins. Indeed, the word "rorqual" comes from the Norwegian word *rorhval*, which means furrow. The precise number of these furrows depends on the species but ranges from a minimum of 12 in humpback whales *Megaptera novaeangliae* to a maximum of 100 in fin whales *Balaenoptera physalus*. Their purpose is to allow a dramatic expansion of the throat— rather like the unfolding of a concertina—which increases the mouth capacity during feeding.

The amount of food required for the growth and maintenance of the huge rorquals, such as the fin whale and blue whale *Balaenoptera musculus*, is extraordinary. A blue whale, for example, probably eats about 4 percent of its own body weight every day during the feeding season which, for the largest individuals, equates to a daily consumption of 6–8 tonnes. The animals therefore have to ingest vast amounts of seawater from which to filter krill or small fish.

Rosemary Chastney/Ocean Images, Inc./Planet Earth Pictures

Rosemary Chastney/Ocean Images, Inc./Planet Earth Pictures

RIGHT: The impressive size of the blue whale becomes evident when it is compared (at a scale of 1:30) with a range of other mammals, down to the tiny field mouse.

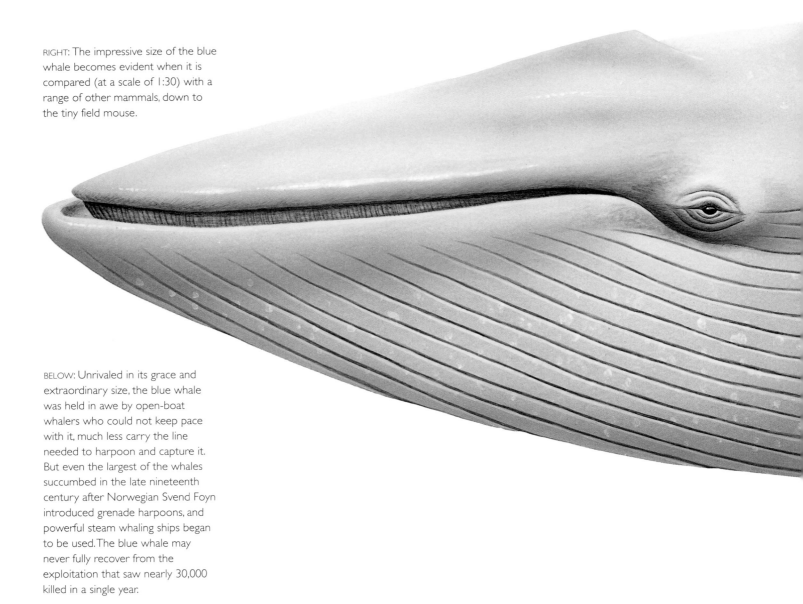

BELOW: Unrivaled in its grace and extraordinary size, the blue whale was held in awe by open-boat whalers who could not keep pace with it, much less carry the line needed to harpoon and capture it. But even the largest of the whales succumbed in the late nineteenth century after Norwegian Svend Foyn introduced grenade harpoons, and powerful steam whaling ships began to be used. The blue whale may never fully recover from the exploitation that saw nearly 30,000 killed in a single year.

Francois Gohier/Auscape International

Rorquals are active, relatively fast swimmers and most undergo extensive migrations from cool temperate or polar waters, where they feed, to warm temperate or subtropical waters, where they breed. Humpback whales undertake the most predictable migrations but, while the other species normally do migrate, we know considerably less about their precise movements and destinations.

The blue whale is the largest of the rorquals and, indeed, the largest animal ever to have lived on earth. Its heart alone is the size of a small car. It has been known to reach a maximum length of more than 33 meters and a maximum weight of 190 tonnes, although the norm is nearer 24–27 meters and 100–120 tonnes. These huge animals could produce many tonnes of valuable oil and, as technology improved, they became the prime target of twentieth-century whalers.

It has been estimated that more than 350,000 blue whales were killed, many of them in the waters surrounding Antarctica. In one whaling season alone (1930–31) no fewer than 28,325 blue whales were killed around the world. Not surprisingly, the blue whale is now an exceedingly rare animal and, although population estimates vary widely, there could be as few as 6,000–14,000 survivors.

After a gestation period of about 11 months, the female blue whale gives birth to a single calf some 6–8 meters long and weighing an incredible 2.5-4 tonnes. This giant baby drinks about 350 liters of fat-laden milk every day and grows at a phenomenal rate. By the time it is seven months old, and ready to be weaned, it is about 15 meters long. It will be another five years or more before it is sexually mature and ready to breed itself; the exact age of sexual maturity seems to depend, at least in part, on the availability of food. It is hard to estimate how long a blue whale can live, but most experts believe that it can reach an age of at least 70 years. However, in the twentieth century, few have been given the opportunity to live out their natural lives to the end.

The blue whale feeds almost exclusively on krill, which are captured primarily by speed: the

Francois Gohier/Auscape International

whale simply swims so fast that the krill do not have a chance to react and escape. There is some evidence that blue whales in the Northern Hemisphere also feed on shoals of pelagic red crabs, but this is believed to be rare.

In both hemispheres, most blue whales migrate to warmer waters for mating and calving. However, in some tropical areas they are observed year-round, which suggests either that they are permanently resident or that two different populations are using the same areas at different times of the year. Little is known about the routes taken by the migrating populations, or the precise locations of their preferred breeding grounds. They certainly seem to avoid close proximity to major shorelines, which makes tracking them rather difficult. It is most likely that the animals are widely dispersed across the oceans during the breeding phase.

There is one population of blue whales which, against all the odds, seems to be thriving. Approximately 2,000 animals live in the seas off

the coast of California, in the eastern North Pacific, and the number seems to be growing steadily. Sadly, elsewhere in the world, the news is not so good and blue whales are still struggling to survive.

The fin whale is second in size only to the blue whale. It reaches a length of about 18–22 meters (although, in exceptional circumstances, it can grow to more than 26 meters) and weighs anywhere from 30 to 80 tonnes. Also known as the finback, or razorback, it has a sharply defined ridge along the upperside of the tailstock behind the prominent dorsal fin. The relatively small pectoral fins are narrow and pointed. It is unusual among mammals in having assymetrical pigmentation: on the righthand side, the lower "lip," mouth cavity and some of the baleen plates are white, but on the lefthand side they are all uniformly gray. No one knows why this should be the case, but it is possible that fin whales use the bright white of the right lower jaw to startle and herd their prey more tightly.

ABOVE: Similar in appearance to blue and sei whales, at least at a distance, the fin whale is nevertheless a much faster swimmer. Dubbed the "greyhound of the sea," it can reach burst speeds of over 30 kilometers per hour.

Nigel Merrett/Seaphot Limited/Plant Earth Pictures

ABOVE: Different whales were pursued at different times during the history of commercial whaling. Their popularity depended on the market value of their products, the whaling techniques available at the time, and the availability of the species. The sei whale was at one time aggressively pursued.

After a gestation period of about 11–12 months, the newborn fin whale calf is about 6–6.5 meters in length and weighs some two tonnes. Like the blue whale, it is sexually mature at about five or six years, and probably lives in excess of 70–80 years. Fin whales are more cosmopolitan in their diet than blue whales and, although they feed mainly on krill in the Southern Ocean, they also eat a wide variety of small schooling fish. They are among the fastest of whales and, while they are feeding, can attain burst speeds of 30–40 kilometers per hour. At least half a million fin whales were killed by the commercial whaling industry and, in terms of sheer numbers killed, they were probably the favorite quarry of twentieth-century whalers. They were hunted in the North Atlantic until as recently as 1989.

The sei whale *Balaenoptera borealis* reaches an average length of 12–16 meters (although individuals as long as 21 meters have been recorded) and weighs some 20–30 tonnes. Its name comes from the Norwegian word *seje*, which means pollack or coalfish, and refers to one of its favorite items of prey. The sei is a versatile feeder and, in addition to small schooling fish, will also eat krill, copepods and some squid. It has a distinctive, falcate dorsal fin and the standard rorqual overall shape, but the bristles on the inside of the baleen plates are considerably finer than those of its larger relatives. Sei whales migrate between cold water feeding grounds in the summer (although they do not appear to penetrate into particularly high latitudes) and warm water breeding grounds in

the winter (where they seem to be well dispersed in offshore waters). Their migrations are not as predictable as in some other whales and, strangely, they sometimes appear in an area for a few days, weeks or months, and then disappear completely for years at a time. It has been estimated that as many as a quarter of a million sei whales were killed by commercial whalers and, although their population has been severely reduced, their numbers today are unclear.

The minke whale *Balaenoptera acutorostrata* is the smallest of the rorquals, reaching an average length of 7–10 meters and a weight of some 5–10 tonnes. It is found virtually worldwide, from the tropics right up to the edge of the pack ice in both hemispheres—individuals are even observed pushing their sharply pointed snouts through cracks between ice floes. They are usually more common in higher latitudes during the summer and lower latitudes during the winter, but their migrations appear to vary from region to region and from year to year. Minkes have a gestation period of 11–12 months and the calves are weaned when they are as young as five months. While krill is the favored food in the Southern Hemisphere, they feed on a variety of schooling fish and even copepods in the Northern Hemisphere. Minke whales were too small to be of much interest to commercial whalers until this century, but more than 150,000 have been killed in recent years and nearly 1,000 continue to be hunted annually by Norway and Japan combined.

Unlike the other rorquals, Bryde's whale *Balaenoptera edeni* does not penetrate into polar waters but is found mainly in tropical, subtropical

RIGHT: Bryde's whale is one of the smaller rorquals. Its limited distribution has tended to protect it from overexploitation, although some populations were depleted by whaling. Unusually for the true rorquals, it is often seen close to land, where it hunts coastal fishes.

Bernie Tershy and Craig Strong/Earthviews

Francois Gohier/Ardea London Ltd

and some warm temperate waters worldwide. It only appears in higher latitudes where there are warm water currents. Migrations are probably quite limited, although some offshore animals appear to migrate from tropical waters in winter to warm temperate waters in summer. Bryde's whales probably feed year-round on schooling fish while offshore animals, at least, also feed on krill. The inshore form is unique among baleen whales in breeding year-round, while the offshore form is a seasonal breeder. The gestation period is about 11–12 months and the newborn calf is 3.4–4 meters in length and a little under a tonne in weight.

It is almost impossible to tell how many Bryde's whales were killed by commercial whalers, since so many were incorrectly logged as fin whales or sei whales, but it is believed that at least 20,000 have been killed during the twentieth century. It does not appear to be in trouble and probably escaped the worst excesses of commercial whaling.

For a number of reasons, the highly distinctive humpback whale has become the best known and most intensively studied of all the large whales. Its scientific name, *Megaptera novaeangliae*, means "big-winged New Englander"—after the distinctive pectoral fins, or flippers, and the type specimen which came from New England. Indeed, its very large flippers, which are larger than those of blue whales more than twice its length, are probably its most distinctive feature. Each flipper can be up to a third of the animal's length—as much as 5 meters in some individuals. The humpback is distinctive in many other ways too and, while it belongs to the same family as the other rorquals, it is sufficiently different to justify classification in a separate genus. It is a very active animal at the water surface and can frequently be seen breaching, lobtailing and flipper slapping. Sometimes it will lift one or both flippers out of the water and lie upside-down to wave them in the air, like flags.

ABOVE: The humpback whale's scientific name, *Megaptera novaeangliae*, literally means "big-winged New Englander." The flippers are so long that they really do resemble wings—and the first scientifically described humpback was stranded, during the eighteenth century, on the New England coast.

DISTINCTIVE WHALE BLOWS

BRYDE'S WHALE
The hazy blow produced by Bryde's whale is variable in height, although, it rises to about 3–4 meters. It is rarely distinctive, especially if the whale exhales before breaking the surface.

SEI WHALE
The sei whale's blow appears as a single, narrow cloud. It resembles the blows of fin and blue whales, but reaches a height of only about 3 meters. Nor is it as dense as the fin or blue.

SPERM WHALE
The sperm whale's unique angled blow is extremely distinctive, and projects to a height of 2 meters or more. The blow is projected forward and to the left.

BOWHEAD WHALE
With two widely separated blowholes, the bowhead whale produces a rather bushy, V-shaped blow. The two diverging clouds of spray rise directly upward to a height of about 7 meters.

FIN WHALE
The fin whale's strong, straight blow appears as a tall, narrow column of spray. It is usually 4–6 meters high, and can be seen quite distinctly from a considerable distance.

RIGHT WHALES
The right whale produces a distinctive V-shaped blow, having widely separated blowholes like the bowhead. The plumes rise to a maximum height of about 5 meters.

BLUE WHALE
Blowing as soon as its head begins to break the surface, the blue whale produces a spectacular column of spray rising to 9 meters or more. It is the tallest and strongest blow of all whales.

GRAY WHALE
The gray whale's bushy blow is normally described as V-shaped, but sometimes the two plumes meet in the middle and produce a distinctive heart shape. They normally rise to 3–4.5 meters.

HUMPBACK WHALE
Rising to a height of about 2.5–3 meters, the single bushy blow of the humpback whale is surprisingly visible and distinctive. It is usually wide relative to its comparatively low height.

Duncan Murrell/Oxford Scientific Films

Humpbacks reach an average length of 11.5–15 meters and a weight of 25–30 tonnes. While they are comparable in length to some of the other rorquals, they are much more rotund and heavily built. After a gestation period of 11–12 months, the newborn calf is about 4–5 meters long and weighs 1–2 tonnes. The youngster is not weaned until it is about a year old, and sexual maturity occurs some four or five years later. The lifespan is unknown but probably exceeds 50 years.

Humpbacks are found from the poles to the tropics worldwide. However, they divide their year into four distinct periods: the summer is spent on high-latitude, cold water feeding grounds; the autumn on migration; the winter on low-latitude, warm water breeding grounds; and the spring on migration. Some of the distances they travel are enormous. One particular population migrates all the way from its feeding grounds around the Antarctic Peninsula to its breeding grounds off the coast of Colombia, which is north of the equator; others travel from as far afield as Norway, Iceland, Greenland, Newfoundland and the Gulf of Maine to their breeding grounds in the Caribbean.

In antarctic waters humpbacks feed mainly on krill, but in the Northern Hemisphere they also take a variety of small schooling fish such as herring, sand lance and capelin. They are gulp-feeders and lunge into a prey school with their mouths wide open. However, within this basic framework, they employ an ingenious variety of feeding techniques depending on the location and prey. In some places, they even stun the krill or fish with slaps of their flippers or flukes.

Some of the most extraordinary feeding techniques involve the use of bubbles: either bubble clouds, which somehow trap or concentrate the prey, and are most common in the North Atlantic, or bubble nets, which are more commonly seen in the North Pacific. In bubblenetting, the animals circle below the concentration of prey and, as they slowly spiral toward the surface, gently expel air. The resulting bubbles rise to the surface and gradually form a screen, or net, with the prey animals trapped inside. When the net is complete, the whales then swim toward the surface with their mouths wide open and engulf the food. As many as 20 humpbacks may work together to form a single bubble net and, almost rubbing shoulders, can be seen emerging from the surface together—a spectacular sight as they rise 5 or 6 meters into the air with their mouths wide open and hundreds of fish leaping for their lives.

ABOVE: The number and length of throat pleats in rorquals vary between species. Humpbacks have no more than 36, while fin whales may have up to 100 pleats.

ABOVE: The humpback whale has been studied in the wild for more than two decades and is now one of the better known species of large whale. Long-term studies continue in many parts of the world, from Alaska to Antarctica.

The humpback whale suffered badly during the whaling era, when as many as a quarter of a million were killed. Being a slow swimmer, and often coastal in its habits, it made a relatively easy target. Huge numbers were killed in the Northern Hemisphere, but the greatest damage was done in the Southern Ocean, around Antarctica, where more than 200,000 have been killed during this century alone. The humpback received official protection in 1966, but many thousands have been killed illegally since. Overall, it has been estimated that 95 percent of the original population was wiped out, leaving a small remnant population struggling for survival.

Fortunately, the humpback is one of the few species making a strong comeback in many parts of the world and, while today's population is still well below its pre-exploitation levels, there could be as many as 20,000 and the numbers continue to grow. Nevertheless, it is not safe yet—and faces many new threats ranging from pollution to entanglement in fishing nets—but it has a fairly promising future.

The islanders of Bequia, an island belonging to St. Vincent and the Grenadines, in the Caribbean, are permitted to take two humpbacks every year in a small native fishery which persists to this day.

Humpback whales are often studied with the help of the distinctive black and white markings on the underside of their tail flukes. They usually lift their flukes before a deep dive and, consequently, it is possible to see these markings quite clearly. They range from almost all black to almost all white and include myriad patterns of black and white in between. A tail with a predominantly black background, for example, may have a variety of distinctive blotches, spots, lines and other patterns in white. No two humpbacks have identical markings—making these individual colors and patterns the equivalent of our own fingerprints.

With experience, it is possible to tell one animal from another simply by peering underneath its tail but, since the risk of human error is still high, most whale biologists do not rely merely on sight and memory. They prefer to take photographs of the markings instead, a technique known as photo-identification. Over several decades thousands of individual humpbacks have been photo-identified by their fluke markings and have been included in catalogs of whales in the North Atlantic, North Pacific and in the Southern Hemisphere. In this way, it is possible for biologists to follow the movements and activities of individual whales over a long period.

BALEEN WHALE PARASITES

A variety of organisms attach themselves to the skin of whales and even more live inside their bodies. Not all of them are parasitic, and some appear to do no serious harm.

Copepods, protozoans, algae and diatoms (which form a thin, yellow-green film) all live on the skin of whales. But the two most common external parasites on baleen whales are whale lice and barnacles. Despite their name, whale lice are not related to the lice of land animals but are actually cyamid crustaceans. The number of whale lice found on a whale seems to be inversely proportional to its swimming speed—more are found on slow-swimming right whales than on any other species. Barnacles are not usually species-specific, although they tend to avoid the fast-moving rorquals. There are three different kinds: acorn barnacles, stalked or ship barnacles, and pseudo-stalked barnacles. They all derive nourishment from the host (although the pseudo-stalked is the only one which actually burrows into the skin) yet none of them appears to cause any infection or inflammation.

Gray whales are probably more heavily infested with external parasites than any other whale—indeed, a large gray may carry several hundred kilograms of barnacles alone. Barnacles are embedded in the hide, especially on the head, back and tail, while whale lice (each up to about 2.5 centimeters long) infest barnacle clusters and folds of skin over much of the whale's body. The skin of humpback whales is also covered in barnacles, which live even along the leading edges of the pectoral fins.

But perhaps the most noticeable parasites live on the callosities on the heads of northern and southern right whales. These remarkable patches of rough skin are covered in whale lice. The lice make the callosities appear whitish yellow, orange or pink. Barnacles and parasitic worms also live

on these growths which, strangely, occur in the same areas as hair in humans: on the top of the head, above the eyes, on the upper "lip" and on the chin. On some species of baleen whales, an infrequent but sometimes conspicuous parasite is a modified copepod, called *Pennella*, which burrows into the blubber with its abdomen protruding and hanging down rather like a long streamer.

Whales are also afflicted by a great many internal parasites, including roundworms in the stomach, mites in the lungs, nematodes in the kidneys and urino-genital system, parasitic flukes in the brain, and tapeworms and thorn-headed worms in the intestines. Severe infestations of these parasites can cause weakness or even death. One study concluded that over half the natural mortality of fin whales was the result of a nematode in the liver, causing renal failure. If this is fairly typical, then mortality from parasites could be signficant.

LEFT: Parasites and commensals commonly evolve in concert with their hosts: each of the great whales has its own population of specialized barnacles. These barnacles hitch a free ride to good feeding areas and then filter small plankton or the whales' own scraps from the water around them.

BELOW: "Whale lice"—which are actually crustaceans—are found in folds around the eyes, flippers and throat grooves, and commonly infest barnacle gatherings and wart like callosities.

LEFT: "Whale lice" can feed on shedding skin or unhealed wounds. This afflicted injured northern right whale may have been entangled in a rope or net.

BALEEN WHALE SONGS

For centuries, open-boat whalers were aware that baleen whales made sounds. But biologists were not convinced, and wrongly assumed that they were mute because anatomical studies of the whales had revealed that none of them possessed vocal chords. In recent years, it has been suggested that baleen whales use the larynx to produce sound although, in the absence of vocal chords, it is still not clear exactly how. It is also unclear how they hear sound. The ear canal, which in humans and other mammals is open, is closed by a wax plug in baleen whales—and the sound-receiving pan bone in the lower jaw of toothed whales is absent.

The earliest recordings of large whales were made by accident in the early 1950s by the military, listening underwater off Bermuda and Hawaii, when long underwater moans and complicated sounds were recorded. At the time, they could not be identified. But later, William Schevill, who helped to pioneer the recording of toothed whales both in the field and in studies in captivity, managed to identify some of the recordings as humpback whales. These days, high-tech underwater microphones, or hydrophones, are used as an integral part of whale studies around the world—and are proving invaluable in increasing our knowledge of whale biology, ecology, movements and numbers. Perhaps the most exciting development in this field came recently from the US Navy, which gave whale biologists access to a vast network of top-secret hydrophones in the North Atlantic and North Pacific. The hydrophones were originally established to listen for Soviet submarines, but are now being used to listen for whales over entire ocean basins and to track individual animals over hundreds or even thousands of kilometers.

Sound can be better for long-distance communication than sight. It travels nearly five times faster in water than in air, and low frequencies may travel very long distances indeed (hundreds or even thousands of kilometers in some cases). Baleen whale sounds include rather low-frequency moans, belches, bellows, snorts, bubbling, knocks, grunts and yelps.

The blue whale has the loudest and deepest voice in the animal kingdom. Vocalizing at frequencies as low as 10 Hz—which is far below our range of hearing—the volume can be as high as 180 decibels. Whether or not blue whales use these sounds to communicate over entire oceans is unclear. An alternative explanation is that they use them as a form of long-distance echolocation, enabling the whales to map large areas of ocean for navigational purposes. Even if they are communicating over shorter distances of 10 or 15 kilometers this has some interesting repercussions, since it could mean that blue whales traveling a relatively long distance apart may actually be part of a single group. Fin whales also have deep, loud voices that travel long distances underwater.

The most extraordinary baleen whale songs are made by humpback whales. In the early 1970s, their low grunts, chirps, squeals, whistles and wails made them the only animals to have achieved a hit record in the pop charts—when a recording of their unearthly sounds was released to an unsuspecting world for

the first time. Even today, we continue to marvel at their complexity and attempt to understand their purpose.

A singing humpback hangs almost upside-down in the water, with its head pointing toward the seabed. It may sing throughout the day and night—and may continue for 24 hours or longer with hardly a break. A song can last anything from a few minutes to as

Al Giddings/Seaphot Limited/Planet Earth Pictures

long as half an hour. As soon as the whale has finished, it pauses briefly to catch its breath and then goes back to the beginning and sings the same song all over again. Each song consists of between two and nine main components, which are always sung in the same order but are forever being refined and improved. This means that the song heard one day is quite different from the one being sung several months later. Which whales initiate these changes, and why, is still a mystery. All the humpacks in one area sing broadly the same song, incorporating each other's

improvizations as they go along. In this way, the entire composition changes over a period of about five years. Even more extraordinary is the fact that humpbacks in other parts of the world sing very different compositions.

Since most of the singing takes place at the breeding grounds, and is conducted exclusively by males, it is probably used to attract females and to warn away unwanted competition from rival males. But it is also possible that the songs have more subtle meanings and nuances that we do not yet understand.

TOOTHED WHALES

The feature that unites all of the toothed whales is the possession of teeth. Unlike baleen whales, which have developed whalebone to sieve enormous numbers of prey animals from the water, toothed whales have perpetuated what was apparently the feeding mode employed by the earliest whales more than 45 million years ago: selecting and capturing individual prey. In more highly evolved toothed whales the trend has been toward simplification of all the teeth to single roots and conical crowns as well as an increase in the number of teeth. However, some highly evolved species of toothed whales have lost most of their teeth or developed specialized teeth. The narwhal Monodon monoceros has even developed a tusk. Some of the species that have undergone tooth loss have developed horny thickenings on the palate or the gums instead.

It is interesting that the same specialized changes in dentition have occurred independently in several different families of toothed whales. Thus we see reduction or loss of the upper jaw teeth in species as different as the sperm whale, most of the beaked whales, and Risso's dolphin as an adaptation to eating squid.

BELOW: Separated from the baleen whales by the obvious distinction of possessing teeth, the odontocetes or toothed whales are generally fast swimmers and feed by chasing individual fish and squid. They are widespread in a great variety of habitats, from freshwater rivers to deep oceans.

A DIVERSE GROUP

The most remarkable thing about toothed whales is their diversity. They demonstrate an incredible range of forms, behavior and lifestyles that reflect their long evolutionary history and the variety of environments in which they live. There are toothed whales that are exclusively marine, some that live exclusively in fresh water, and some that can move between the two.

Interestingly, the habit of living in fresh water has evolved independently in several different groups. First, the river dolphins—four out of five species in three closely related families—are exclusively freshwater-dwelling. Second, the finless porpoise *Neophocaena phocaenoides* likes mangroves and estuaries, but has a strictly freshwater population in China's Yangtze River. Third, the Irrawaddy dolphin *Orcaella brevirostris* is at home both in rivers and in the ocean. Last, there are two other members of the dolphin family—the Indo-Pacific humpback dolphin *Sousa chinensis* which moves between salt and fresh water, and the tucuxi *Sotalia fluviatilis*, which has both marine and

exclusively freshwater populations (including one population in the Amazon Basin). It is remarkable that so many species are able to live in both salt and fresh water, and more remarkable that some can move between these differing environments.

The diversity of the toothed whales extends to every facet of their biology and ecology. Reproductive strategies, migration patterns and even daily activities vary greatly among species—allowing different species to occupy the same areas while minimizing competition for resources. Nevertheless, a rich source of food will attract many species of toothed whales, especially dolphins. It is possible to see massive feeding aggregations out at sea that may include bottlenose dolphins *Tursiops truncatus*, long-finned pilot whales *Globicephala melas*, Risso's dolphins, rough-toothed dolphins *Steno bredanensis* and other species.

THE HUMAN PROBLEM

The numerous and diverse adaptations of toothed whales have not helped them to escape the many

Bernd Würsig

ABOVE: A typically active coastal inhabitant of cool temperate waters around New Zealand, southern Africa and South America, the dusky dolphin has up to 144 simple, conical teeth with which to grasp its prey.

THE REMARKABLE SPERM WHALES

WILLIAM H. DAWBIN

There are three species of sperm whale—the "great" sperm whale *Physeter macrocephalus*, the pygmy sperm whale *Kogia breviceps* and the dwarf sperm whale *Kogia simus*. The two smaller species were once rarely seen at sea, but there have been many more sightings in recent years. Their larger relative is one of the better known cetaceans, although many aspects of its life are still shrouded in mystery.

The three species differ greatly in size, ranging from the 15–18-meter male and 11–12-meter female sperm whale to the 3-meter pygmy sperm whale and the 2.1–2.7-meter dwarf sperm whale. But they share a number of features that are not found in other cetaceans. The top of the head projects well beyond the tip of the narrow lower jaw, which fits into a grovelike channel above and carries the only functional teeth. In the front of the head, above the upper jaw, there is a spermaceti organ containing a unique waxlike substance that differs markedly from the oils of baleen whales. This probably plays a role in adjusting buoyancy during the changing pressures encountered on deep dives, and may also be used to focus sonar clicks. The spermaceti organ in the pygmy and dwarf sperm whales is smaller in scale but of similar chemical structure to that of the larger sperm whale.

The sperm whale has a triangular or rounded hump and a series of "knuckles," instead of a dorsal fin, while the two smaller species have small fins. The sexes are very different in size, in sperm whales, and they live separately for much of the year. There is no size difference between the sexes in the dwarf and pygmy sperm whales, and they are normally solitary or form small groups. All three species are deep divers—the sperm whale may be able to reach depths of 3,000 meters—and they feed mainly on squid.

The sperm whale produced the finest and most valuable oil, not from its blubber, but from the spermaceti organ inside its huge, cavernous head. Known as spermaceti oil, it was initially used to make high-quality candles but later became a sought-after lubricant. Not surprisingly, the sperm whale became a major target of commercial whalers and was hunted from 1714 until it received official protection in 1984. More sperm whales were killed than any other large whale species, yet their population was never reduced to the critically low levels of most of the baleen whales. It is still present in fairly substantial numbers in all oceans.

The gestation period in sperm whales is exceptionally long—at 16–17 months it is considerably longer than that of any baleen whale. The calves are normally nursed for about two or three years, although nursing has been documented in animals as old as 12 years. Sexual maturity is reached at 8–12 years in females and more than 10 years in males.

Although not their only food, deepwater giant squid form a major part of the diet of sperm whales in some parts of the world. They also eat a variety of other squid species, as well as octopus and various kinds of fish. Their deep dives in search of food are remarkable—in tropical waters, for example, a dive will range from 25° Celsius in sparkling sunshine at the surface to just above freezing and total darkness near the seabed.

pygmy sperm whale

P.S. Hammond/Sea Mammal Research Unit

ABOVE: In the past 35 years, commercial tuna fishing in the eastern tropical Pacific has been responsible for the deaths of more dolphins—as many as half a million every year—than any other human activity. The recent introduction of new regulations has reduced the scale of the slaughter to several thousand every year, though it is still too many.

Robert Pitman/Earthviews

ABOVE: Pantropical spotted dolphins sometimes gather in herds of several thousand individuals and commonly associate with yellowfin tuna.

threats posed by humans, which include hunting, destructive fishing methods and pollution.

Hunting has been a major problem in the past and, for some species, is still a serious threat. Toothed whales are killed for a variety of reasons but, in modern times, it is usually to provide meat for human consumption or as scapegoats for badly managed fisheries. Species such as the sperm whale and the long-finned pilot whale have been the focus of intensive whaling operations. An estimated one million sperm whales were killed by commercial whalers before 1984, when they were given official protection, and they are probably still being killed illegally by pirate whalers. Pilot whales have been hunted around the Faeroe Islands, a group of Danish islands in the northeast Atlantic, for several centuries— and, even today, an average of 1,200 are killed every year.

Some species have been hunted for more unusual but often valuable products: the narwhal *Monodon monoceros* for its ivory, for example; and the Amazon river dolphin *Inia geoffrensis* for its eyes and reproductive organs, which were dried and sold as an aphrodisiac.

Commercial fishing is probably the greatest threat today—and around the world accounts for the deaths of hundreds of thousands, or even millions, of toothed whales every year. Driftnets— probably the most indiscriminate method of fishing ever devised—and coastal gillnets are largely to blame. In the past 35 years, however, the tuna-fishing industry probably killed more dolphins than any other human activity: it was directly responsible for the deaths of some six to 12 million pantropical spotted dolphins *Stenella attenuata* and long-snouted spinner dolphins *Stenella longirostris*, and several other species. Industry regulations were introduced a few years ago and, fortunately, the death toll has dropped dramatically.

Pollution seriously threatens the future of cetaceans around the world. Ever-increasing quantities of industrial waste, agricultural chemicals, untreated sewage, radioactive discharges, oil, plastic debris and a huge variety of other pollutants are dumped into seas and rivers every day. Some of them cause immediate death, while others are more subtle in their effects and may be responsible for prolonged suffering. While few places are free of pollution, species living in rivers and partly enclosed waters such as the Baltic Sea, Black Sea and North Sea are particularly hard hit. Belugas living in the Gulf of St. Lawrence, in Canada, for example, have such high levels of mercury, PCBs, DDT and other pollutants in their bodies that when they are washed ashore they are effectively toxic waste.

Not all human interactions with toothed whales are hostile. For example, fishermen in a number of countries cooperate with dolphins, which help to drive fish into their nets; the dolphins are then rewarded with a share of the catch. Meanwhile, at Monkey Mia, in Western Australia, a small group of wild bottlenose dolphins has been greeting tourists in shallow water at the beach for more than 30 years.

BEAKED WHALES

The beaked whales, family Ziphiidae, are small to medium-size pelagic whales that feed primarily on squid. Many members of the family appear to be rare or, at least, they are rarely seen; little is known about their biology or population sizes. Most species have a small dorsal fin set far back on the body and, unlike the majority of other cetaceans, they usually lack a notch in their tail flukes.

The general evolutionary trend in beaked whales has been toward a reduction in the number of teeth. The females of most species have no teeth at all, or at least their teeth remain invisible. In most males, there are no teeth in the upper jaw and just two or four teeth in the lower jaw—and these are generally quite large and often extravagant in shape. In some species, they have developed into tusks and in one, the strap-toothed whale *Mesoplodon layardii*, they grow over the top of the upper jaw and sometimes even meet in the middle. The main exceptions are Shepherd's beaked whale *Tasmacetus shepherdi*, the only member of the family with a full set of functional teeth, which occur in both jaws of both sexes, and Gray's beaked whale *Mesoplodon grayi*, in which both sexes have rows of tiny vestigial teeth in the upper jaw and the male has a single pair of large teeth in the lower jaw.

Baird's beaked whale *Berardius bairdii* is one of the better known beaked whales and, since it is capable of reaching a length of more than 12 meters, is probably the largest member of the family. It forms organized herds normally consisting of three to 30 animals, including adults of both sexes and their young, and appears to live in tight

strap-toothed whale

Sowerby's beaked whale

LEFT: Two species of beaked whales, genus *Mesoplodon*. While Sowerby's was the first to be described, it remains one of the most elusive. The strap-toothed whale reaches 6 meters and is one of the largest beaked whales.

social groups. It is a deep diver and, although it can probably stay underwater for more than an hour, dives of 25 to 35 minutes are more common. This species was being hunted even before it had been officially recognized and classified by scientists; the Japanese still take 40 to 60 every year, in an area near Tokyo and off Hokkaido Island. Baird's beaked whale is confined to the North Pacific. The similar Arnoux's beaked whale *B. arnuxii* occurs only in the Southern Hemisphere, below 34° South.

Cuvier's beaked whale *Ziphius cavirostris* is probably one of the most widespread and abundant members of the family and is found worldwide in tropical, subtropical and temperate waters. Also known as the goose-beaked whale, because of the strange shape of its head, it is sometimes seen on whale-watch trips in the Mediterranean, the Canary Islands, Hawaii and in the Drake Passage between southern South America and Antarctica. The older males are often heavily scarred from the teeth of other males.

The largest genus of beaked whales is *Mesoplodon*, which includes a total of 15 species. Most of them are rare and poorly known. Sowerby's beaked whale *M. bidens* was the first of the beaked whales to be discovered, when a lone animal was found stranded in Scotland in 1800; it was formally described four years later. Blainville's beaked whale *M. densirostris* was formally described a few years later, in 1817, from a small piece of jaw. The bone structure is extremely dense—even denser than elephant ivory—which gives it its other common name: the dense-beaked whale. The male is very distinctive, with a pair of massive teeth, like horns, that grow from huge bulges in the lower jaw. The most prominent feature of the aptly named strap-toothed whale *M. layardii* is a pair of enormous teeth up to 30 centimeters long, which occur only in the male and project upward and backward from the lower jaw. These prevent older animals from opening their mouths properly.

There have been a number of confirmed sightings of Gray's beaked whale *M. grayi* at sea, although most available information is from stranded animals. Found in the cool temperate waters of the Southern Hemisphere, it probably forms small herds, although up to 28 animals have been known to strand together. Hector's beaked whale *M. hectori* is one of the smaller beaked whales, and appears to be extremely rare since it is known from only about 20 stranded specimens

in the Southern Hemisphere and the eastern North Pacific. Gervais' beaked whale *M. europaeus* was first recorded in the English Channel in the 1840s—hence its Latin name—although it is mainly known from the western North Atlantic.

Andrew's beaked whale *M. bowdoini* and True's beaked whale *M. mirus* are known mainly from a small number of strandings. Stejneger's beaked whale *M. stejnegeri* is also poorly known, but has been observed at sea. The males are quite distinctive, with two massive, laterally compressed teeth in the center of a strongly arched mouthline. The ginkgo-toothed beaked whale *M. ginkgodens* also has strange teeth. As its name suggests, the teeth of the male are shaped like the leaves of the ginkgo tree—a common tree in Japan. Hubb's beaked whale *M. carlhubbsi* is another strange-looking animal—the male has a strongly arched lower jaw and a raised white "cap" around the blowhole. It is found in the cold temperate waters of the eastern and western North Pacific.

Longman's beaked whale *M. pacificus* is perhaps the rarest of all the beaked whales, and indeed of all whales. Believed to occur in deep tropical waters of the Indian and Pacific oceans, it is known from only two beached skulls, one in Australia and the other in Somalia, and one confirmed sighting.

Several new *Mesoplodon* species have been discovered in recent years. The most recent was Bahamonde's beaked whale *M. bahamondi*, which is known only from a strange skull found on Robinson Crusoe Island, in the Juan Fernandez islands off Chile; it was officially named in 1996. The so-called unidentified beaked whale *Mesoplodon species* "A" could possibly belong to the same species, since it is known only from about 30 sightings in the eastern tropical Pacific. Unfortunately, no stranded or dead specimens have been found, so it has yet to be properly named. The Peruvian beaked whale or lesser beaked whale *M. peruvianus* is also found in the eastern tropical Pacific; it is known only from a few specimens and was officially named in 1991.

ABOVE: The two teeth in the lower jaw of the male strap-toothed whale grow up and over the upper jaw, sometimes wrapping right around it. These teeth may be a sexual characteristic to help determine the fittest males for mating.

There are two species of bottlenose whale. The northern bottlenose whale *Hyperoodon ampullatus* is found in the cold temperate waters of the North Pacific and is the better known of the two. Its counterpart in the colder waters of the Southern Hemisphere is the southern bottlenose whale *H. planifrons*. The two animals are very similar in appearance, with huge, bulbous foreheads and distinct dolphinlike beaks. Northern bottlenose whales have been hunted more than any other beaked whale, and tens of thousands have been killed during the past century. The southern bottlenose whale is rarely observed at sea and has never been heavily exploited.

WHITE WHALES

The family Monodontidae includes the narwhal *Monodon monoceros* and the beluga *Delphinapterus leucas*. Some researchers also include the Irrawaddy dolphin *Orcaella brevirostris* which, indeed, looks a little like a beluga and shares a number of characteristics in common; however, it has many features which put it in the oceanic dolphin family.

Narwhals and belugas live in the cold waters of the Arctic and subarctic. They are similar in size—reaching a maximum length of about 5 meters—and in shape. They have blunt,

rounded heads and very short beaks. Both species lack a dorsal fin (but they have a low ridge along the center of the back) and their pectoral fins are small and rounded.

The beluga, or white whale, gives the family its common name, although its all-white body color can also appear yellowish and young animals are much darker. The seasonal movements of belugas are highly variable, depending on the location and ice conditions, but most populations do not make extensive migrations. In winter they tend to form small groups of five to 20, but in summer they gather in enormous herds of 1,000 or more in estuaries and major rivers. They have been known to swim hundreds of kilometers up rivers and have little fear of shallow waters.

Belugas are among the most vocal of all cetaceans and their diverse range of sounds includes loud clicks, yelps, squeaks and shrill whistles. They can be heard through the hull of a boat, or from above the surface of the water, and are sometimes called "sea canaries."

Belugas have been hunted by native peoples in many parts of the Arctic for centuries, and there has been over-hunting by commercial operators during the twentieth century. In some parts of their range, they are threatened by oil and gas exploration and pollution. The total

BELOW: Belugas in the shallows of Somerset Island, in the Canadian Arctic. Whale-watching expeditions have made these whales much more accessible.

Doug Allan/Oxford Scientific Films

Fred Bruemmer

world population is estimated to be between 50,000 and 70,000 animals. There are five main populations: in high arctic Canada and Greenland; Hudson Bay and James Bay, Canada; the Gulf of St. Lawrence, Canada; the Svalbard area; and in the Bering, Chukchi and Okhotsk seas.

The narwhal is best known for the tusk of the male. Resembling a gnarled and twisted walking stick, it is unlike any other cetacean feature. It is actually a tooth: when the male is about one year old, one of only two teeth in the upper jaw—the

left-hand tooth—erupts and grows to a length of 2–3 meters. Very occasionally, females have tusks and males have two tusks. For many years, narwhal tusks were sold as the horns of the legendary unicorn. Many interesting theories have been proposed for the purpose of the tusk, including spearfishing, grubbing for food and even drilling through ice (it has since been discovered that the forehead is used to break through sea ice and form breathing holes). In fact, it is primarily for display and is used to compete for females—in a similar

ABOVE: The narwhal's bizarre tusk has inspired steady hunting pressure since the Middle Ages. Until early in the seventeenth century, the tusk was sold for an exorbitant price as the horn of the legendary unicorn. Canadian and Greenland Inuit still hunt narwhals, with a combined annual quota of several hundred.

way to deer using their antlers. It is estimated that about one-third of adult males have broken or damaged tusks. Narwhals form small family pods of up to 25 individuals, although aggregations of as many as several thousand move seasonally with the advancing and retreating sea ice.

The narwhal has been hunted for centuries by European and Inuit peoples, and is still hunted in northern Canada and Greenland. The world population is estimated to be 25,000–45,000. Both narwhals and belugas are preyed upon by orcas and polar bears.

PORPOISES

There are six different porpoises in the family Phocoenidae. They are sufficiently different from the dolphins (family Delphinidae) to warrant a separate family, and are typically smaller and more robust. Porpoises have no distinct beak, a small, rounded head, small flippers and, in all species except the finless porpoise, a well-defined dorsal fin. They live mainly along the coast, although finless porpoises *Neophocaena phocaenoides* also occur in major rivers and spectacled porpoises *Australophocaena dioptrica* and Dall's porpoises *Phocoenoides dalli* can be seen offshore as well as in their coastal environment.

Dall's porpoise behaves more like a hyperactive dolphin than a shy, retiring porpoise and will often race around boats or ride the bow waves. Striking black and white in color, it is found in the northern North Pacific. Its vertebral column is one of most highly evolved of any cetacean: the numerous vertebrae are extremely compressed front to rear with exceptionally long spines. This increase in the number of vertebrae is commensurate with increased trunk muscle mass, and undoubtedly explains why Dall's porpoise is one of the fastest, strongest swimmers of all cetaceans. Capable of reaching speeds of more than 50 kilometers an hour, it is easily recognized by the distinctive spray of water, known as the "rooster tail," that comes off the forehead as it surfaces.

Dall's porpoises are found in small schools of up to 20 animals, although several hundred may gather together in large feeding aggregations. They eat a variety of small schooling fish, such as hake, herring, mackerel and capelin, as well as squid. Their population is unknown, although they are probably numbered in hundreds of thousands. The number has been depleted in recent years as a direct result of various Japanese, Taiwanese and South Korean fishing operations. Some are killed incidentally in salmon and squid nets, but in some parts of the world they are killed specifically for human consumption.

The harbor porpoise *Phocoena phocoena* is seen singly, in pairs or in small groups of up to a dozen animals; occasionally, several hundred may gather together on good feeding grounds. Although the most commonly seen and best studied member of

ABOVE: Strikingly marked, the Dall's porpoise has a vertebral column extensively modified to give it extraordinary speed: this species of the northern North Pacific can reach burst speeds of more than 50 kilometers per hour.

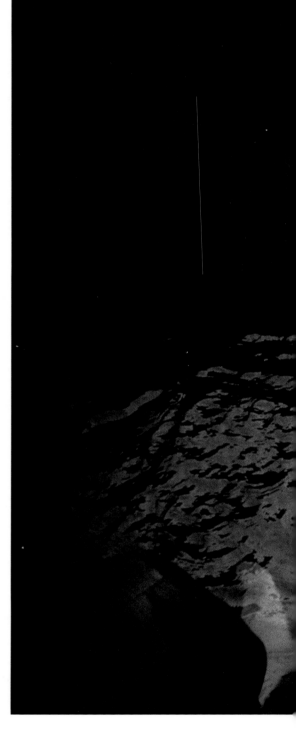

the family, it is difficult to observe closely and is typically wary of boats. It may make arc-shaped leaps when chasing prey, but otherwise does not leap out of the water and remains fairly inconspicuous. Found mainly in cool, coastal waters in the Northern Hemisphere, it faces many threats and its numbers have declined in some parts of the range. It gets caught in fishing nets, suffers habitat loss and disturbance near urban areas and in shipping lanes, and is still hunted in some areas. It is probably the shortest lived cetacean, and rarely survives longer than about 12 years.

Ken Balcomb/Earthviews

The harbor porpoise's two closest relatives are the vaquita *Phocoena sinus* and Burmeister's porpoise *Phocoena spinipinnis*. Burmeister's porpoise, found off the east and west coasts of South America, is a shy and little-known animal. Although it is easy to overlook, it may be one of the most abundant small cetaceans living around southern South America. It is best distinguised from all other cetaceans by its small size, dark appearance at sea and backward-pointing dorsal fin. Burmeister's porpoises are hunted for food and crab bait and are caught incidentally in gillnets. The vaquita, or Gulf of California porpoise, is under even greater threat and is now one of the rarest and most endangered of all cetaceans. Found only in shallow lagoons in and around the Colorado River delta in the northern Gulf of California, Mexico, it is also one of the smallest of all cetaceans and grows to a maximum of 1.5 meters. Its population continues to decline as a result of incidental catches in gillnets and habitat destruction, and there may be fewer than 200 survivors. In 1993, the Mexican government established the Upper Gulf of California Biosphere Reserve to protect the vaquita and its habitat—but this urgently needed protection may be too little too late.

ABOVE: The finless porpoise is one of the smallest cetaceans. It is rarely seen more than 5 kilometers from shore and often penetrates fresh water, with populations far upstream in several major rivers in Asia.

Nicholas Tapp/Seaphot Limited/Planet Earth Pictures

ABOVE: The Atlantic white-sided dolphin is a large and robust animal, frequently seen in the cool temperate and subarctic waters of the northern North Atlantic. It is a fast swimmer and can sometimes be seen bow-riding in front of large whales.

The finless porpoise inhabits tropical and temperate coastal waters, and estuaries and rivers in the Indian Ocean and southwest Asia. Rarely found more than five kilometers from shore, it can be seen alone or in small schools of up to 10 individuals. These schools may aggregate into groups of up to 50 on good feeding grounds. There is a permanent population of finless porpoises in the Yangtze River, China, where they occasionally associate with Yangtze river dolphins; these particular animals are restricted to fresh water. Many finless porpoises live near large population centers in Asia and, consequently, suffer badly from shipping traffic, dams and pollution.

The spectacled porpoise is poorly known, mostly from strandings. Found along the southern Atlantic coast of South America, and certain offshore islands in the Southern Hemisphere, it is rarely sighted at sea. However, it is believed to be more common than this would suggest.

DOLPHINS AND OTHER SMALL TOOTHED WHALES

With a total of 33 different species, the Delphinidae is the largest and most diverse cetacean family. It includes all the oceanic dolphins as well as orcas, pilot whales and their relatives.

Most delphinids feed on fish or squid, or both, although some also take cuttlefish and octopus, a variety of crustaceans and even marine mammals. Extinct species were mainly generalists and had snouts of intermediate length and width. But modern species have a wide variety of skeletal, dental and other physical adaptations reflecting their varied diets and lifestyles.

Some extreme anatomical adaptations have evolved in members of this family. They range from the tiny black dolphin and the equally small Hector's dolphin, each as little as 1.2 meters in length, to the male orca, which can attain a length of up to 9.8 meters. Some species are highly conspicuous, with spectacular spots, brightly colored stripes or striking black and white markings, while a few are relatively drab and gray. Some are long and slender and have prominent beaks, while others are much stockier and have poorly defined beaks. Some have enormous dorsal fins, others have scythe-shaped fins or triangular fins, and two have no fins at all.

The Indo-Pacific humpback dolphin *Sousa chinensis* is interesting because it does not always have a humped back: individuals found west of Sumatra, in Indonesia, do have an elongated hump in the middle of the back, while those living in the east have a more prominent dorsal fin but no hump. The closely related Atlantic humpback dolphin *Sousa teuszii* lives in the coastal waters of tropical West Africa. It is well known for cooperating with Mauritanian fishermen by driving fish toward their nets. Unlike the Indo-Pacific humpback, all Atlantic humpback dolphins have a conspicuous hump.

The tucuxi *Sotalia fluviatilis* is found in both salt and fresh water, occurring in the shallow coastal waters and rivers of northeast South America and eastern Central America. It is one of the few delphinids with permanent freshwater populations—one of which is found no less than 2,500 kilometers up the Amazon River. There are many different age and color variants of the tucuxi,

some of which were once considered to be separate species, and riverine animals are usually paler and smaller than those living along the coast.

Perhaps the best known dolphin—and one of the best known cetaceans—is the bottlenose dolphin *Tursiops truncatus*. Trained bottlenose dolphins are often seen in marine parks and zoos and have been the stars of several television shows and films. In the wild they are found worldwide, from cooler temperate to tropical waters, and occur both inshore and offshore. Inshore animals are mostly found in small schools of up to 10 animals, but larger schools of up to 500 animals sometimes occur offshore. They are fairly active swimmers, frequently leaping from the water, and are often seen riding the bow waves and in the wake of ships. Many of the so-called "friendly" dolphins that have mixed with humans over the years, such as Fungie in Ireland, and the dolphins at Monkey Mia, Western Australia, are bottlenose dolphins.

The rough-toothed dolphin *Steno bredanensis* superficially resembles a bottlenose dolphin but, on closer inspection, its narrow head and unusually large eyes give it a rather reptilian appearance. Found in warm waters worldwide, its name comes from the fine, vertical ridges on its teeth.

Risso's dolphin *Grampus griseus* is found in all oceans of the world, from the tropics to cool temperate waters. A large delphinid, reaching

Peter Corkeron

ABOVE: One of the most familiar of all the dolphins, the widely distributed bottlenose is found in many parts of the world, from cold temperate to tropical seas. There are two distinct forms— one occurring offshore (and around oceanic islands) and the other mainly inshore.

WHAT'S IN A NAME?

M.M. BRYDEN

Whales, dolphins and porpoises are all members of the order Cetacea. In theory, whales are the largest, dolphins are medium-size, and porpoises are the smallest. But splitting them in this way can be confusing, because there is a great deal of overlap in size between the three groups and, most importantly, these size distinctions have no real scientific basis.

The order Cetacea is divided into three suborders: the archaeocetes (which are all extinct); the mysticetes (baleen whales); and the odontocetes (toothed whales). Each suborder is further divided into families, genera and, ultimately, species.

All 11 mysticetes are referred to as "whales" and every species has "whale" in its name: blue whale, minke whale, Bryde's whale, gray whale and so on. However, the odontocetes are referred to as "whales," "dolphins" or "porpoises," depending on many different factors, and include no fewer than 70 widely differing species. The sperm whale, northern bottlenose whale, striped dolphin, Yangtze river dolphin, beluga and harbor porpoise are all odontocetes—so there is no uniformity in their common names. The porpoise family, Phocoenidae, is perhaps the most readily categorized because all six members have distinctive, spade-shaped teeth. But some odontocete families can be quite confusing: the dolphin family, Delphinidae, for example, includes six species with "whale" in their names: killer whale, short-finned and long-finned pilot whales, melon-headed whale, false and pygmy killer whales.

Consequently, while "whale," "dolphin" and "porpoise" will always remain popular, it is more useful to consider modern cetaceans in terms of the two scientifically recognized groups: odontocetes or toothed, and mysticetes or baleen whales.

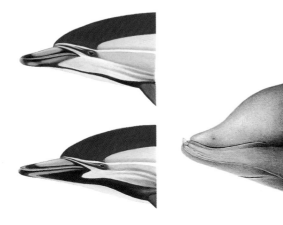

LEFT: Popular names can be confusing in identifying groups and species of whales, dolphins and porpoises. The short-beaked and long-beaked common dolphins (far left) and Cuvier's beaked whales (left) are all odontocetes, or toothed whales.

a length of up to 3.8 meters, it is unusual in having no teeth in the upper jaw and only 4–14 teeth in the lower jaw. Instead, it has corrugations on the palate to help hold its prey, usually squid, cuttlefish or octopus. Older Risso's dolphins are easy to identify at sea because they develop a battered appearance, due to extensive scarring from the teeth of other Risso's dolphins.

The white-beaked dolphin *Lagenorhynchus albirostris* and its close relative the Atlantic white-sided dolphin *Lagenorhynchus acutus* have almost identical ranges in the cool temperate and subarctic waters of the North Atlantic. They can both be seen in enormous schools of more than 1,000 animals, although much smaller groups are usually more common. The Pacific white-sided dolphin *Lagenorhynchus obliquidens* is also sometimes found in large schools, particularly offshore, within its range of temperate waters of the northern North Pacific. There are three other members of this genus: Peale's dolphin *Lagenorhynchus australis*, which is fairly common around the southern tip of South America and in the Falkland Islands; the hourglass dolphin *Lagenorhynchus cruciger* of the cold waters of the Southern Hemisphere, which really does have an hourglass pattern on its flanks; and the dusky dolphin *Lagenorhynchus obscurus*, which is found in coastal temperate waters of Australasia, southern Africa and South America.

The two spotted dolphins—pantropical spotted *Stenella attenuata* and Atlantic spotted *Stenella frontalis*—are quite similar in appearance

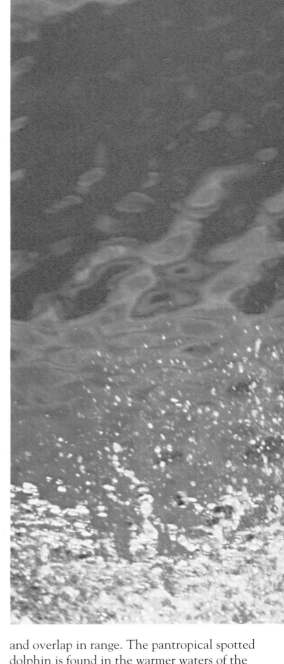

BELOW: Named for its spectacular spinning leaps, the long-snouted spinner dolphin hunts small fish and squid in the tropical and subtropical Atlantic, Pacific and Indian oceans. Hundreds of thousands—and, possibly, millions—were killed by tuna fisheries in the eastern tropical Pacific, causing a great decline in the population of this area in recent years.

Bernd Würsig

and overlap in range. The pantropical spotted dolphin is found in the warmer waters of the Indian, Pacific and Atlantic oceans, while the Atlantic spotted dolphin inhabits only the warm waters of the Atlantic. Both species vary enormously in size, shape and color. Newborn animals are unspotted and develop dark spots on the underside and light spots on the upperside as they grow older.

Marc Webber/Earthviews

The long-snouted spinner dolphin *Stenella longirostris* belongs to the same genus and is one of the most acrobatic of all cetaceans. It is named for its spectacular aerial displays, which involve leaping into the air and then spinning around rapidly on the longitudinal axis. Spinner and pantropical spotted dolphins frequently associate with one another, particularly in the eastern tropical Pacific, where they also associate with

tuna. Tuna-fishing operations have killed millions of these two species in recent decades.

The short-snouted spinner dolphin, or clymene dolphin *Stenella clymene* was long considered to be one of the many variations of its long-snouted relative, but was officially classified as a separate species in 1981. It sometimes leaps into the air and spins longitudinally, as its name would suggest, but most individuals are not as

ABOVE: Since 1959, an estimated 6 to 12 million dolphins have been killed by the tuna-fishing industry in the eastern tropical Pacific—and pantropical spotted dolphins were among the hardest hit. Conservation regulations have recently reduced the death toll to about 4,000 dolphins annually.

Francois Gohier/Ardea London Ltd

ABOVE: The common dolphin varies enormously in appearance and, for many years, its single species status was doubted by many experts. Recently, it was split into two separate species: the long-beaked common dolphin and the short-beaked common dolphin. The long-beaked has a longer beak and is slimmer in profile.

acrobatic as the more common and widespread long-snouted spinner dolphin. The short-snouted spinner dolphin is found in warm waters of the Atlantic, while the long-snouted spinner is found in warm waters around the world.

The fifth member of this genus is the striped dolphin *Stenella coeruleoalba*, which is another striking acrobat. This dolphin breaches, porpoises upside-down, performs back somersaults, tail-spins, and occasionally bow rides. It may travel in schools of several hundred individuals, although smaller groups are also common, and is found in warm waters around the world.

Until recently, only one species of common dolphin was recognized but, in 1995, the genus was split and now there are two distinct species: the short-beaked common dolphin *Delphinus delphis* and the long-beaked common dolphin *Delphinus*

capensis. These show many subtle genetic, physical and behavioral differences, but can still be very difficult to tell apart at sea. Even with two species, there are many different variations, although they all have the distinctive hourglass pattern of white, gray, yellow and black on their sides. Common dolphins are found worldwide in warm temperate, subtropical and tropical waters. Sometimes their schools—which can be 2,000-strong—are so acrobatic and boisterous that the noise of their approach can be heard several kilometers away.

The northern right whale dolphin *Lissodelphis borealis* is a streamlined animal and probably the sleekest of all cetaceans. Traveling in smooth, low leaps, it can be mistaken at a distance for a sea lion or fur seal—although it can swim much faster and has been known to attain speeds of up to 45 kilometers an hour. Because it has no dorsal fin, it is unlikely to be confused with any other species in its range. Its closest relative is the southern right whale dolphin *Lissodelphis peronii* of cool waters of the Southern Hemisphere; surprisingly, it was discovered 50 years before its counterpart was first noticed in the temperate waters of the North Pacific. The southern right whale dolphin also lacks a dorsal fin (like its much larger namesake the right whale) but it has more white on its body. Both species feed on fish and squid.

Fraser's dolphin *Lagenodelphis hosei* was first described in 1956 and was not seen in the wild until the 1970s. However, it is much better known these days and can even be seen on some whale-watching trips in the Caribbean and the Philippines. Found mainly offshore, it occurs in deep tropical and warm temperate waters around the world.

There are four species in the *Cephalorhynchus* genus: Commerson's dolphin *Cephalorhynchus commersonii*, Hector's dolphin *Cephalorhynchus hectori*, the black dolphin *Cephalorhynchus eutropia* and Heaviside's dolphin *Cephalorhynchus heavisidii*. They all have relatively short, indistinct beaks, smoothly sloping foreheads and fairly robust bodies. Their dorsal fin shapes are very distinctive: fairly rounded in Commerson's, rounded and backward-sloping in Hector's, very large and rounded in the black, and triangular in Heaviside's. They all occur in coastal waters, but there is little overlap in their range. Commerson's is found mainly in southern Argentina, as well as the Falkland Islands and Kerguelen Island in the Indian Ocean; the black dolphin occurs mainly in southern Chile; Heaviside's dolphin lives in western South Africa and Namibia; and Hector's dolphin is found in New Zealand.

Ken Balcomb/Earthviews

The Irrawaddy dolphin *Orcaella brevirostris* is sometimes considered to be the oddest member of the Delphinidae and, indeed, is occasionally classified with the narwhal and beluga as a member of the Monodontidae. It certainly looks a little like a beluga, but it shares many characteristics with other oceanic dolphins. Found in warm waters of the Indian and western Pacific oceans, it lives in coastal waters and major rivers, and feeds on a variety of fish, squid and crustaceans.

Among the largest members of the dolphin family are the long-finned pilot whale *Globicephala melas* and the short-finned pilot whale *Globicephala macrorhynchus*. These two species are very similar in appearance but, as its name suggests, the long-finned has longer pectoral fins (flippers); in most individuals, it also has more teeth than the short-

ABOVE: Narrow, tapered and streamlined with no vestige of a dorsal fin, the medium-size northern right whale dolphin is a striking dolphin. It is probably the sleekest of all cetaceans and can swim very fast. When traveling at speed, it leaves the water in low-angled leaps and looks as if it is bouncing on and off the surface of the water.

LEFT: The bottlenose dolphin is the archetypal dolphin, found around the world from cooler temperate to tropical waters. They are mostly gray, with a short beak and prominent melon.

ABOVE: Distinctive in size and appearance, the orca is an efficient predator of virtually all marine vertebrates, from relatively small fish to the largest of baleen whales. Orcas are skilled cooperative hunters with a complex social system and live in close-knit family groups, known as pods.

finned. Both species live in deep waters, usually offshore, but they are separated geographically: the short-finned pilot whale lives in warm temperate and tropical waters around the world, but the long-finned pilot whale lives in cold temperate waters in the North Atlantic and Southern Ocean. The short-finned normally lives in groups of 10–30 animals and, while the long-finned normally lives in groups of 10–50 animals, there are reports of thousands being seen together. Because of their strong social ties, long-finned pilot whales are prone to mass strandings. They have been heavily exploited over the years.

The false killer whale, or pseudorca *Pseudorca crassidens*, is also prone to mass strandings. A distinctive animal, with a long, slender head and slim body, it normally lives in family pods of 10–50 animals—although several hundred are sometimes seen together. It is active at the surface and frequently leaps clear of the water, spyhops, lobtails, bow-rides and wake-rides. Although it eats mainly fish and cephalopods, it has been reported attacking dolphins escaping from tuna nets and there is one case of false killer whales attacking a humpback whale calf near Hawaii. They live in warm waters worldwide.

Relatively little is known about the melon-headed whale *Peponocephala electra* and pygmy killer whale *Feresa attenuata*, which are among the smallest cetaceans with "whale" in their names. The melon-headed reaches a maximum length of 2.7 meters, while the pygmy reaches 2.6 meters. Both species are found in subtropical and tropical waters and eat squid and small fish.

The largest and most striking member of the dolphin family is the orca or killer whale *Orcinus orca*. With its jet-black, brilliant white and gray markings, it is unmistakable. The male also has a distinctive tall dorsal fin, which can reach a height of 1.8 meters. It is found in all seas, from the equator to the polar ice, and feeds on fish, squid, turtles, seabirds, marine mammals and a variety of other prey. Orcas live in long-term family groups for life—which is an average of 29 years for males and 50 years for females.

RIVER DOLPHINS

There are five species of river dolphins belonging to three different families: Iniidae—Amazon river dolphin; Pontoporiidae—baiji and franciscana; Platanistidae—Indus and Ganges river dolphins. Despite their collective name, they are not all exclusively riverine animals—the franciscana lives in shallow coastal waters—nor are they the only cetaceans living in rivers. It is uncertain whether they are all closely related because, although they share many features and have broadly similar habits, they may simply have adapted to life in large, muddy rivers in similar ways through convergent evolution.

The Amazon river dolphin or boto *Inia geoffrensis* is the largest member of the group. Normally found alone or in pairs, it is occasionally seen in groups of up to 15 individuals in the dry season or on good feeding grounds. During the wet season, Amazon river dolphins spread out into the flooded forest. They inhabit all the main rivers of the Orinoco and Amazon basins in South America, and at the surface are the most active members of the group. They leap into the air, sometimes spyhop, and may even ride in the bow waves and wake of passing boats. Although more common than its Asian relatives, the Amazon river dolphin's population is declining as a result of rainforest destruction, damming and hunting.

The baiji *Lipotes vexillifer* has many different common names: Chinese river dolphin, whiteflag dolphin, whitefin dolphin, Yangtze river dolphin, beiji and several others. It is probably the most endangered of all cetaceans, with a surviving population of fewer than 50 animals. Some experts believe there may be no more than a couple of dozen left and fear that it could be the first cetacean species to become extinct in modern times. Despite conservation efforts, it continues to decline. The Yangtze River is one of the world's busiest waterways and, not surprisingly, the dolphin faces a great many threats—including the effects of damming, agricultural and industrial pollution, riverine development and increased boat traffic and fishing.

A close relative of the baiji is the marine-living franciscana or La Plata dolphin *Pontoporia blainvillei*. Unlike the other river dolphins, it does not inhabit rivers but prefers shallow coastal waters. It lives in eastern South America. Franciscanas feed near the seabed and normally occur alone or in small groups of up to five individuals. Until recently, there were few records of live animals in the wild, but there have been many more sightings in recent years and several populations are now being studied.

The Indus river dolphin *Platanista minor* and Ganges river dolphin *Platanista gangetica* are almost identical. Only recently have they come to be considered separate species. The Indus river dolphin lives only in the Indus River in Pakistan and is the rarer of the two, numbering fewer than 500 individuals. The Ganges river dolphin lives in the Ganges, Brahmaputra and Meghna rivers of India, Bangladesh, Nepal and Bhutan and its population is estimated at 4,000–6,000 individuals. They face many threats including damming, pollution, fishing, disturbance and hunting. Also known as susus, the two species are the only cetaceans without proper eye lenses which, effectively, makes them blind, although they can probably detect the direction and, possibly, the intensity of light. They hunt and navigate in the muddy river waters using echolocation.

Institute of Hydrology, Academia Sinica Wuhan, P.R. China

ABOVE: The baiji is the world's rarest cetacean. It is believed that fewer than 50 survive in their natural home in the Yangtze River, China. Baiji face a barrage of threats, from overfishing to dam construction. Like the other river dolphins, they are highly specialized animals, superbly adapted to life in turbid, silty water.

LEFT: Largest of the river dolphins, the Amazon river dolphin, or boto, is widely distributed in all the main rivers of the Amazon and Orinoco basins. Its body color is highly variable according to age, water clarity, temperature and location, and may be bluish-gray, off-white or even vivid pink.

RIGHT: In an effort to stimulate public awareness of one of the most endangered large mammals in the world—the baiji—the Chinese government has issued stamps depicting this dolphin. There is even a Baiji brand beer.

FACING PAGE: The riverside city of Tongling has adopted the baiji as its municipal mascot and has constructed a seminatural reserve in the neighboring Yangtze River in the hope that it may be possible to establish a small breeding population of these severely endangered dolphins.

THE BAIJI

KAIYA ZHOU

Like the giant panda, the baiji or Yangtze river dolphin *Lipotes vexillifer* is a national treasure of China, and deserves worldwide recognition. This rarest of the world's cetaceans is a graceful animal with a very long and narrow snout. It can also be identified by the low triangle of its dorsal fin. In China, it is usually known by the name "baiji," which means "white dolphin." The name dates from classical times and is to be found in the ancient dictionary *Erh Ya* (Anonymous) published as long ago as 200 BC.

The baiji has previously been classified in the same family as the Amazon river dolphin, but is now included in a separate family with the franciscana. One of its closest relatives is a fossil, *Prolipotes yujiangensis*, which is about 15 million years old and known from the bank of the Yujiang River in southern China. The ridges on the crowns of the teeth show a similar pattern in both the living species and the fossil.

In 1986, the baiji was recognized by the Species Survival Commission of the World Conservation Union (IUCN) as one of the 12 most endangered animals in the world—and its status has worsened considerably since then. There are probably fewer than 50 survivors left in the Yangtze River, and the population still appears to be declining. In theory, it occurs along a 1,700-kilometer stretch of the river, but it is very rare above Zhicheng and below Nanjing. There is one individual in captivity, a male called Qi-Qi, which has been held in a concrete tank in the city of Wuhan for many years. Qi-Qi has been a crucial source of information on his species since his capture in 1980.

The baiji faces many threats, including entanglement in fishing gear, overfishing, heavy boat traffic, agricultural and chemical pollution, riverine development and dam construction. The Yangtze River itself is one of the planet's busiest waterways and the Yangtze Basin is one of the most populated regions anywhere in the world. In the past, as many as half the dead dolphins found in the Yangtze have been killed accidentally by multiple-hook lines and other illegal fishing gear. Many of the individuals entangled on such hooks are killed, but others manage to free themselves and escape with inevitable injuries: one critically ill female, taken from the river in 1982, had a total of 103 hook scars of different sizes. Occasionally, the dolphins are killed or injured by ships' propellers, particularly in the lower reaches of the river where the level of traffic has been doubling every 10 years. The enormous Three Gorges Dam, currently under construction, could be the final nail in the baiji's coffin.

The dolphin has been protected in China since 1975 and, since the late 1980s, there has been an intensive campaign to save it from extinction. But little, if any, progress has been made. Indeed, the situation in the Yangtze has seriously worsened and the dolphin population has decreased to a very dangerous level. Unfortunately, it is virtually impossible to control threats such as illegal fishing and heavy boat traffic. In recent years, there has been general agreement that the animal's best hope of survival is in semi-captivity. The plan is to establish large reserves on the river—in areas where the baiji can be self-contained—in order to build up the population through an intensive breeding program. Several of these semi-natural reserves have been established, including ones at Tongling and Shi-Shou, but it has proved virtually impossible to capture the dolphins. After a huge amount of effort, a female was captured and transferred to Shi-Shou, but she died after only six months.

Even if a breeding population can be established, the future of the baiji looks extremely bleak. Establishing semi-natural reserves may be a short-term solution but it does not rescue the dolphin in the long term. The worst fear is that, if the Yangtze River continues to deteriorate at an alarming rate, there will never be a secure home for these dolphins in the wild.

Kaiya Zhou

LEFT: The baiji has disappeared from most stretches of the Yangtze River in the face of pollution, competition for food, accidental capture by fishermen, dam construction and riverbank development.

DISTRIBUTION AND ECOLOGY

ABOVE: The bowhead is the only large whale to be living exclusively in the Arctic. With a layer of blubber up to 70 centimeters thick, and an ability to create its own breathing holes by breaking through the ice, it can live right up to the edge of the pack ice.

PETER CORKERON

*W*here are different cetacean species found? Why do some species occur worldwide, while others have restricted ranges? Why do some species regularly move according to the seasons while others remain confined to a limited home territory? These are some of the questions that the study of distribution and ecology attempts to answer.

On an evolutionary time scale, historical zoogeography (the study of how species distributions have changed with time) is affected by complex factors, such as climatic change and continental drift, as well as the evolutionary response to these by animal groups. But on a more immediate time scale, there are many ecological factors that can affect distribution. These include water temperature, depth, salinity and the topography of the seafloor, as well as factors such as the availability and abundance of food.

The distribution of cetaceans is often related to the temperature of the surface water and, for easy reference, the world can be divided into distinct temperature zones. Polar waters are the high latitude zones, around the Arctic and Antarctic. Moving toward the equator from these waters, there are the subarctic and subantarctic zones, cold temperate, warm temperate, subtropical and, finally, tropical zones. But cetacean distribution also relates to many other factors, from water depth to the proximity of land. Among the different habitats available are the coastal zone, the sublittoral zone or continental shelf, and the pelagic or offshore zone over deep ocean basins.

RIGHT: Although the divisions between zones of surface water temperature are not always well defined—subtropical waters, for example, vary in extent from season to season and according to local currents—the distribution of many cetaceans follows a pattern related to water temperature.

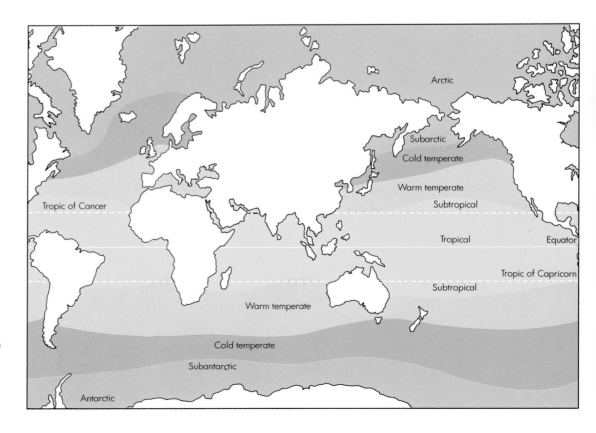

DISTRIBUTION OF BALEEN WHALES

As a group, baleen whales are found in all the oceans of the world and, while some have fairly limited distributions, others occur worldwide.

The bowhead whale has the most restricted natural distribution since it is rarely found far from the edge of the cold arctic pack ice. Northern right whales were once fairly widespread in the North Atlantic and North Pacific, although nowadays the remnant population of about 300 animals is found almost exclusively in the western North Atlantic; there may be a handful of survivors left in the eastern North Atlantic and the North Pacific. Closely related southern right whales are faring considerably better and have breeding

populations across the Southern Hemisphere, in southern South America, South Africa and Australasia. From a limited number of strandings and observations, the pygmy right whale appears to be fairly widely distributed in the temperate waters of the Southern Hemisphere.

Gray whales are found mainly along the eastern North Pacific: they feed in Alaska and breed in Mexico, migrating thousands of miles along the west coast of North America in between. A small population also survives in the western North Pacific.

The minke whale is among the most widely distributed baleen whales and is found worldwide in tropical, temperate and polar waters of both hemispheres. The closely related

ABOVE: The open ocean may seem a featureless and barren place to humans, but to the minke whale, smallest of the rorquals, it is a rich and varied environment of underwater prairies and mountain ranges stretching from the tropics to the poles.

RIGHT: Common dolphins are among the most widespread and abundant small cetaceans and inhabit virtually all tropical, subtropical and warm temperate seas from the Mediterranean and the Black Sea to the Pacific, Indian and Atlantic oceans.

BELOW: Closely related species may have overlapping or complementary distributions. Short-finned pilot whales (top) are restricted to tropical and warm temperate waters, while the physically similar long-finned pilot whale (bottom) hunts similar prey—principally squid—in cool temperate and subpolar waters.

Jacki Kilbride/Earthviews

Paul Ensor

sei whale is also widely distributed, although its distribution is very patchy and it does not occur as far north or as far south as the minke whale. Fin whales and blue whales occur worldwide as well, but they both prefer colder waters and the distribution of blue whales is particularly patchy. Humpback whales are also worldwide but divide their time between cold water high-latitude feeding grounds and warm water low-latitude breeding grounds. The last of the rorquals, Bryde's whale, has a comparatively smaller range and occurs mainly in tropical, subtropical and some warm temperate waters throughout the world.

TOOTHED WHALES WITH A WORLDWIDE DISTRIBUTION

A considerable number of toothed whales have a worldwide distribution, although many of them appear to have particular pockets of abundance and are absent from large areas within their overall range.

Pygmy sperm whales and dwarf sperm whales are both found in deep temperate, tropical and subtropical waters around the world, but there are vast areas where they have never been recorded. The sperm whale is more widely distributed, although it also has a patchy distribution; males frequently occur in polar waters but females and calves do not.

As a group, the beaked whales have a worldwide distribution, although few individual species are found in all oceans. Unfortunately, our knowledge of the distribution of most species is severely limited and much more information is needed before we can really be sure of their full ranges. The only species which appear to be truly worldwide are Blainville's beaked whale, which probably has the widest distribution of any *Mesoplodon* species, and Cuvier's beaked whale, which is absent only from polar waters in both hemispheres. But even these widely spread species appear to have patchy distributions.

Arnoux's, Shepherd's and Gray's beaked whales, the strap-toothed whale and the southern bottlenose whale appear to be found across the Southern Hemisphere. Hector's beaked whale is also found mainly in the Southern Hemisphere, although it may occur in the eastern North Pacific as well.

Baird's, Stejneger's and Hubb's beaked whales are found only in the North Pacific. The northern bottlenose whale and Sowerby's beaked whale are found only in the North Atlantic. The so-called unidentified beaked whale (*Mesoplodon* "A") and the Peruvian beaked whale are found in the deep waters of the eastern tropical Pacific. Andrew's beaked whale occurs in the cool temperate waters of Australasia. True's beaked whale seems to have

Don Croll

ABOVE: Resident in deep temperate waters of the northern North Pacific, the Pacific white-sided dolphin is separated from the Atlantic white-sided dolphin by the continent of America.

FACING PAGE: One of the most acrobatic of all the dolphins, the dusky dolphin is found mainly close to shore in cool temperate waters of the Southern Hemisphere—in Australasia, southern Africa and South America.

a strange distribution in the North Atlantic, southeastern Africa and Australasia. Longman's beaked whale and the gingko-toothed beaked whale probably occur in the warmer waters of the Indian and Pacific oceans. Gervais' beaked whale is found in deep subtropical and warm temperate waters of the Atlantic.

The "blackfish"—six toothed whales in the oceanic dolphin family—have broadly worldwide distributions. However, only the orca is truly worldwide; it is particularly common in polar waters, but is actually found in all oceans of the world. The pygmy killer and melon-headed whales occur worldwide but only in tropical and subtropical waters. The short-finned pilot and false killer whales have a similar worldwide range and extend into warm temperate waters as well. Interestingly, the long-finned pilot whale occurs almost wherever its close relative, the short-finned pilot whale, is absent. It is found in cold temperate and subpolar waters of the Atlantic and throughout the Southern Hemisphere, although it is not present in the North Pacific.

Some of the "true" oceanic dolphins also have a worldwide distribution. The most widely distributed is probably the bottlenose dolphin, which is found everywhere except polar waters. Common and Risso's dolphins occur in warm temperate, subtropical and tropical waters worldwide. Striped, rough-toothed and pantropical spotted dolphins are worldwide, although they are usually absent from cool temperate and polar waters. Similarly, the long-snouted spinner dolphin is found in tropical and subtropical waters.

TOOTHED WHALES WITH A RESTRICTED DISTRIBUTION

Like the bowhead, the narwhal and beluga are predominantly arctic species, and both are circumpolar in distribution. The beluga is most common in areas which are seasonally ice-covered, while the narwhal is found mainly in association with the pack ice.

Many of the "true" oceanic dolphins have a fairly restricted distribution. As its name suggests, the Pacific white-sided dolphin is found only in the North Pacific. The northern right whale dolphin also inhabits the same region, while its close relative, the southern right whale dolphin, is found only in the Southern Hemisphere. The hourglass dolphin is another Southern Hemisphere species. The dusky dolphin is found in coastal waters of the Southern Hemisphere. Atlantic white-sided and white-beaked dolphins are both restricted to the northern North Atlantic. The tucuxi occurs only near the coasts of southeastern Central America and northeastern South America. Peale's dolphin occurs only in southern South America. The Indo-Pacific humpback dolphin is found mainly in the Indian Ocean, but also in the western South Pacific. The Atlantic humpback dolphin is restricted to the coastal waters of tropical West Africa. Short-snouted spinner and Atlantic spotted dolphins are also found in tropical West Africa, but their ranges extend right across the Atlantic. Fraser's dolphin occurs around the equator, mainly in the Pacific, and in a few other widely scattered areas. The Irrawaddy dolphin lives in warm coastal waters and rivers of southeast Asia.

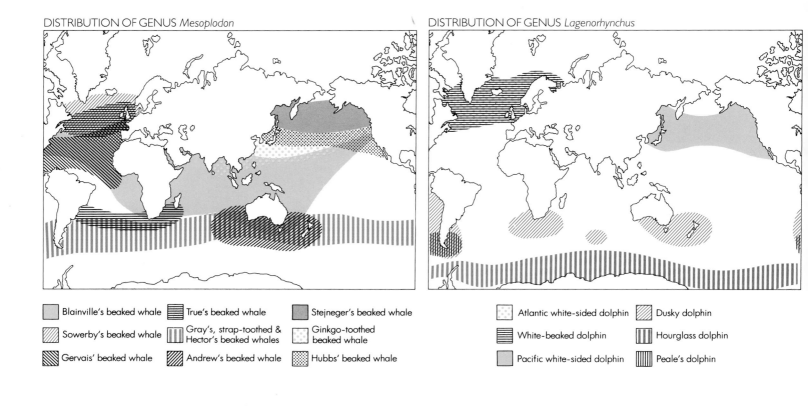

DISTRIBUTION OF GENUS *Mesoplodon*

DISTRIBUTION OF GENUS *Lagenorhynchus*

Blainville's beaked whale | True's beaked whale | Stejneger's beaked whale
Sowerby's beaked whale | Gray's, strap-toothed & Hector's beaked whales | Ginkgo-toothed beaked whale
Gervais' beaked whale | Andrew's beaked whale | Hubbs' beaked whale

Atlantic white-sided dolphin | Dusky dolphin
White-beaked dolphin | Hourglass dolphin
Pacific white-sided dolphin | Peale's dolphin

RIGHT: Small and distinctively marked, Commerson's dolphin is found only in the cold waters of southern South America, including the Falkland Islands, and around Kerguelen Island in the Indian Ocean. It feeds on small fish, squid and shrimps, mainly close to shore.

Francisco Erizo/Bruce Coleman Limited

Stephen Leatherwood/Earthviews

ABOVE: Dall's porpoise is another striking animal, although its black and white markings are quite unlike those of Commerson's dolphin.

Members of the *Cephalorhynchus* genus have very restricted ranges: Commerson's dolphin is found only in southern South America (including the Falkland Islands) and Kerguelen Island in the Indian Ocean; the black dolphin is restricted to the coastal waters of Chile; Heaviside's dolphin occurs only along a small stretch of coast from central Namibia to southern South Africa; and Hector's dolphin is found only in the coastal waters of New Zealand.

The river dolphins all have restricted ranges. The boto, or Amazon river dolphin, occurs in all the main rivers of the Orinoco and Amazon basins, in South America. The franciscana, or La Plata dolphin, is another South American species, inhabiting temperate coastal waters in eastern South America. The baiji, or Yangtze river dolphin, is found only along a 1,700-kilometer stretch of the Yangtze River, in China. The other two Asian species are the Indus and Ganges river dolphins (sometimes

referred to as susus). The Ganges river dolphin is found in the Ganges but also in several other major rivers of India, Pakistan, Bangladesh, Nepal and Bhutan; however, the Indus river dolphin occurs exclusively along a small stretch of the Indus River, Pakistan.

The porpoises also have restricted ranges. The harbor porpoise probably has the widest range, and is found in cold temperate and subarctic waters of the Northern Hemisphere. At the other extreme, the vaquita, or Gulf of California porpoise, probably has the most limited distribution of any marine cetacean; it is found only in the extreme northern end of the Gulf of California, or Sea of Cortez, in western Mexico. The finless porpoise inhabits coastal waters and all major rivers of the Indian Ocean and the western Pacific. Burmeister's porpoise occurs in the temperate and subantarctic coastal waters of South America. Dall's porpoise is found only in the northern North Pacific and, finally, the spectacled porpoise has a patchy coastal distribution in parts of the Southern Hemisphere.

THE HARBOR PORPOISE IN THE BAY OF FUNDY

Extensive surveys of the harbor porpoise in the Bay of Fundy, eastern Canada, have taught us much about the ecological factors that can affect the distribution of a species on a local scale.

The Bay of Fundy, between Nova Scotia and New Brunswick, is well known for having the highest tides in the world. This causes extraordinary rip tides, and very tricky currents, and contributes to the famous "Fundy fog." Such bad conditions may have discouraged whalers in the past, and today the region is a critically

DISTRIBUTION OF GENUS *Cephalorhynchus*

DISTRIBUTION OF PORPOISES, FAMILY PHOCOENIDAE

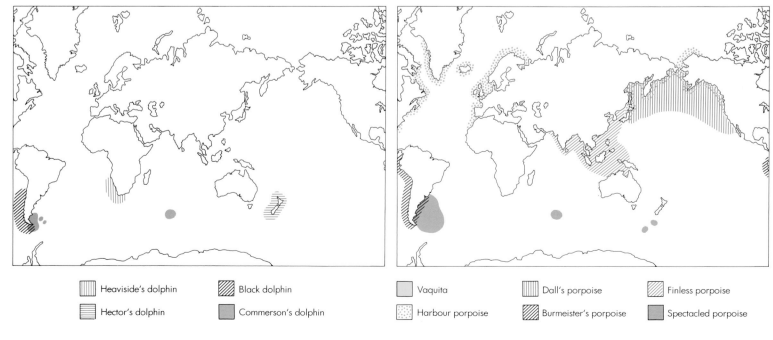

Heaviside's dolphin

Hector's dolphin

Black dolphin

Commerson's dolphin

Vaquita

Harbour porpoise

Dall's porpoise

Burmeister's porpoise

Finless porpoise

Spectacled porpoise

Fred Bruemmer

LEFT: The narwhal occupies one of the most northerly habitats of any cetacean—it is found mostly above the Arctic Circle and right to the edge of the ice cap. The unique spiraling tusk of the male was, until early in the seventeeth century, thought to have been the horn of the legendary unicorn.

BELOW: The beluga is another arctic species, with a circumpolar distribution from the subarctic to the high arctic. In the summer, it frequently enters extremely shallow water where it is able to swim in depths barely covering its body.

important refuge for cetaceans. It is home to northern right, humpback, fin and minke whales, and during the spring and summer the western side of the bay is famous for high concentrations of harbor porpoises (although large numbers have been caught and drowned in gillnet fisheries in recent years).

Harbor porpoises are small cetaceans, with the adults reaching a maximum size of about 1.9 meters, and they live mainly in cool waters. They are also capable of annual reproduction. This suggests a relatively high turnover of energy reserves and, indeed, harbor porpoises need to eat up to 10 percent of their body weight every day. Their main prey in the Bay of Fundy is herring, which is a relatively unpredictable food source, and so the porpoises tend to concentrate in areas where the herring are most common.

The precise distribution of porpoises was determined through carefully designed surveys and then compared with a variety of physical and biological variables, including water temperature, current speed, water depth and the availability of food. It was discovered that their distribution and density appeared to be directly linked with the distribution and energy content of herring, which accounts for as much as 80 percent of their food intake in the region. The fat content of herring can range

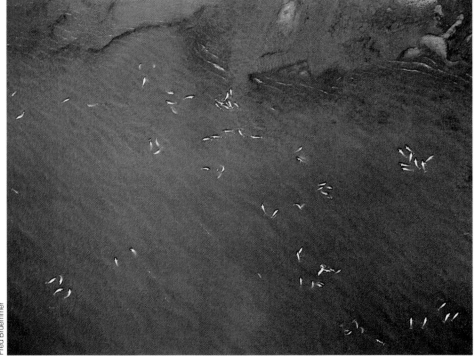

Fred Bruemmer

from 1 to 25 percent and varies from one season to the next as well as from one place to the next. In turn, the distribution of herring is dependent upon the distribution of planktonic prey such as *Calanus*, which can also vary enormously in biomass from one year to the next. It seems that harbor porpoises may require a continuous proximity to a reliable food source—with the consequence that their distribution may reflect the distribution of their prey more than for any other cetacean.

SHARING SPACE

Many parts of the world are home, permanently or temporarily, to more than one cetacean species. In most cases, they have little or no effect on one other. For example, when migrating baleen whales pass through the range of coastal dolphins there is no real conflict of interest. In some cases, such as the mixed schools of long-snouted spinner and pantropical spotted dolphins in the eastern tropical Pacific, different species actually seem to benefit from living together. But how do they coexist successfully?

In a study off the coast of Patagonia, in Argentina, bottlenose dolphins and dusky dolphins were found to space themselves in both geography and time. The bottlenose spent more time in shallower water than the duskies and, although they frequently fed in the same area, they did so at different times of day. Interestingly, the two species did not mix regularly, yet both interacted with other marine mammals such as whales and seals.

Two studies have compared aspects of the ecology of bottlenose and Indo-Pacific humpback dolphins. The first, off the southeast coast of

South Africa, found that the humpback dolphins occurred in smaller groups than the bottlenose and spent most of their time closer to shore. Food preferences of the two species also varied: the humpback dolphins apparently took mostly reef fish while the bottlenose dolphins fed on both reef and open-water fish. The two species interacted occasionally, and sometimes they appeared to play together.

In the second study, in a bay off southeast Queensland, Australia, the humpback dolphins were again found in shallower water than the bottlenose and they spent most of their time on the mainland side of the bay. The humpback dolphins appeared to be less perturbed by human activities and were found in shipping lanes, in small boat harbors and also in the vicinity of a major sewerage outlet. Both species fed behind fishing boats, often side-by-side, although they did not actually mingle and no amicable social behavior was observed. These two studies revealed quite different patterns of interaction between the two species. In one area the bottlenose and humpback dolphins shared a food source (fish discarded by the fishing boats), yet did not appear to interact socially. In the other, they interacted, but fed on different types of prey.

Very similar species may also avoid direct competition by geographical separation. The two pilot whales—long-finned and short-finned— are a good example. They are both similar in

BELOW: Long-snouted spinner dolphins are widespread in tropical and warm temperate waters of the Atlantic, Pacific and Indian oceans. They are often found in the company of other species of dolphins, such as the pantropical spotted, although their ecological requirements appear to be complementary rather than competitive.

appearance; both occur mainly in deep, offshore waters; both feed mainly on squid; and both are highly social animals that live in tightly knit family groups. Their range overlaps in a few temperate waters but, for the most part, the two species do not cross paths. Long-finned pilot whales inhabit two distinct regions of cold temperate to subpolar waters: one in the North Atlantic and the other in a band across the Southern Hemisphere. Intriguingly, their short-finned relatives inhabit the warm temperate and tropical waters in between.

The ocean appears to us to be a uniform environment. However, dolphins living in the deep oceans show patterns of distribution that can be correlated with a variety of oceanographic conditions and with the topography of the ocean floor.

Extensive surveys of the waters of the eastern tropical Pacific Ocean have been undertaken as part of the United States government's research on the dolphin stocks affected by tuna purse-seining. These surveys have shown that two communities, both consisting of several dolphin species, can be found in the area, and that these communities are associated with two quite different masses of water. In one water mass, where tuna fishing occurs, there is relatively little variation in the temperature of the surface water, and spotted and spinner dolphins predominate. In the other water mass, there is much greater variation in the surface water temperature, and striped and common dolphins predominate. Both communities contain several other dolphin species as well.

Detailed analysis of the distribution and abundance of dolphins in the area where tuna fishing occurs has demonstrated further division of dolphin groupings. In oceanic waters relatively close to shore, pilot whales, bottlenose and Risso's dolphins (and, to a lesser degree, common dolphins) predominate. Further offshore, spotted and spinner dolphins are the main species.

SIMILAR BUT DIFFERENT

Many cetacean species have a worldwide distribution, or a broad distribution within a single hemisphere or a particular ocean. However, an individual whale or dolphin does not range all over the world and, in most cases, does not even move from one ocean to another.

Humpback whales, for example, are found in all oceans from the poles to the tropics. But while they are inveterate travelers and migrate enormous distances between high and low latitudes, even they do not travel worldwide. Some individuals spend their entire lives in the North Atlantic, some in the North Pacific, and others in the Southern Hemisphere. Even within one ocean, there appear to be separate stocks. Several thousand humpbacks from all over the North Atlantic gather on their Caribbean breeding grounds over shallow banks off

Peter Corkeron

the coasts of the Dominican Republic, Puerto Rico and the Virgin Islands. But then they split into separate feeding "stocks"—large groups of animals found in geographically definable areas—in the Gulf of Maine, and off Newfoundland, Greenland, Iceland and Norway. These are all believed to be discrete—although there is limited movement between them during summer and, of course, they all mix at the breeding grounds during winter.

In some species, there is a huge amount of variation between individuals in different parts of their range. Indo-Pacific and Atlantic humpback dolphins are an interesting example. Their classification is still in dispute, although most authorities currently recognize two separate species. However, there appear to be two distinct stocks of the Indo-Pacific humpback dolphin: one found in the waters west of Sumatra, Indonesia, and the other to the east and south of the island. Individuals around South Africa, in the extreme west of their range, have the pronounced hump

LEFT: Bottlenose dolphins vary greatly in size, shape and color—in length alone, they range from as little as 1.9 meters to as much as 3.9 meters. However, only two main varieties are recognized: a smaller, inshore form and a larger, more robust form that lives mainly offshore.

BELOW: Striped dolphins are highly social animals. They pursue a variety of prey, mainly offshore, in tropical, subtropical and warm temperate waters around the world. However, they do not appear to be evenly distributed and are absent or uncommon in some parts of their range.

Robert Pitman/Earthviews

TUNA FISHING AND DOLPHIN SAFETY

In the waters of the eastern tropical Pacific, a stretch of ocean extending from southern California to Chile, yellowfin tuna *Thunnus albacares* are often found in association with groups of dolphins. The main species involved are pantropical spotted dolphins *Stenella attenuata*, long-snouted spinner dolphins *S. longirostris* and, less frequently, common dolphins *Delphinus delphis* and Fraser's dolphins *Lagenodelphis hosei*. The dolphins and tuna feed on the same small fish, and often swim together, although the precise reason for this partnership is still unclear.

Until comparatively recently, tuna fishermen posed little threat to the dolphins in the region. But, in 1959, the US introduced a particular form of purse-seining that has since killed more dolphins than any other human activity before or since. Purse-seine fishermen began to use the presence of dolphins to find shoals of tuna—the dolphins are much easier to find than tuna simply because they have to keep surfacing for air—and then to set their enormous nets around the two animals together. Once both the tuna and the dolphins are surrounded, the bottom of the net is closed underneath to form a bag (like a purse—thus the name). Then the drawstring is pulled tight and the net dragged toward the side of the seiner with the complete catch inside.

In the worst period, during the 1960s and early 1970s, it has been estimated that between 200,000 and 500,000 dolphins were being killed in the eastern tropical Pacific every year. The record-breaking year was 1961, when some 534,000 were recorded as being killed. In total, over a period of about 35 years, some 6–12 million dolphins have died. To put these figures into perspective, about 42,500 great whales were officially killed by whalers in the 1972–73 whaling season, but at least 380,000 dolphin were killed "incidentally" in the 1972 tuna-fishing season.

The killing continues, although nowadays it is on a significantly smaller scale. One possible reason is that there are now far fewer dolphins in the eastern tropical Pacific than in the 1960s and 1970s. Indeed, some populations have been reduced by as much as 80 percent. But it is more likely that the introduction of crucial rules and regulations to govern the tuna-fishing industry has had the greatest impact.

First of all, a special panel called the Medina Panel was introduced. This works as a kind of escape hatch within the net that allows trapped dolphins to be released. In 1972, use of the Medina Panel was made compulsory for all US-registered vessels. The same legislation ruled that official observers had to be on board to count kills and report any infractions. But US President Ronald Reagan submitted to the powerful economic and political lobby of the tuna industry, and relaxed the regulations, while more than half the US-registered tuna boats avoided them altogether by "going foreign."

Then the body responsible for managing the tuna-fishing industry in the eastern tropical Pacific—the Inter-American Tropical Tuna Commission (IATTC)—was forced to take action of its own. In 1986, it introduced an official observer program that allows experts to be placed on all vessels capable of fishing for tuna. Some of the objectives of the observer program included developing techniques for catching tuna that do not harm dolphins; providing training for crews of the international tuna-fishing fleet; and gathering information necessary for the introduction of "dolphin-safe" or "dolphin-friendly" labels now used by some tuna processors. Finally, in 1992, IATTC member governments signed the Agreement for the Conservation of Dolphins, commonly known as the La Jolla Agreement, which was established specifically to reduce the annual mortality of dolphins without harming the tuna resources of the region or the fisheries which depend on them.

Although the number of dolphins being killed was still high as recently as the late 1980s and early 1990s, the number of mortalities has decreased dramatically since then. The La Jolla Agreement included a target reduction in dolphin mortality in the eastern tropical Pacific from 19,500 in 1993 to less than 5,000 by 1999. It has been an enormous success: the death toll has already dropped below the target figure.

In the meantime, the dolphins themselves have altered their behavior around fishing boats, which has probably contributed to the reduction in mortalities. In areas where fishing effort has been heavy for many years, they flee from approaching boats, and have become difficult to set nets around. If they do get trapped, experienced dolphins wait, apparently calmly, near the Medina Panel where they know they will be released.

The dolphins of the eastern tropical Pacific can be divided into separate stocks, and these have been affected to differing degrees by tuna fishing. The most heavily exploited stock, the eastern stock of the long-snouted spinner dolphin, was reduced to approximately 17 percent of its initial (pre-1959) numbers.

BELOW: Tuna and dolphins are encircled in a net, and the bottom is drawn up to trap the animals. The Medina Panel provides an escape route for the dolphins.

that gives the species its name. But individuals around Australia, in the extreme east of the range, lack the hump and have a more prominent dorsal fin instead.

Bottlenose dolphins provide another good example of stock separation. Inshore and offshore populations living in the same general area tend to be quite different in body shape and behavior. The inshore form is generally smaller, and lives in groups of 1–10 individuals. The offshore form is normally larger and more robust, and lives in groups of 25 individuals or more. There is also a great deal of variation in appearance from one region to another: indeed, it is sometimes hard to believe that the sleek, long-beaked animals living in Western Australia, for example, really belong to the same species as the robust, short-beaked animals living in the Moray Firth, in Scotland. It is not surprising that taxonomists still debate the number of species of bottlenose dolphin—

in particular, whether some stocks are sufficiently different to be considered separate species.

In the eastern tropical Pacific Ocean, regional differences in the body shape and coloration of spinner dolphins allow them to be divided into stocks. These dolphin populations demonstrate the necessity to recognize that species exist in discrete stocks. Different stocks have been variously affected by the tuna purse-seining industry. In the past 20 years, some stocks have been reduced dramatically, while others have been less affected.

The best known examples of cetacean stocks are those of the baleen whales. Blue, fin, sei, Bryde's, minke and humpback whales are found in both hemispheres. Their migrations are timed so that whales from the Northern Hemisphere are at their low-latitude breeding grounds at different times of the year to whales from the Southern Hemisphere. Consequently, they never meet "in the middle."

ABOVE: Deep-diving pilot whales are seen mainly over submarine canyons, around volcanic islands or in other areas of deep water.

Michael Bryden

ABOVE:: Indo-Pacific humpback dolphins in the west of their range have a distinctive hump in the middle of the back, while those in the east have a more prominent dorsal fin but no hump.

David Rootes/Seaphot Limited/Planet Earth Pictures

As a result of this separation, Northern Hemisphere whales are different in size, and sometimes in appearance, to whales from the Southern Hemisphere. Rorquals in the Southern Hemisphere, for example, tend to be larger than their Northern Hemisphere counterparts. Minke whales in the Northern Hemisphere have a white band on their pectoral fins, but this is absent on many Southern Hemisphere animals. The two right whales, northern and southern, are considered sufficiently different to be classified as distinct species.

Much is still to be learned about the distribution and ecology of cetaceans. Even species that are relatively well studied, such as gray and humpback whales or bottlenose dolphins, are still shrouded in mystery. There are so many possible factors involved in determining the distribution of a species that a better understanding of the marine environment, and more long-term field studies, are essential before we can fill in many of the gaps in our knowledge.

LEFT: Spyhopping by southern right whales in the Southern Hemisphere is also seen in northern right whales in the Northern Hemisphere. These two animals are officially recognized as separate species, but are virtually identical and may be no more than geographically isolated populations.

THE RAREST CETACEANS

SPECIES AND DISTRIBUTION	POPULATION	NOTES
Yangtze river dolphin or baiji Yangtze River, China (middle and lower reaches)	Fewer than 100 (possibly fewer than 50)	Now very little chance of rescuing this species. It is likely to become the first cetacean to become extinct in historical times.
Vaquita or Gulf of California porpoise Extreme northern end of the Gulf of California (Sea of Cortez), Mexico	Fewer than 200	Has the most restricted distribution of any marine cetacean; most commonly seen around the Colorado River delta.
Northern right whale Western North Atlantic (occasional records from eastern North Atlantic and eastern North Pacific)	Fewer than 320	Officially protected for more than 60 years, it has never recovered from being hunted almost to extinction by commerical whalers.
Indus river dolphin or bhulan Indus River, Pakistan (mainly along 160-kilometer stretch between Sukkur and Guddu barrages, or dams)	Fewer than 500	Since the 1930s, barrages have split the dwindling population into isolated pockets.
Heaviside's dolphin Coastal waters of western South Africa and Namibia	Fewer than 1,000	The world's rarest marine dolphin, with an extremely restricted distribution.
Ganges river dolphin or susu Ganges, Meghna, Brahmaputra and Karnaphuli river systems of India, Bangladesh, Bhutan and Nepal	Fewer than 4,000	The population is split in two by the Farakka Barrage.

WHALE MIGRATION

BALEEN WHALES

Baleen whales undertake some of the longest migrations in the animal kingdom. The distribution and abundance of food and the availability of sites suitable for reproduction are the factors that motivate these migrations.

They spend the summer months in high-latitude, cold water feeding grounds, gorging themselves on small shrimp-like organisms, called krill, as well as a variety of other invertebrates and fish. But they spend the winter months in low-latitude warm water breeding grounds. During the spring and autumn, they have to migrate between their two widely separated homes. The distance they travel depends largely on their food preferences and breeding requirements. In the Southern Hemisphere, blue, fin, humpback and minke whales feed almost entirely on krill. Southern right whales eat even smaller crustaceans, called copepods, while sei whales feed on a variety of crustaceans and fish. Because of their different food preferences, southern right and sei whales are not found as far south as the other species. In the Northern Hemisphere, only the blue whale feeds entirely on krill; the other baleen whales feed on a variety of crustaceans and fish.

The longest and most regular migrations are undertaken by humpback and gray whales. Grays commute up to 10,000 kilometers along the entire length of the North American coastline, between their feeding grounds in Alaska and their breeding grounds in Mexico, and back again every year. Humpbacks travel between different feeding and breeding grounds all over the world, depending on the stock: the longest journey is undertaken by humpbacks that feed in the Southern Ocean, around the Antarctic Peninsula, and breed north of the equator in Colombia.

Other species appear to migrate in a more haphazard manner, without such a well-defined procession of animals moving north or south at specific times of the year. Bryde's whales, for example, live in tropical or warm temperate waters in all seasons. Presumably their diet is sufficiently varied that they can find enough areas of high productivity (perhaps around oceanic upwellings) to meet their food requirements all year round. Sei whale migrations are also fairly diffuse and, if ecological conditions are suitable, these whales may invade areas where they are infrequently seen. Similarly, bowhead whale migrations depend on the conditions of the arctic pack ice, which varies considerably from year to year. Even some humpbacks and grays do not complete their journeys if they find sufficient food en route.

Whatever their migrations, the precise details are poorly known for most species. How do they know when to leave, and when to return? How do they find their way? Do they stop to rest or feed? Do they swim near the surface, or travel at depth?

SPERM WHALES

Regular long-distance migrations are virtually unknown in toothed whales. They are typically nomadic rather than migratory. But there is one major exception—the sperm whale. Older males commonly migrate huge distances between high-latitude feeding grounds and the low-latitude warm temperate and tropical waters that are preferred by the females and calves year-round.

Nursery groups consist of adult females and their calves, including males up to about six years old; they live mainly in latitudes lower than 35 degrees. Mature males, however, live alone or in all-male groups and live mainly in latitudes higher than 45 degrees (55 degrees in the North Pacific). The males migrate to polar waters to feed on vast quantities of squid, rejoining the nursery schools in winter to breed.

FACING PAGE: Humpback whales undertake extensive migrations.

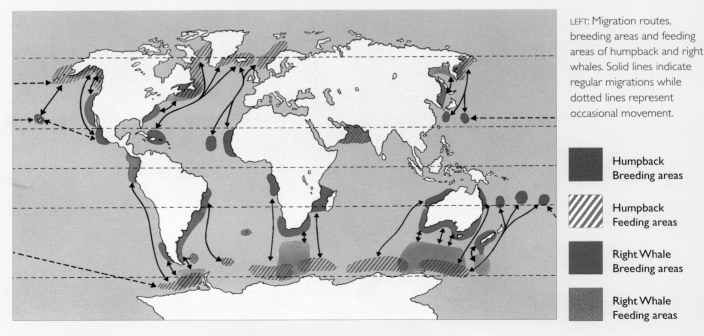

LEFT: Migration routes, breeding areas and feeding areas of humpback and right whales. Solid lines indicate regular migrations while dotted lines represent occasional movement.

Humpback Breeding areas

Humpback Feeding areas

Right Whale Breeding areas

Right Whale Feeding areas

G.L. Kooyman

ABOVE: An audience of penguins
watch as an orca surfaces for air.

WHALES UP CLOSE

A MARINE MAMMAL

M.M. BRYDEN

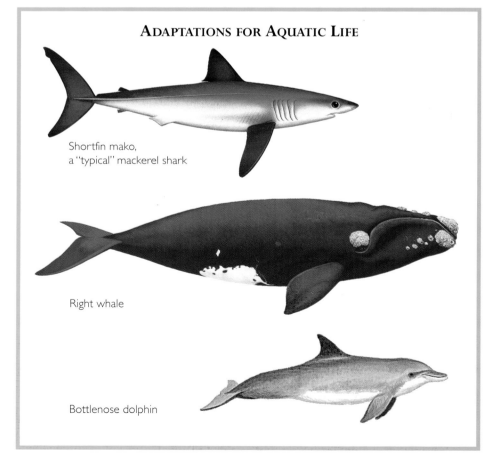

ABOVE: Several adaptations have enabled whales to take advantage of very cold but nutrient-rich polar waters.

G.L. Kooyman

BELOW: The similar body shapes of a shark (a fish), right whale and bottlenose dolphin (both mammals) are evolutionary responses to the need for streamlining to reduce friction in an aquatic environment.

Whales evolved from land-dwelling mammalian ancestors. For warm-blooded, air-breathing creatures, this "new" aquatic environment presented particular difficulties. Water is much denser and more viscous than air, making movement in it more difficult. Compared with air, water absorbs heat faster, transmits sound faster and with significantly less attenuation, and absorbs light more readily.

But although water—particularly very cold water—is an alien and, in some ways, hostile environment for mammals, living in it also has some obvious advantages. Buoyancy in water counteracts gravitational pull on the body and effectively makes an animal weightless. There are also vast exploitable resources in the oceans. A great many mammals feed on aquatic life or seek protection in water, including such seemingly unlikely candidates as some cats, bats, pigs, primates and, of course, humans. It should not be surprising that these advantages led to greater aquatic specialization in certain mammals, especially since the basic mammalian plan is readily adapted to the requirements of aquatic life; the polar bear, for example, is partially aquatic and yet is similar in appearance to other bears.

Marked modifications of form and function became necessary only when mammals evolved to live semi-permanently or permanently in water. These modifications are greatest in the dugongs and manatees (order Sirenia) and whales, dolphins and porpoises (order Cetacea)—the only mammals to have become totally aquatic.

ADAPTATIONS FOR AQUATIC LIFE

Shortfin mako, a "typical" mackerel shark

Right whale

Bottlenose dolphin

BODY SHAPE AND SIZE

The external form of cetaceans is a strong reflection of their watery environment. Because water is denser and more viscous than air, streamlining of the body became an advantage, and as evolution progressed, the shape of whales became more like that of other marine vertebrates. Superficial comparison of small whales, sharks, and extinct fishlike reptiles (ichthyosaurs) reveals a remarkable similarity of form. This is an example of convergent evolution.

Whales, dolphins and porpoises are all comparatively large mammals. The baleen whales, in particular, are enormous—the blue whale *Balaenoptera musculus*, which can grow to more than 30 meters in length and a maximum weight of 190 tonnes, is the largest animal that has ever lived on earth.

There are significant metabolic advantages to being so large—an important consideration, since many large whales live in very cold seas. Like humans, whales must maintain a constant body temperature of around 37° Celsius, but the temperature of the sea can be as low as –1.7° Celsius. Water is an excellent conductor of heat and can suck heat out of a typical mammalian body many times faster than air. However, the rate at which heat is lost

depends on the surface area of the body which, comparatively, decreases as body size increases. Since the surface area of a large mammal is relatively less than that of a small one, large whales have a considerable advantage because they lose heat more slowly.

Because whales live permanently in water, their size is not limited by the effects of gravity, as it is with land mammals. Their bodies are weightless in water and their limbs do not have to support their body weight. Instead, the forelimbs have been flattened to form pectoral fins, or flippers, and are used for steering and maneuvering, temperature regulation, touch and other purposes. In most cases, in order to decrease the surface area and for streamlining,

the forelimbs are reduced in size and the hind limbs have been lost altogether (although they have been replaced to some extent by the development of flukes).

Whales propel themselves with their paddle-like tail flukes. Although their flippers are also paddle-shaped, they are used not for propulsion, but as balancing planes. The upward movement of the tail is the power stroke, driving the animal forward, while the downward movement is the recovery stroke.

ON THE MOVE

Traveling through water is much harder than traveling through air. Water provides resistance against movement, producing turbulence and

ABOVE: The streamlining of the body does not reduce drag sufficiently to account for the extraordinary swimming speeds attained by some cetaceans. As it accelerates through the water, this bottlenose dolphin creates a laminar flow of water over its body to further reduce turbulence.

1

2

HOW A DOLPHIN SWIMS

In a paper published in *Nature* in 1948, James Gray described experiments (carried out using a rigid model of a dolphin) indicating that in order to maintain the observed swimming speeds of living dolphins, the propulsive force of the tail would require the muscles to develop about 10 times as much power as the muscles of other mammals. This was considered unlikely, but no other explanation could be advanced until the work of Peter Purves was published in *Nature* in 1963.

Put simply, as the tail is moved upward in the water by the action of the propulsive muscles (the "power stroke"), water is forced from the upper to the lower surface of the flukes, setting up turbulence and forming a vortex at the trailing edge of the flukes. An area of low pressure is created beneath the flukes as the upstroke continues, causing the blades of the flukes to bend down and drawing water backward from the surface of the head and body. This causes the dolphin to move forward and downward against the hydroplaning action of the flippers.

As a result of this forward and downward body movement, further upward movement of the flukes accelerates the passage of water obliquely over the body and down the back, and the vortex at the trailing edge of the flukes is washed away.

The blades of the flukes relax before the downstroke of the tail begins. As the tail is pulled downward by the recovery muscles (the "recovery stroke"), the flukes begin to curl upward

ABOVE: Just as the bulbous bow of large ships reduces drag, the bulbous forehead of some fast-swimming whales appears to contribute to their speed in the water.

frictional drag at the skin surface. To minimize this problem, a whale's body is perfectly streamlined, with all the protruding parts, such as hair, external ear pinnae, mammary glands and reproductive organs reduced or tucked away.

A whale's skin is also silky smooth and has a number of extraordinary adaptations. It sheds and renews its outer cells rapidly (every couple of hours compared with every 18 hours in human skin) and exudes tiny droplets of oil that are believed to act as a lubricant. Cetaceans also have a large number of glands in their eyelids that produce a copious mucous secretion, easily visible as a stringy material starting from the eye and passing back along the body toward the shoulders. This may have a similar function to the fine film of mucus secreted by fish as they swim. There is also a system of dermal ridges beneath the skin, similar to the ones that form our fingerprints, which seems to correspond to

patterns of water flow. The skin surface is even believed to shift in folds and ripples as a response to changes in pressure on different parts of the body. These subtle alterations in shape at the skin surface probably eliminate turbulence before it is fully formed.

The most important factor helping whales attain such high swimming efficiency—they easily outperform laboratory models—is the way their tail flukes create a "laminar flow" of water over the body. This greatly reduces drag and enables whales to swim relatively fast and for long periods with relatively little exertion.

Dolphins, and some other small cetaceans, also save energy when they are swimming fast by "porpoising" or leaping clear of the water. This is the most efficient way to travel in terms of energy. Since air offers less resistance to movement than water, every time they need to breathe they leave the water altogether.

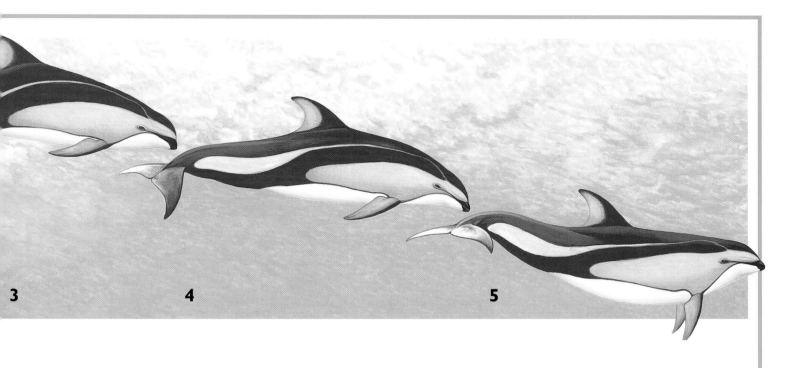

3   **4**   **5**

and spill water sideways instead of accelerating it to the rear. The buoyancy of the head and thorax, enhanced by the large amount of oil and fat contained in them, causes the head to rise while the downstroke of the tail continues. The water flow over the rear of the body is similar to that during the propulsive stroke, but without positive acceleration.

The positive acceleration of water over the body during the power stroke allows laminar (non-turbulent) flow to occur at speeds well above those at which turbulent flow develops. A condition of laminar flow exists over the majority of the dolphin's body surface during swimming, thereby reducing greatly the power needed for high-speed swimming.

DOLPHIN PROPULSION

1. The flukes start descending to begin the downstroke.

2. The downstroke continues.

3. The downstroke is completed.

4. The upstroke then begins.

5. The dolphin completes the upstroke and prepares for the next downstroke.

CONTROLLING BODY TEMPERATURE

Whales are warm-blooded creatures and therefore face particular difficulties in maintaining a steady body temperature (homeothermy) in an environment with considerably lower temperatures. Water has a much greater capacity to absorb heat, and it does so much more rapidly than air. Heat exchange in water is consequently many times greater than in still air at the same temperature.

Whales are unable to conserve body heat by behavioral means in the ways that some terrestrial mammals do—by curling up, building nests, huddling together, seeking shelter in protected places or seeking out warm, sunny areas. For whales, all the water available is at more or less the same temperature and, in the polar regions, for example, this is extremely cold.

To avoid excessive body heat loss, whales, like other aquatic mammals, have a heavy blanket of

fat, called blubber, in the deepest layer of the skin, which acts as an insulator as well as an important energy store. Blubber varies greatly in thickness within and between individual whales and whale species, but it has been recorded up to 50 centimeters thick in one species, the bowhead whale *Balaena mysticetus*.

Blubber has been shown to be an effective insulator, and it is clear from direct observation that whales in good physical condition do not suffer greatly from the cold. However, it is not a complete insulator. Consequently, whales in very cold water do lose more heat than those in warmer water, and therefore require more energy from food to survive.

Although conservation of body heat is largely taken care of by the development of the blubber layer, there is a potential problem of overheating when a whale engages in bursts of activity. This is overcome by the presence of many large arteries

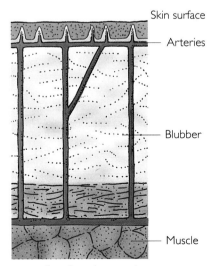

ABOVE: Forming a layer up to 50 centimeters thick, the dense blubber that lies beneath a whale's skin insulates the body.

David Rootes/Seaphot Ltd/Planet Earth Pictures

BELOW: Blood traveling from the heart to an extremity flows through a central artery (shown in red) at 37° Celsius and exchanges heat with surrounding veins to maintain a stable temperature gradient. Cool venous blood (shown in blue) flowing from an extremity is warmed gradually from as low as 4° Celsius to 37° Celsius as it approaches body cavities.

running up through the blubber to the skin. If large volumes of blood are pumped through these vessels, the skin is warmed by all this blood and the heat is quickly dissipated to the surrounding water. The flow through the arteries is controlled by nerves. When the volume is decreased almost to zero, the blubber serves its normal function as an insulator.

But how is heat conserved in those parts of the body that lack blubber: the flippers, the flukes and the dorsal fin? These regions must receive some blood to supply their tissues with oxygen, but blood flowing through them at body

temperature would cause significant loss of body heat. A modification of the blood vessels minimizes this loss by an elegant mechanism called "countercurrent heat exchange." The basic arrangement is present in many terrestrial mammals, including humans, where the deeply placed major arteries supplying the extremities are accompanied by two or more veins. Heat is transferred between artery and veins so that the blood is cooled as it approaches the extremity and warmed again as it leaves it. In the whale, the arrangement has been modified so that the arteries are completely enclosed in a plexus (bundle) of veins, increasing the efficiency of the countercurrent heat exchange.

The return of venous (deoxygenated) blood from the flippers, flukes and dorsal fin is controlled by a simple mechanism. If the flow of blood to these extremities is increased, the arteries

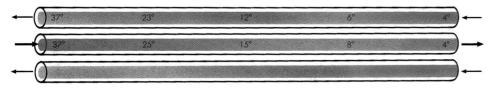

increase in diameter to accommodate the extra flow. This in turn puts pressure on the surrounding venous plexus, restricting the blood flow in it (and hence preventing the cooling of the arterial blood) and forcing the blood to return to the body in surface veins. These are not accompanied by arteries, so heat is now lost from the relatively warm venous blood to the surrounding water.

This intriguing system can control the amount of heat lost from the surface of the extremities—heat is conserved when required by the countercurrent mechanism, or dissipated when this mechanism is closed off, in conditions (such as during physical exertion) where surplus heat is produced.

DIVING SKILLS

All whales are skilled divers and hunt for food underwater in their natural environment. But,

as mammals, they must surface at intervals to breathe. Until just a few years ago, the only information about the diving capabilities of whales had been obtained either indirectly (by dissection of specimens or by examination of whales entangled in nets or other structures underwater) or directly (but not experimentally) from observers attached to research expeditions and whaling vessels.

Although such observations have been recorded for a long time, it was not until the 1950s that detailed studies of the diving physiology of cetaceans began, stimulated by the development of ways to catch and maintain small cetaceans in captivity. These were extended later by training dolphins to dive in the open ocean, following specific commands, and then returning for further examination. Another method involves the use of radio and satellite

ABOVE: A thick layer of blubber and a variety of physiological adaptations help to regulate heat loss. Many whales that live in high latitudes grow to an enormous size, thus reducing their surface area relative to their mass and making protection from cold waters even more efficient.

Marty Snyderman

telemetry. A dolphin is captured at sea, fitted with a device to record information about the dive and a signaling device to record the animal's whereabouts, and then released. Observers pick up signals transmitted by the equipment every time the dolphin surfaces to breathe. The recording device is attached to the animal with a corrosive coupling designed to dissolve in seawater, and the equipment falls off after a time. It can then be recovered and reused.

Diving ability varies greatly among different whale species, but all are impressive divers. Sperm whales *Physeter macrocephalus* and bottlenose whales, genus *Hyperoodon*, are probably the most accomplished, although some other beaked whales may also be capable of impressive dives. One sperm whale, being studied in the Caribbean, was recorded on a dive which lasted an incredible 2 hours and 18 minutes. Rorquals, family Balaenopteridae, rarely dive for more than 40 minutes, while the bottlenose dolphin *Tursiops truncatus* normally dives for less than 15 minutes, and the two common dolphins *Delphinus delphis* and *Delphinus capensis* dive for only about three minutes.

It is striking just how briefly a whale is at the water surface when it breathes. The nostrils, at the front of the head in most other animals, have in the course of whale evolution become a single blowhole (in toothed whales) or a double blowhole (in baleen whales), normally at the highest point of the head. Therefore, only a small part of the head region and back needs to break the surface during respiration, and the animal can exhale and inhale remarkably rapidly while swimming at speed.

LEFT: The amount of time spent underwater varies greatly among different species but these spotted dolphins, like all cetaceans, require a remarkably brief time at the surface to take in air, partly due to the convenient location of their blowholes on the top of the head.

BELOW: Diving and breathing patterns vary between species. Each small "crest" in the diagram represents the whale surfacing in order to breathe. Sperm whales may dive to 3,000 meters (not shown to scale in the diagram). The horizontal scale shows the time elapsed during the dive.

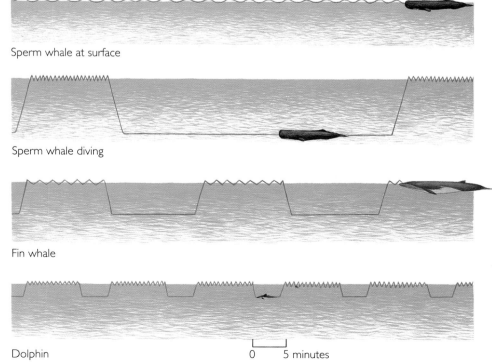

Sperm whale at surface

Sperm whale diving

Fin whale

Dolphin

0   5 minutes

Some whales, particularly sperm whales, dive to phenomenal depths—certainly in excess of 2,000 meters and possibly as deep as 3,000 meters or more. But how do they avoid the problems inflicting human scuba divers, such as decompression sickness or, as it is more popularly known, "the bends"?

Whales do not suffer the bends—a potentially fatal condition caused by nitrogen bubbling out of the blood—because, unlike scuba divers, they do not breathe compressed air. Human divers breathe in copious quantities of compressed air when they are underwater, and more and more of the nitrogen in this air dissolves in their blood. As the diver rises to the surface, the pressure decreases, and the nitrogen begins to come out of solution. If the nitrogen comes out too quickly, bubbles form in the blood vessels and tissues— just like the bubbles of carbon dioxide released in a bottle of pop when the top is removed and the internal pressure is released. These nitrogen bubbles can lodge in joints, causing severe pain, or in vital blood vessels, causing paralysis or even death.

Cetaceans, on the other hand, are breath-hold divers. They take down only the air contained in their lungs and respiratory passages after a single breath. Therefore, there is relatively little nitrogen to dissolve in the blood and tissues and so cetaceans do not suffer the bends. Also, when a whale dives, the hydrostatic pressure, which increases at a rate of about 1 atmosphere for every 10-meter increase in depth of seawater, is transmitted to all parts of the body. Since a large proportion of the whale's body consists of water, which is practically incompressible, most of its body is not deformed by the increased pressure. But the air in its lungs and respiratory passages is compressible and with increasing pressure, the lungs collapse and much of the air is forced into the thick-walled windpipe and nasal passages leading to the blowhole. The blood vessels supplying these passages are fewer and further from the surface than in the lungs, which means that gas exchange from air to blood is drastically reduced.

There is another relatively large air space surrounding the tiny structures of the middle ear. Only a small pressure difference between this cavity and the tissues and blood vessels lining its wall would be needed to make the vessels swell and rupture. The pain in the ears caused by such disequilibrium is appreciated by any diver. The whale is protected against this by having extensive vascular sinuses in the lining of the middle ear space. Under pressure, these swell with

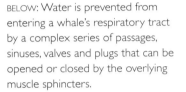

BELOW: Water is prevented from entering a whale's respiratory tract by a complex series of passages, sinuses, valves and plugs that can be opened or closed by the overlying muscle sphincters.

blood and reduce the volume of the cavity. This simple mechanism, which is automatic, always keeps the middle ear at the same pressure as the outside environment—whatever the dive depth.

CATCHING THEIR BREATH

Whales have to obtain all the oxygen they need for a dive during the brief period when they surface to take a breath. But how can they stay underwater for so long and still breathe less frequently than land mammals? Proportionately, their lungs are not significantly larger than those of land mammals and some of the better diving whales have relatively smaller lungs. In fact, the air in them plays a surprisingly minor role in long, deep dives—although they do use it very efficiently. They exchange much more of their lung volume with each breath (dolphins exchange an incredible 80–90 percent of their lung volume, compared with only 5–15 percent in humans). They also extract much more of the oxygen present in the air (nearly 90 percent in some cases). However, lung capacity does not explain how whales can store sufficient oxygen to hold their breath for minutes or even hours at a time.

Many of the other more unusual features of the respiratory system of whales are merely adaptations to prevent water entering the airways: the nasal passages are complex and convoluted, and the larynx (the upper end of the respiratory tube) extends up into the nasal cavity rather than opening into the throat.

Whales have increased their capacity to store oxygen in the body not by enlarging their lungs, but by modifying their circulatory system and the chemistry of their muscles. Blood makes up 10–15 percent of the body weight of whales, compared with about 7 percent in humans. It also contains many more red cells—the cells responsible for transporting oxygen—and therefore can carry much more oxygen.

A significant amount of oxygen is also contained within the muscles, thanks to the presence of a protein called myoglobin, which acts as a highly efficient oxygen reservoir. Myoglobin has a greater affinity for oxygen than the equivalent protein in blood, known as hemoglobin, so oxygen carried in the blood is readily given up to the muscles. Myoglobin

ABOVE: Whales use air more efficiently than other mammals, extracting a greater amount of oxygen and exchanging more air with each brief breath—up to 90 percent of the lungs' contents compared with the 15 percent exchanged by humans.

is more abundant and more concentrated in whales than in land mammals, giving the muscles a characteristic dark color.

Even taking all these different oxygen collection and storage techniques into account, theoretically they cannot explain how so many cetaceans can dive for so long. Clearly, other mechanisms must be operating during a dive—or the animals would quickly run out of oxygen.

In 1870, the French physiologist Paul Bert described a phenomenon of profound slowing of the heart beat, or bradycardia, when ducks were submerged. This has since been termed "diving bradycardia," and is the most familiar cardiovascular response in diving animals, including whales. Observations of bottlenose dolphins have revealed that the heart rate fluctuates continually in concert with the respiration. While the dolphin is underwater, between breaths its heart rate is fairly constant at 33–45 beats per minute, but when it takes a breath at the surface the rate rises sharply for a brief time to 80–90 beats per minute. The longer it has been submerged, the more the heart rate rises when it breathes.

In many aquatic animals, diving bradycardia is accompanied by a redistribution of blood flow so that only essential organs are supplied with oxygenated blood. Blood flow to vital organs, such as the brain and the heart wall is maintained during dives, whereas the arteries supplying other organs, such as the stomach, intestines, kidneys, and muscles may constrict to the point where blood flow is cut off almost

completely. Large volumes of blood are stored in the veins (which are enlarged to form sinuses) in the abdominal and thoracic cavities.

Similar mechanisms to these may operate in cetaceans. The veins in the body cavities of whales are large and distensible, indicating that redistribution of blood flow does occur during dives. Of course, distension of the veins may also have the added advantage of filling space in the body cavities as respiratory air is compressed during a dive.

Animals produce the energy they need for life and movement by breaking down glycogen. This is normally accomplished by the process of aerobic metabolism, which uses oxygen and produces carbon dioxide plus non-toxic waste products. The function of the respiratory system is to supply the oxygen to the blood and take away the unwanted carbon dioxide.

When insufficient oxygen is available for the complete breakdown of glycogen—for example, in a diving animal—the reaction is interrupted at an intermediate stage, producing toxic lactic acid. This is called anaerobic metabolism. In this case, the animal incurs an "oxygen debt," which can only be settled when it returns to the surface and breathes, replenishing its oxygen stores.

Increased tolerance to lactic acid and carbon dioxide is another important adaptation to diving. Terrestrial mammals tolerate only low levels of lactic acid, but seals, for example, accumulate large amounts of these chemicals in their blood during a dive. While cetaceans can breathe and store enough oxygen to permit most of their dives to be

THE WONDERFUL NETS

The blood system of whales is complex, and the full functional significance of all its features is not yet understood. Among the most intriguing structures are the "retia mirabilia," or "wonderful nets." These are massive plexuses, or bundles, consisting of contorted spirals of tiny blood vessels that form great blocks of tissue on the inside wall of the chest near the backbone and elsewhere. How these retia function is not fully understood, although several possibilities have been suggested.

All of the blood flowing from the heart to the brain passes through a large rete mirabile in the upper part of the chest wall, so one possibility is that this arrangement has a pressure-damping function for the blood flowing to the brain. Another suggestion is that the retia mirabilia play a crucial role in dealing with the bends, since the largest of them are found in the upper parts of the body cavity and are well placed to trap bubbles of nitrogen as they form.

Other speculations on the functions of the retia suggest that they may help to maintain steady blood flow, equalize pressure differences, act as temporary reservoirs of oxygenated blood, act as temperature-regulating devices in countercurrent heat-conserving systems, or simply as stores used to help the redistribution of blood during diving.

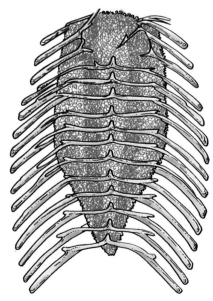

ABOVE: One of the most intriguing features of whale anatomy is the existence of the large retia mirabilia ("wonderful nets"), massive structures composed of blood vessels beneath the backbone and ribs.

aerobic, during very long dives at least some tissues must be depleted of their oxygen stores and depend upon anaerobic metabolism. It has been suggested that during the latter part of a deep dive, a whale has barely enough oxygen remaining in the body to maintain the heart, and that even the brain may be capable of some anaerobic metabolism.

REGULATING BUOYANCY

Most whales swim with a slight negative buoyancy. Their bodies become denser with increasing depth as the air in their lungs is compressed. This is of little consequence in many species because they do not dive to great depth, but it is extremely important in the very deep-diving species, such as the bottlenose whales and the sperm whale.

The most striking characteristic of the sperm whale is its remarkable head—that huge, rather square structure usually depicted in diagrams or cartoons of the "typical" whale. The spermaceti organ in the whale's head contains a yellowish wax, which is very rich in oil. It is different in composition from the oils in blubber and in other parts of the body. A 30-tonne sperm whale may have as much as 2.5 tonnes of spermaceti. Above 30° Celsius this oil is a clear, straw-colored liquid, but at lower temperatures it becomes cloudy, and

eventually solidifies. The spermaceti organ is a huge component of the sperm whale's body; this fact, and the fact that it is present as a similar although less complex organ in other deep-diving whales, suggests that it must serve an important function—or maybe several important functions.

One possible function, suggested by biologist Malcolm Clarke, is that it serves as a buoyancy regulator. By altering the temperature (and therefore the density) of the wax as the whale dives, it could help the animal to sink or float with the minimum of effort. Clarke argues that, as the whale descends in the ocean, it experiences colder and colder water, which cools the spermaceti organ. Cooling of the wax changes its physical condition—it contracts and increases in density— while the increasing pressure as the whale dives adds to this density increase. Consequently, as the spermaceti becomes denser, buoyancy decreases. Because so much spermaceti is present, a variation in temperature of only a few degrees would provide a sufficient change in density for the whale to regulate its buoyancy as it dives.

By no means do we have all the answers about how whales, as mammals, cope with life in the sea. While many fascinating aspects of their lives are known to us, many more mysteries remain.

ABOVE: The oil contained in the spermaceti organ inside the sperm whale's massive head may act as a buoyancy regulator. As the oil becomes cooler and denser during a deep dive, it may have the effect of reducing buoyancy and therefore reducing the amount of energy required to hunt at depth.

WHALE ANATOMY

C etaceans are remarkable among mammals in that they are fully aquatic and have been so for more than 40 million years. They seem superbly adapted to life in water. But, upon close study, cetacean anatomy is full of compromise—there is no perfect anatomical design. Rather, the anatomy of whales and dolphins reflects a mix of factors: some features have been inherited relatively unchanged from mammalian ancestors; some are recently evolved in response to the demands of aquatic life; and some reflect the dictates of geometry.

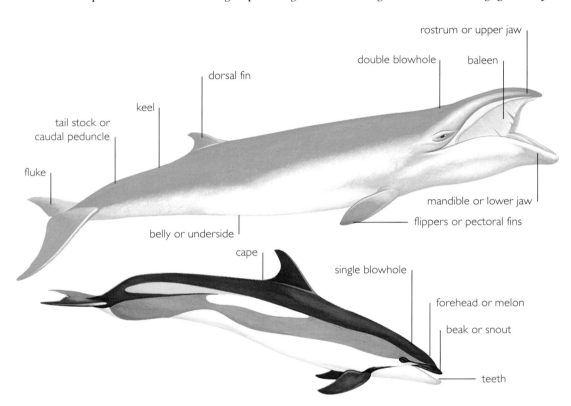

RIGHT: The pygmy right whale (top) has characteristics typical of a baleen whale. These differ markedly from the features of the Atlantic white-sided dolphin (below), which typify the toothed whales.

THE MAMMALIAN HERITAGE

Many features of cetaceans were inherited with little modification from distant ancestors, reflecting the warm-blooded and air-breathing active lifestyle of mammals. For example, cetaceans have hair (albeit vestigial, and mainly in juveniles and in baleen whales); a four-chambered heart supplying both lungs and body; and a diaphragm to aid breathing. Reproduction and parental care are complex: the genitals and anus are separate; young are nourished by a placenta in the uterus; and after birth the young are suckled by the mother.

Body structures related to hearing and feeding show a distinctively mammalian form: there is a single lower jawbone on each side, and the ear contains three small auditory ossicles that transmit sound to the organ of hearing—the cochlea—in a separate periotic bone. The skull articulates at two condyles with the first of seven cervical or neck vertebrae, and the vertebrae of the trunk are separated into those with ribs (thoracics) or without (lumbar vertebrae). Anatomically, then, cetaceans are clearly mammals.

ADAPTATIONS FOR SWIMMING

Cetaceans have a smooth body that is propelled through the water by horizontal tail flukes, aided by foreflippers and a dorsal fin. These features resemble those of other marine vertebrates like sharks and penguins. Streamlining has removed impediments to smooth efficient water flow across the moving body surface. Indeed, in adapting to aquatic life, cetaceans have lost some characteristic external structures usually seen in mammals, such as significant body hair, sweat glands, an external ear lobe, a projecting nose, and externally projecting genitals, scrotum and mammary glands. Remnants of the hindlimbs are internal, but very rarely a tiny vestigial leg occurs as an evolutionary throwback. Body outlines vary markedly between species. The extremes of profile are understandable—for example, the slender right whale dolphins *Lissodelphis* spp. are fast-moving, while the tubby bowhead *Balaena mysticetus* is a slow swimmer with thick, heat-conserving blubber.

All cetaceans have well-developed forelimbs or flippers placed behind and below the head. The foreflippers are stiff, without the movable elbow joint seen in most mammals, and there is little visible external evidence of their internal structure. Yet these flippers have the same basic internal form as a human arm and presumably

help in steering. Proportions vary greatly from species to species, but it is not clear what this variation means in terms of function. In some species, the flippers are held rather rigidly out from the body, while in others (such as the humpback whale *Megaptera novaeangliae* and the finless porpoise *Neophocaena phocaenoides*) they are quite mobile, and may be used for slow-speed sculling, maneuvering and perhaps display. Internal variation involves the number of "fingers" (four or five digits); the number of phalanges—individual bones—in each digit (some species show extreme increase, or hyperphalangy); and the degree of splaying of the digits.

SMALL, BIG AND BIGGEST

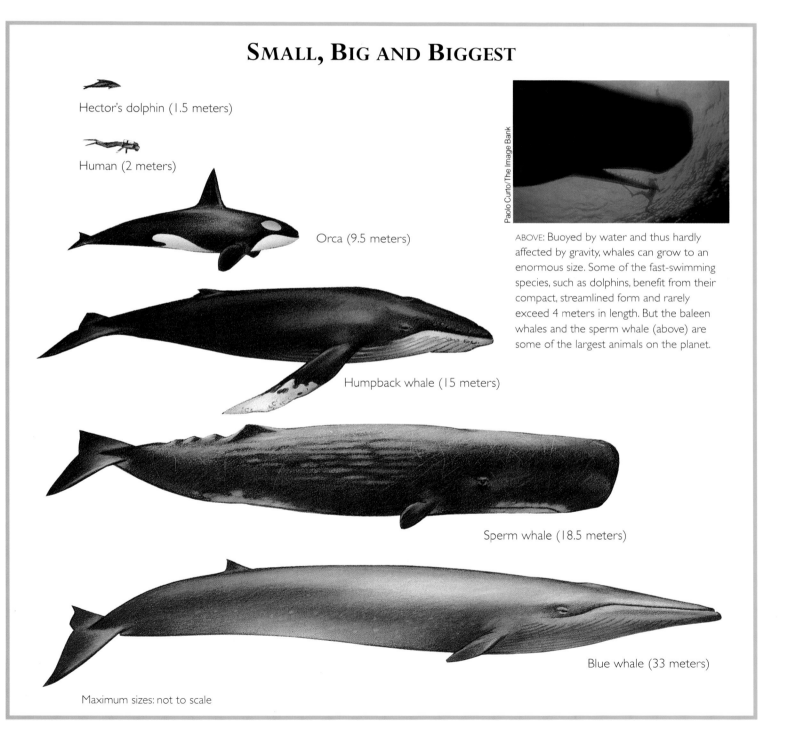

Hector's dolphin (1.5 meters)

Human (2 meters)

Orca (9.5 meters)

Paolo Curto/The Image Bank

ABOVE: Buoyed by water and thus hardly affected by gravity, whales can grow to an enormous size. Some of the fast-swimming species, such as dolphins, benefit from their compact, streamlined form and rarely exceed 4 meters in length. But the baleen whales and the sperm whale (above) are some of the largest animals on the planet.

Humpback whale (15 meters)

Sperm whale (18.5 meters)

Blue whale (33 meters)

Maximum sizes: not to scale

ABOVE: The remarkable narwhal tusk is, in fact, an erupted tooth that can grow to a length of 3 meters.

BELOW: The distinctive throat pleats of the humpback whale and other rorquals allow a tremendous expansion of the mouth cavity, forming an expandable pouch below the throat and thorax.

Most cetaceans have a prominent dorsal fin on their back, at or behind mid-length in most species. This fin is supported not by skeleton, but by tough fibrous tissue inside it. Its size, shape and position vary, although it is not clear what this means in terms of controlling body orientation during swimming. It has been suggested that the dorsal fin also has a second role: regulating the temperature of reproductive organs.

Behind the anus the body tapers into the laterally compressed tail stock or peduncle and the stiff horizontal flukes at the tip of the tail. The flukes are supported internally by tough interwoven tendons. Power comes from large muscles which dominate much of the body, particularly above and below those vertebrae behind the abdomen. Power is transmitted from these muscles through the peduncle to the terminal tail vertebrae and tail flukes via strong tendons lying close to the vertebrae.

Movement is a basic up-and-down body flexing, essentially the same as the undulation seen in a running land mammal. The beating flukes, which pivot most around a specialized internal joint at the "ball vertebra," provide swimming thrust. Although the body is most flexible in a vertical plane, most cetaceans can also bend from side to side. There are many variations on this basic pattern of swimming apparatus—in relative size of swimming muscles, proportions of vertebrae, and size and shape of flukes. While the broad patterns of swimming are understood reasonably well, research is needed to understand how anatomical differences between species relate to different swimming styles.

KEEPING WARM

Cetaceans, like other mammals, are warm-blooded animals with a fast metabolism. A constant fast metabolism brings advantages—it allows quick responses in feeding and flight from threat—but at the cost of needing a large energy input from food. Further, warm-blooded mammals must conserve body energy against the heat-sapping effects of water.

Cetaceans have several heat-conserving systems. One is the intrinsic geometry of their body. As any animal increases in size, the ratio of its surface area to volume decreases markedly, with major implications to heat loss. Cetaceans, which are huge compared with most mammals, have a low surface area-to-volume ratio which helps to retain heat. Blubber insulates against the chill of water, and there are heat-conserving "counter-current exchange" systems which conserve heat in blood that circulates in

Francois Gohier/Auscape International

LEFT: The shape and size of dolphin dorsal fins varies enormously: some are falcate, others are triangular and a few are rounded, while several species have little or no dorsal fin at all. The functional significance of these different designs is uncertain.

Minke flipper banding

Long-finned pilot whale flipper

Short-finned pilot whale flipper

ABOVE: Distinctive flipper shapes and patterns provide a useful way to identify cetaceans. Minke whales usually have a white band on the flippers although in some parts of the world their flippers are all black..

appendages—flippers, dorsal fin and flukes—and near the surface. These exchange systems can also radiate excess heat at times of exercise, and they may operate constantly to keep some parts of the body a little cooler than surrounding tissues. For example, the internal testes and uterus in the bottlenose dolphin may be cooled by blood that circulates near the dorsal fin.

THE HEAD AND SKULL

The two groups of living cetaceans—baleen whales or mysticetes and toothed whales or odontocetes—can be separated immediately based on the appearance of the head and skull. Differences between these groups reflect different feeding behaviors: baleen-assisted filter-feeding in mysticetes and echolocation-assisted predation in odontocetes. In each group, the feeding method is closely linked with unique soft tissues and skull form. Often, the skull in both mysticetes and odontocetes is described as "telescoped," because in each group some bones overlap each other in a way not seen in other mammals. But "telescoping" is a confusing term which refers to the results of several different processes and is best avoided. Details of the anatomy of the head and skull (the cranium) are reviewed below for both the mysticetes and odontocetes. First, though, some general points of cranial anatomy are noteworthy.

All cetaceans have a prominent upper jaw or rostrum which protrudes in front of the eyes. In bulbous-headed species, the rostrum cannot be seen externally, but is apparent on the skull. Many species seem to wear a permanent smile, but this reflects mouth shape rather than

emotional expression. Under the skin, the head has a layer of blubber which prevents major muscles of the face reaching the surface. With the expressive face typical of land mammals largely obscured, cetaceans cannot use facial movements and hair patterns in social signaling. Perhaps body color patterns or sexually dimorphic features like dorsal fins and tusklike teeth have assumed a role in social communication to compensate.

Most land mammals have forward-facing nostrils, but the equivalent blowhole in living cetaceans is on top of the head. There is no obvious snout and, indeed, the sense of smell is reduced in mysticetes and apparently absent in odontocetes. Most cetaceans have only a short and rather inflexible neck. However, some species, like the Irrawaddy dolphin *Orcaella brevirostris* and the finless porpoise *Neophocaena phocaenoides*, exhibit great mobility of the head.

Cetacean eyes are rather small and expressionless. They lie on the sides of the head, just behind the gape of the mouth. There are no eyebrows or lashes. Further backward behind and below the eye, a dimple or small hole on the side of the head marks the position of the ear. There is no external ear flap or lobe, and in many species, sound is probably transmitted to the ears through soft tissues rather than through the reduced ear canal. Nevertheless, hearing appears to be very sophisticated.

CRANIAL ANATOMY OF MYSTICETES

A dominant feature of the head of mysticetes is the large upper jaw which carries a rack of baleen or "whalebone" on each side. The baleen is used

WHALE HEADS

BOTTLENOSE DOLPHIN
Tursiops truncatus
This familiar dolphin has a well-formed melon separated from the stocky snout by a crease. It has up to 108 small, pointed teeth and feeds on small fish, squid and octopus.

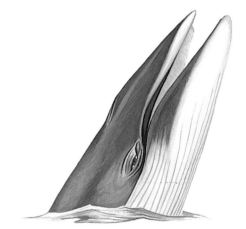

MINKE WHALE
Balaenoptera acutorostrata
The minke whale has a pointed head and prominent median ridge. 460–720 baleen plates, each 20–30 centimeters long, hang from its upper jaw. It feeds on krill, small fish and, occasionally, free-swimming mollusks.

SOUTHERN RIGHT WHALE
Eubalaena australis
This whale has up to 540 baleen plates in its upper jaw. It feeds on krill, copepods and other zooplankton. The head and body are marked with callosities.

SPERM WHALE
Physeter macrocephalus
Largest of the toothed whales, the sperm whale has up to 50 teeth in the lower jaw only. It feeds on squid, including giant squid, fish and cephalopods. The massive head makes up one-third of total body length.

in filter-feeding. Each rack contains scores or hundreds of horny baleen plates which hang down from the roof of the mouth like long parallel strings. Each plate is oriented from side to side, perpendicular to the body axis, and only a few millimeters from its neighbor. A baleen plate is formed from tough flexible organic tissue rather like fingernail, which arises from a narrow base in the gum tissue, and hangs far down into the mouth. As the plate grows, its inner edges become frayed into a mat of tough fine hairs which collectively form a filter to trap food inside the mouth. Adult mysticetes do not have teeth, but multiple simple teeth occur in embryos. These teeth are resorbed as baleen develops before birth. They are a reminder of the distant toothed ancestry of baleen whales.

The baleen filter-feeding system is linked with other anatomical features. Bones in the upper jaw are loosely attached to each other and to the skull, probably to help absorb the shock when the jaws close after gulping plankton-loaded water. Part of the upper jaw thrusts back under the eye region to extend the roof of the mouth, perhaps increasing the food-processing area. The main jaw-closing or temporal muscles attach above the eye, rather than behind or under it.

Baleen whales do not show the diversity of cranial structure seen in odontocetes. Species differ most obviously from one another in the proportions of the upper jaw, and in shape, color and number of baleen plates. These features are linked in turn with skull form and feeding behavior. In the slow-swimming and plankton-skimming right whales, long and narrow baleen arises from a narrow high-arched upper jaw. Lower lips curve up to meet the arched upper jaw, covering the baleen. Associated with the unusually arched upper jaw, the frontal bone, which forms the orbit at its outer margin, descends far below the level of the blowholes. Thus, the eyes lie far down on the side of the head.

Rorquals have rather short baleen and a flat upper jaw. These are gulp-feeders, which drop the lower jaw far open to engulf huge mouthfuls of water and food. Externally, the throat has conspicuous concertina-like grooves or pleats, which allow it to expand enormously when food is engulfed. Above the eyes, the frontal bones are abruptly depressed to form large origins for the temporal muscles that close the lower jaws.

Mysticetes have widely separated lower jaws which are toothless and lack baleen. They typically bow outward, and at the front they are not fused together but are attached to each other by ligaments. This flexible joint presumably allows some independent movement of the jaws during feeding. Other distinctive features of the head and skull include the double blowhole and the lack of enlarged facial muscles and nasal sacs. In contrast to odontocetes, the braincase is not expanded markedly upward.

CRANIAL ANATOMY OF ODONTOCETES

Externally, odontocetes show more variation in cranial structure than mysticetes. Generally the jaws are narrow and toothed; there is a bulbous "melon" associated with facial muscles and nasal sacs above the eyes and upper jaw; and a single blowhole opens high on the elevated forehead. Variations may include a bulbous forehead which obscures the jaws; broad and short rather than long and narrow jaws; a tooth complement which varies from hundreds (in some river dolphins) to none (in most female beaked whales); and an anterior blowhole (in sperm whales).

Despite this variation in external features, odontocetes are unified by aspects of skull anatomy around the nasal region and the skull base. The posterior parts of the maxilla (the main tooth-bearing bone of the jaw) and premaxilla (the jawbone that carries the incisors) extend backward and upward above the eye region to cover the front of the braincase. Commonly, the left and right maxilla and premaxilla are asymmetrical. This pattern of the maxilla and premaxilla is linked with the ability to echolocate using high-frequency sound. The expanded and backward-shifted maxilla holds a large volume of facial muscles, equivalent to those that in humans help move the lips and flare the nostrils. These facial muscles focus upward and in toward the blowhole. Here they are attached to a series of sacs in the soft tissues of the nasal passage between the external blowhole and the bony nasal openings on the skull. Apparently, the facial muscles help to produce echolocation sounds in the complex soft tissues of the nasal passages, inside the forehead between the skull and the blowhole. In front of the nasal passages, a large internal fat body, the melon, helps to transmit sound forward into the water.

Other skull features in odontocetes probably help to produce and receive echolocation sounds. For example, the reduced cheekbone presumably isolates the sound-producing front from the sound-receiving back of the skull. In each ear, the middle ear cavity is expanded into a complex sinus on the skull base. These sinuses perhaps compensate for increased pressure on the ear during diving. They may help to isolate the right and left ears from each other, making it easier to identify the direction of a sound source. The periotic—the earbone with the organs of hearing and balance—is loose in the skull, probably to eliminate spurious transmission of sound through the adjacent skull bones. The external ear canal is vestigial. Sound is probably not transmitted from the water to the internal earbones via the vestigial ear canal. Rather, it travels through a dense thin receiving area, the pan bone, in the lower jaw and then through a fatty channel to the ear.

BELOW: Although the embryos of baleen whales have vestigial teeth, these disappear before birth. Instead, the whales use hundreds of baleen plates, which hang down from their upper jaws and form a sieve to filter food out of the seawater.

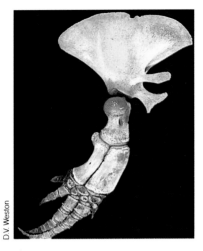

D.V. Weston

ABOVE: Greatly altered in length, the bones of the forelimb have been transformed to form a pectoral fin or flipper. A reduction in the number of "fingers" is common, although each finger usually has a greater number of individual bones.

RIGHT: All whales, such as this male common dolphin, share anatomical features with other mammals. However, they have become superbly adapted for life in their aquatic environment.

All odontocetes have teeth, sometimes vestigial, which differ from those of other mammals. Many dolphins, for example, have dozens of simple conical teeth on both sides of each jaw—far more than the typical number for mammals. There is only one set of teeth, whereas most mammals have two (milk and permanent teeth). In most odontocetes, the teeth are undifferentiated or homodont, with the same shape throughout the jaw, in contrast to the differentiated or heterodont teeth of most mammals, including archaic fossil cetaceans. Sometimes, teeth may be strangely elaborate, presumably for a display function, as in the tusk of the narwhal *Monodon monoceros* or strap-toothed whale *Mesoplodon layardi*. Squid-eating odontocetes usually have reduced numbers of teeth. Most beaked whales, family Ziphiidae, do not use teeth, but capture prey by suction-feeding.

BEHIND THE HEAD
The cetacean postcranial skeleton also differs markedly from that of land mammals. Cervical vertebrae are foreshortened, and may be partly or wholly fused. The form of ribs in the thorax reflects aquatic life—the body is buoyed by water, without the need for the body support required by land animals. For their size, the ribs are rather delicate, and not strongly attached to the spine or sternum. Indeed, the sternum is vestigial in mysticetes. Thoracic structure will not support the weight of the body on land, which is why cetaceans often die when they strand.

There is considerable variation in form and number of vertebrae between species, but we have only a crude understanding of what this means in terms of function. The vertebrae in ziphiids have tall spines which reflect a large mass of swimming muscles, perhaps linked to deep-diving. In Dall's porpoise *Phocoenoides dalli* the vertebrae are short and greatly increased in number—perhaps related to the fast swimming speed of the species. In all cetaceans, lumbar vertebrae pass into caudal or tail vertebrae without a distinct pelvis. Only a remnant of the pelvic girdle remains, suspended below the spine.

THE BRAIN AND OTHER ORGANS
Generally, cetacean brains are large compared to their body size, and the brains of large whales may be heavier than those of any other animals. Are these proportions meaningful? The sperm whale has one of the largest brains of any animal, but its brain is tiny compared to overall body mass. In many species, the cerebral hemispheres are impressively large and folded, with a

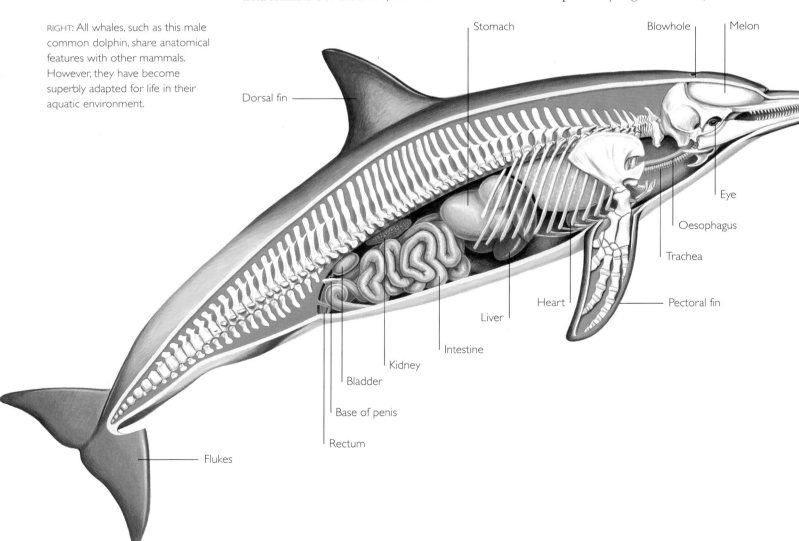

Stomach

Blowhole | Melon

Dorsal fin

Eye

Oesophagus

Trachea

Heart | Pectoral fin

Liver

Intestine

Kidney

Bladder

Base of penis

Rectum

Flukes

well-developed outer layer. Similar patterns are seen in humans. It is tempting to ascribe these similarities to "higher" intelligence in cetaceans, but their function is not clear. Blood supply to the cetacean brain is not by the normal mammalian route of the carotid arteries, but instead by way of blood vessels associated with the spinal cord. Also here are the retia mirabilia, a complex network of blood vessels which may help store blood and regulate its pressure during diving.

The internal organs of cetaceans deserve a long account, for it is here that so many of the critical physiological adaptations for an aquatic lifestyle can be identified. Yet, because of the difficulty of studying the physiology of living water-dwelling animals, we know less about how cetaceans work than for most mammals. Cetacean stomachs are chambered, usually with

a large fore-stomach followed by a main stomach and smaller duodenum. This arrangement is like that of ruminant hoofed mammals, although cetaceans do not chew their cud. The alimentary tract varies widely between species. Cetaceans lack a gall bladder and appendix, and the liver is not lobed. Lungs, which lie near the heart, are supplied by a short and often wide trachea. The kidneys are large with many separate lobes—each effectively a small kidney in itself.

Whales, dolphins and porpoises are difficult to study in the wild, and studies of dead or captive animals are unsatisfactory, so we still do not understand the function of many structures. Several centuries of study have given a tantalizing insight into the remarkable marine adaptations of much of cetacean anatomy— adaptations that overprint but never fully hide the distant land ancestry of these animals.

ABOVE: Cetaceans are difficult animals to study. They often live in extremely remote areas far out to sea, spend much of their lives diving to great depths underwater, and then show little of themselves when they rise to the surface to breathe. Not surprisingly, we still know very little about many aspects of their lives at sea.

A REMARKABLE SENSORY WORLD

ROBERT J. MORRIS

*W*hales and dolphins evolved from a group of land mammals. We can assume that their ancestors had the same five senses as us—sight, touch, taste, smell and hearing— and that these senses were adapted, as they are in other land mammals, to receive messages through the medium of air rather than water. As the early cetaceans moved into the sea it was vital for their survival that these aerially adapted senses became quickly readapted to life underwater. And if any sense could not be modified to function effectively underwater it was necessary to develop a new one to replace it.

FACING PAGE: The eyes of these spinner dolphins must be capable of adapting quickly to intense light at the surface, and to hunting and navigating in the twilight world below. Some deep-diving whales may be able to detect the bioluminescent organs of their prey at great depths.

Mike Osmond/Pacific Whale Foundation

ABOVE: This humpback whale has eyes that are mobile and well adapted to life in the sea. At depth the pupils are very large, enabling the eyes to make maximum use of the low light intensity; at the surface they are reduced to narrow slits.

VISION

Being air-breathing mammals, cetaceans need to be able to see both underwater and in air. The cetacean's eye was originally adapted only for sight in air, and important evolutionary developments occurred that allowed it to operate successfully in both media. One of the major problems is that light travels more slowly in water than in air and refracts, or bends, when it passes from air to water. Because of this, an eye adapted for focusing in air loses its focusing power in water. We humans have overcome the problem by wearing face masks when we dive, to keep our eyes in air

when we are underwater. Whales have overcome the problem by means of a physiological change. During the course of their transition and evolution into marine animals they have developed strong muscles around the eye that can change the actual shape of the lens in the eye to suit either air vision or underwater vision.

The intensity of light is another problem in using the eye both at the surface of the sea and at depth. Underwater, particularly at depth, light levels are very low, while at the surface the light is very strong. Cetaceans have adapted to these extremes of lighting by developing an eye with a large pupil. This pupil can collect large amounts of light so that the animal can see even in very low light. In bright light, however, the pupil can be closed right down to a narrow slit, so it can also be used for vision at the surface under the sort of lighting conditions for which our own eyes are designed.

When viewing objects, whales and dolphins often turn on their side and use a single eye which can readily be moved around to give a wide range of vision. This behavior is often seen both underwater and at the surface. They can, however, also focus on objects quite close in front of their mouths using binocular vision.

It has been suggested that one effect of their living underwater might be that whales have a limited color vision. Red or yellow light is quickly absorbed by water and most underwater objects appear blue-green in color. But in our own studies on wild dolphins we have found a strong preference for yellow and red objects which would indicate that at least some dolphins do have the ability to discriminate between different colors.

The extent to which whales use their eyes at great depths in the ocean is not known. Below about 200 meters, light levels are very low, but many species of toothed whales regularly dive and feed well below these depths. Many of the deep-

sea animals that they catch have light organs. These organs produce light of particular frequencies by a chemical process. Perhaps the deep-diving toothed whales have eyes specifically adapted to detect this "chemical light" underwater.

TOUCH

We normally associate the sense of touch with the use of our hands and fingers, and possibly our feet and toes. By touching or feeling a new object, we get information on its three-dimensional shape, texture and consistency.

Cetaceans no longer have "hands" that they could use in this way, but the sense of touch is still very important to them. They have developed a highly specialized skin that is far more elaborate and contains a complex system of organized, encapsulated nerve endings, which are more abundant in certain regions of greater sensitivity. The skin is soft and easily damaged, though it heals fast. In the wild, older animals often have a battered appearance when viewed close-up as a result of the numerous scratches and wounds the delicate skin suffers during its life.

One important function of the skin is probably to help them swim more efficiently. Cetaceans need to achieve "laminar flow" of water over the body if they are to swim efficiently at high speeds. If turbulence develops anywhere on the body surface the laminar flow is interrupted. Hence the animal's body shape needs to be adjusted constantly while it is swimming. Many species of whales and dolphins appear to be able to do this, and it is thought that they manage it by using their highly sensitive skin as a pressure sensor. By monitoring the entire body surface for pressure or stretching points as it swims, the animal can continually keep its body in the correct shape for laminar flow to occur.

Robert Morris

Particular areas of the skin may have specialized functions. For example, some cetaceans may be able to use the skin surface in the region of the jaw to detect sources of low frequency vibrations. And by sensing pressure build-up in this same region, they may be able to tell how fast they are swimming.

A major problem for air-breathing animals living in the sea is the proper coordination of their breathing so that only air is taken in to the lungs and not a mixture of air and water—we have all coughed and spluttered after breathing in water while swimming. As they adapted to aquatic life, cetaceans developed a much more reliable system when the nostrils moved to the top of the head and powerful muscles developed to close them tightly when underwater. Unfortunately, if the opening for the lungs is on the top of the head, it is difficult to know exactly when it is clear of the water so that it can be used for breathing purposes. Snorkelers are familiar with this problem. We believe cetaceans solve the problem by using a specialized area of skin around the blowhole. Complex nerve endings are found in the skin from this region which sense

ABOVE: The nerve-rich head and jaw region responds to pressure changes and may be able to sense speed as well as low-frequency vibrations that aid navigation and prey detection.

LEFT: Like all mammals, whales will drown if water enters their lungs. Sensitive nerve endings around the blowhole detect pressure changes as the water surface is broken. Powerful muscles close the blowhole when the whale dives.

FACING PAGE: The skin of whales is highly sensitive, not only to touch but possibly also to subtle changes in air pressure, water pressure and density. These changes stimulate minute alterations in body shape and help maintain laminar flow, reducing turbulence as the whale moves through the water at speed.

Robert Morris

ABOVE: Dolphins use the sensitive skin on the lower jaw to investigate small objects in much the same way that humans use their fingertips, but they also make use of other senses that the vast majority of land mammals do not have.

pressure changes so that the animal can know exactly when the blowhole is in the air and can be opened. In calm weather wild dolphins have regularly been seen starting to blow air from their lungs before surfacing and while their blowhole is still 5 to 10 centimeters below the surface. They then take a breath with the blowhole only just clear of the surface.

The behavior of dolphins toward unusual objects in the water also provides clues about other means of touch sensing in cetaceans. A dolphin will often rest the tip of its lower jaw on an object it is investigating, or take the object into its mouth. Both of these behaviors may be associated with touch sensing but as we shall see later, they could be linked to a very different type of sensory system. Finally, there is a most unusual behavior often observed in wild and captive male dolphins—the use of the extended penis apparently to "investigate" an object. Whether the penis, which has abundant sensory nerve endings, is actually being used for touch investigation must remain as conjecture, but if this is what is indeed happening it does seem to be a somewhat hazardous operation!

TASTE AND SMELL

In land animals there is a clear distinction between taste and smell. Smelling (olfaction) is associated with detecting the source of chemical substances dispersed in the air at a distance from the source. Tasting (gustation) is concerned with detecting chemical substances dissolved in water that is brought into contact with the mouth. Both are examples of chemical sensing, which is believed to be the oldest sensory faculty in use by animals.

Underwater, the distinction between taste and smell is less obvious. The transfer of chemical information can only occur by solution in water. It is, however, still meaningful to separate the two as distinct senses. Smell in water is the chemical sense that provides information at a distance (presence of a predator or food) while taste gives mainly chemical information on objects near or in the mouth (generally food).

Water is an excellent solvent for many substances and acts as a good carrier for dissolved materials, which remain detectable for long periods. Many marine organisms rely on chemical sensing (chemoreception) as their major means of finding food or recognizing a potential mating partner. Sharks, for example, have an extremely well developed olfactory system for distance "smell" sensing of waterborne chemicals, and efficient gustatory receptors in their mouths for close-up "taste" sensing.

We know that whales can see in air as well as in water. It seems reasonable, therefore, to ask whether they can also smell in both air and water. In fact, they do not seem to be very good at smelling in either.

Rosemary Chastney/Ocean Images/Planet Earth Pictures

Cetaceans appear to have largely lost the sense of airborne smell that exists in most mammals, as they have very limited olfactory receptors. They may have lost this sense with the repositioning of the nostrils from the front to the top of the head when a number of important changes to the function and operation of organs associated with the nostrils must have occurred. The nostrils (blowhole) are usually closed except when the animal breathes at the surface and the breathing is so

rapid that "air smelling" must be of limited use. Baleen whales appear to have rather more olfactory receptors than the toothed whales and they may still be able to use these receptors to "sniff the winds" in search of plankton-rich waters. Recent research has revealed that plankton produce a distinctive gas, dimethyl sulfide, which might allow them to track their prey by smell.

There is no indication of any system of waterborne smelling in cetaceans equivalent to the olfactory system in sharks. This would have required the development of a completely new sense of smell, but its absence must have put them at a great disadvantage compared with the sharks.

The sense of taste appears to be still present in at least some cetacean species. Dolphins can certainly detect a range of chemicals dissolved in water, distinguishing between what we would describe as sweet, sour, bitter and salty tastes. In addition, what appear to be taste buds are

ABOVE: It is unlikely that humpback whales have anything but the most rudimentary ability to detect odors in the air, but they may be able to "taste" small plankton concentrations in the water, which would make their search for food more efficient.

Christian Petron/Planet Earth Pictures

ABOVE: The function and importance of the outer ear is unknown: certainly its small size and inconspicuous opening, behind and below the eye, suggest it plays only a minor role in underwater hearing but it may be of use when the head is above water.

present on the tongues of several species of toothed whale. Some species have a small sensory organ, known as Jacobson's organ, which occurs at the front of the mouth and may further broaden tasting abilities.

If some cetaceans do have a sense of taste they could use it in a number of ways. Taste might be used to investigate likely food items for signs of decomposition—we have regularly tried to feed wild dolphins on dead fish without success. Waste products of cetaceans (urine and fecal material) will only be dispersed slowly in the water and might be used to provide taste cues for other members of the species. They might, for example, contain sexual pheromones that would indicate readiness for mating, or they might provide trails for others in a herd during periods of migration. Taste might also be used to sense the presence of nearby food in the form of large shoals of plankton or blood from a wounded animal. Thus the gustatory detection of waterborne chemicals

could provide a rich source of knowledge on the local environment and on social matters within a group. Unfortunately the extent to which cetaceans can use such a sense is largely unknown. It does, however, seem certain that this sensitivity to chemicals could not be used as a long-range sensory faculty to rival the olfactory sense of sharks.

HEARING

As with vision, important changes have been made in cetaceans' methods of hearing as they adapted from hearing in air to hearing in water. Sound travels about five times as fast in water as in air owing to the much greater density of water. This density difference between the two also makes it difficult for sound to pass between air and water. There is what is called an "acoustic impedance mismatch" between the two media. As a result of this imbalance, an air-filled ear is useless underwater.

An obvious physical characteristic of cetaceans is the absence of external ears. These have been sacrificed for the sake of a streamlined body shape for efficient swimming. Cetaceans do still have ears but they are barely noticeable, being marked only by a small hole just behind the eye. In the bottlenose dolphin *Tursiops truncatus* the ear hole is 5–6 centimeters behind the eye and is only 2–3 millimeters in diameter.

There is still considerable argument among scientists as to how cetaceans use their ears. The external ears of the baleen whales are filled with a horny wax plug, which is thought to transmit underwater sounds to the inner ear. Because the impedance of the wax plug matches that of seawater, baleen whales are probably deaf in air.

The toothed whales do not have earplugs and there is far more controversy about their hearing. Some scientists believe that the ear channel from the external ear hole to the inner ear is open and filled with seawater, and is fully operational underwater. However, there are reports that some dolphins can hear quite well in air, which, if correct, suggests that the ear channel is air-filled at least at the sea surface. Other scientists are convinced that hearing does not occur via the ear channel at all. They believe that in some dolphin species at least the ear channel is closed off and that during the course of evolution to a marine existence, the ear hole and ear channel have become redundant in the same way as our appendix has lost its function. There is indeed a second sound-receiving organ—the lower jaw. This contains oil-filled sinuses that are believed to be able to channel sound waves directly to the inner ear. It is quite possible, of course, that both the ear and the lower jaw are used for hearing— the ear for receiving atmospheric and communication sounds, the lower jaw for echolocation clicks, for example.

ECHOLOCATION

So far we have dealt with senses familiar to us. Now we come to a sensory faculty with which we and most other land animals are unfamiliar. Only bats, some shrews and a handful of cave-dwelling birds could properly appreciate the developments that have taken place in certain cetaceans relating to sound perception of the environment.

Perhaps the most serious problem for ancestral whales colonizing the sea was that they were entering an environment where other animals had, over the course of many millions of years, already perfected sensory systems ideally suited to the marine environment. Sharks in particular had a highly developed underwater "smell" sense and a well-developed sense of sound detection with the result that they were undoubtedly the most successful predators. For the early whale, the shark must have been a major threat both as a predator and as a competitor for food. The baleen whales

largely solved the problem by growing to enormous sizes and living on small plankton. For the toothed whales it was different. If they were to compete successfully with the sharks they had to develop a new sense faculty to match those of the sharks.

Many of the early whalers were baffled by the survival of the toothed whales that actually had very few teeth but preyed successfully on the fast-moving squid. Most baffling was the great sperm whale *Physeter macrocephalus* which hunted for squid in the depths of the ocean. The sperm whale had teeth only in its lower jaw and the males often had lower jaws so badly damaged from fights with other males as to be quite functionless. In spite of this, sperm whales that

Frans Lanting/Bruce Coleman Limited

had obviously had such injuries for many years were regularly taken by the whalers in good condition and with full stomachs. They could think of only one explanation—the animals had supernatural powers.

The true explanation is that toothed whales had learned to "see with their ears." They developed this unique sensory system based on sound millions of years ago. This faculty enabled them to catch food in the dark depths of the ocean and successfully compete with the shark .

Sound communication in water is both effective and efficient. It is, therefore, not surprising that it has been used by the toothed whales as the basis for one of the most advanced sensory faculties in use on this planet— echolocation.

Echolocation involves an active process of emitting sounds in the form of short broad-spectrum burst-pulses (clicks) and gaining information on the surrounding environment

ABOVE: The apparently featureless ocean provides as much—if not more—information to dolphins as the land does to humans. The presence of efficient, dangerous predators probably stimulated the evolution of new navigational senses such as echolocation and an ability to detect the earth's magnetic field.

(nearby objects, obstructions) by analysis of the returning echoes. Highly accurate echolocation, using a broad band of both low- and high-frequency sound emissions coupled with very sensitive directional hearing, has given toothed whales a sensory system unrivaled in the sea. Their prowess at navigating in turbid water and for locating and identifying objects well out of visual range has been marveled at on many occasions.

When we look at an object with our eyes we are seeing reflected light. When toothed whales "look" at an object with their echolocation system they are hearing reflected sounds from their echolocating clicks. Sound waves carry much more information than light. This is because sound has a more complex interaction with the environment. While light can give color patterns by selective absorption of certain wavelengths, sound by a similar process can give a three-dimensional picture. A target object's material, internal structure and texture will all combine to produce a specific echo. Only in recent years have we appreciated what a powerful sensory technique this is and as a result ultrasonic exploration is replacing x-rays in medical examinations of internal human structures.

Although the various species of toothed whales have developed their own separate types of acoustic faculty, we believe they are all based on the same principle and have all involved major anatomical changes to the basic structure of the animal's head.

All the toothed whales examined so far have been found to contain large deposits of fat in their heads and lower jaws. Such deposits are unique in the animal kingdom and are remarkable for a number of reasons. Firstly, they are large in relation to the size of the animal and represent an immense store of potential metabolic energy, yet they seem not to be used as a source of energy. Second, the chemical composition of these deposits is markedly different from that of the normal body fat and from that of the animal's normal dietary fat intake. Third, the shape and positioning of the deposits has apparently been so important that major changes in the shape and structure of the skull have been necessary in order to accommodate them.

These structures thus represent a major "commitment" on the part of the animal, involving severe metabolic penalties—they tie up large amounts of metabolic energy and valuable

HOW A DOLPHIN ECHOLOCATES

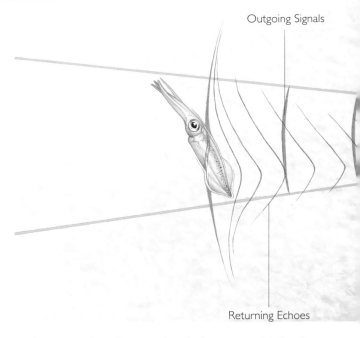

Outgoing Signals

Returning Echoes

The likely sequence of events during a typical dolphin echolocation is as follows:

1. During normal swimming, with no specific target of interest, a general low-frequency echolocation signal of fairly pure tone is used. This acts like a ship's echo sounder, providing the animal with information on the topography of the area including water depth, changes in seafloor profile and position of any coastal features. The scan range will be determined by the time interval between the signals (clicks) and how much energy there is in the signal. For efficient echolocation one individual click must be sent out and the echoes (if any) received before the next click is emitted. Thus, we can estimate the range at which a dolphin is "looking" by measuring the time between clicks. The maximum range is believed to be at least 800 meters. This type of echolocation will also tell the dolphin whether there are any large animals nearby.

2. Once a new echo is received, the first requirement is to determine distance and direction, and to collect more detailed information on the target itself—for example, is it a predator such as a shark, or likely prey? The dolphin emits a series of clicks with a broad frequency band, the echoes of which can give many different pieces of information on the target. The high frequencies give the most detailed

information, but they are absorbed quite quickly by the water and so are useful only at closer ranges.

3. Once the bearing of the target is established, the dolphin focuses the signals on the target. This concentrates the power of the higher frequency components and gives a more detailed picture of the target. It can also scan the target by moving its head from side to side.

fat reserves, and have required significant anatomical modifications. To have evolved they must have an important function that confers great advantages on the animal.

The largest fat deposits are in front of the braincase. In the sperm whale these deposits (their spermaceti organ) are enormous, weighing many tonnes. Most of the other toothed whales have a similar but smaller organ called the melon. The other large fat deposit, in the lower jaw, is strategically placed behind an area of the jaw where the bone is very thin. This deposit is similar in composition to the melon and extends up to the middle ear region. A widely accepted theory regarding their function is that they aid in echolocation. The process is believed to work like this: Sound is produced internally by the animal. The head fat organ focuses this sound into a directional beam. Reflected echoes carrying information about targets are received at the "acoustic window" area of the lower jaw. The sound is then transmitted by the fat organ in the lower jaw to the middle ear and subsequently to the brain for processing and interpretation.

Thus many scientists believe that the fat deposits in the head and lower jaw of toothed whales represent a completely novel physiological and biochemical development that provides the animals with the means to acquire their unique acoustic sensory system.

There are two other structural changes to the head of the toothed whales that are thought to be linked to the development of the acoustic faculty. The first is the reduced number of functional teeth compared to their early ancestors. As the ancestral toothed whales perfected their sense of sound detection, food capture became much easier and teeth were no longer needed so much for this purpose. The second change is the immensely large brain. Echolocation is a highly sophisticated sense and requires much processing of information. We now know that a large part of the brain in toothed whales is involved purely in the storage, processing and interpretation of all the acoustic information that is continually coming in concerning their surroundings.

Toothed whales are the only group of whales to have properly developed sound for use as a sensory faculty. Baleen whales use low-frequency sounds for communication and produce complex "songs." There are some reports of certain species emitting fairly pure-frequency clicks and it has

4. As the range closes between dolphin and target, the dolphin can use much higher frequencies in its echolocation clicks and hence get even more detailed information. At this stage the clicks will start to come very close together, producing what sounds to us like a continuous "creaking."

5. Finally, at very close range, it may be necessary to determine texture or other fine structural information. In this case use of a short-range sonar system with very high frequencies would be necessary. It has been suggested that the habit of resting the tip of the jaw on objects or taking objects into the mouth may be associated with such a close-range acoustic sensory system rather than with the sense of touch.

been suggested that these could have a sonar function for detecting targets or sensing water depth. Certainly such information would be useful. If, for example, they were able to obtain information on the topography of the seafloor during their long seasonal migrations across the oceans, this might enable them to recognize distinctive features (seamounts, underwater mountain chains, deep trenches) and use these features as landmarks However, such baleen whale clicks lack the structured form produced by echolocating toothed whales. The whales themselves lack the complex nasal passages which in toothed whales generate echolocation sounds. Therefore, if baleen whales have an acoustic sense like the toothed whales, it must be, at best, primitive.

THE MAGNETIC SENSE

There is considerable evidence that many organisms, from bacteria upward, have a sensory faculty that can receive directional information from the earth's magnetic field. Small crystals of the magnetic form of iron oxide (magnetite) have been found in certain species of mud bacteria, bees, butterflies, fish, birds, bats and reptiles. They have also been found in some cetacean species. In the higher organisms they are generally located either in the vicinity of the brain or near areas where there is a high concentration of nerve endings.

At present many other animals are being examined for the presence of magnetite crystals in their bodies, and this field of research is at a particularly exciting stage with many new and challenging ideas. In general terms, the magnetite crystals are thought to continually orientate themselves in line with the earth's natural magnetic force fields—just like mini-magnets. By sensing changes in the orientation of these crystals, the host animal is thought to be able to work out the direction in which it is traveling. Such a system would have obvious uses for long-distance navigation and could be used at most points on the earth's surface.

Cetaceans appear to be ahead of most other mammals in developing this unusual sensory faculty. Several species of toothed whales have been found to have magnetic crystals in their external brain tissues. In the marine environment, fixed points that can be used for navigational purposes are scarce. Thus the development of a system of orientation based on the earth's magnetic field would be of great importance to all whales and dolphins—just as the invention of the compass was so important for human navigators.

Normally the natural magnetic force fields run north to south at an even density. In places, however, the field is distorted by certain types of geological formations—for instance those rich in

Steven French

iron. Such distortions are called geomagnetic anomalies. Areas of high or low geomagnetic anomalies are found all over the oceans, particularly in the vicinity of seamounts, in areas where active continental drift is occurring and in some continental shelf areas. The result is a whole series of fixed, reliable landmarks across the ocean if one has the sensory faculty available to recognize them. We believe that at least some of the cetaceans have that faculty by virtue of their magnetic sense.

There is also circumstantial evidence to support this idea. Some live strandings have been closely linked to local magnetic, rather than physical, characteristics of the coastline. They may be the result of serious navigational mistakes by the whales while they are attempting to use their magnetic sense for orientation. Possibly, this is one sensory faculty in cetaceans that is still in its experimental stage.

ABOVE: Geomagnetic anomalies occur where natural magnetic force fields are distorted. In some parts of the world, live strandings of cetaceans are believed to occur in areas where such anomalies occur—serious navigational mistakes can be made while they are attempting to use their magnetic sense of orientation—but in other parts of the world no such correlation has been found.

FACING PAGE: Evidence is growing to support the theory that a sophisticated geomagnetic sensitivity enables whales and dolphins to navigate across vast areas of ocean.

REPRODUCTION AND GROWTH

M.M. Bryden

Most of what we know about the reproduction and growth of whales relates to species that, in the past, have been of commercial and economic value. Investigators attached to whaling stations, ships and museums gained information by observing animals and their collected organs. More recently we have learned a lot about reproduction in certain species that have been killed accidentally in commercial ventures aimed at species other than whales. One major source of information was the tuna-fishing industry in the eastern tropical Pacific—in a period of about 35 years an estimated 6–12 million spotted and spinner dolphins were killed in the purse-seine nets. Gill-netting likewise has imposed heavy mortalities on some inshore species of small whales in various parts of the world.

EXTERNAL SEXUAL DIFFERENCES

During adaptation for a life in water, streamlining of the whale's body has involved modification of the external genitalia. On superficial examination it is difficult to distinguish between the sexes of most species of whales because the penis of the male is retained within a prepuce (except when it is erect), whose opening is a slit (the genital slit), similar in appearance to the female's genital slit or vulva. The only conspicuous difference between the sexes is the distance between the anus and the genital slit: in the male it is about 10 percent of the body length, but in the female the genital slit appears continuous with the anus. Even the mammary glands of the female are difficult to discern. Each nipple, one on either side of the genital slit, is retained within a tiny mammary slit, which is often difficult to see. The nipple protrudes only during suckling, and the mammary gland itself lies beneath the blubber over an extensive area of the ventral body wall. There is no external sign of it except in heavily lactating females.

RIGHT: This calf is reassured and protected by its closeness to its mother. The bond between mother and calf is a strong link in whales' social organization.

Flip Nicklin/Minden

However, there are obvious sexual differences after maturity in some species—for example, the sperm whale *Physeter macrocephalus* and the pilot whales, genus *Globicephala*, in which males are significantly larger than females. As well as being larger, the male orca *Orcinus orca* has a taller and more conspicuous dorsal fin than the female. Male and female beaked whales can also be quite different in appearance—in particular the teeth erupt in males but do not erupt in most females.

COURTSHIP AND MATING

Relatively little is known about mating in whales and dolphins. There have been few observations in the wild, so most of the available information is based on studying smaller species in captivity.

Courtship display and mating in whales may not always be directed toward reproduction. It has been suggested that they may be used in the greeting and bonding of individuals or groups after a period of separation. Certainly a great deal of apparent sexual activity is common in captive groups; even juveniles are quite sexually precocious. Various behavioral signs considered to be associated with courtship, including chasing, nuzzling, rubbing and even erection and intromission, have been observed in sexually immature males.

Whales have little sense of smell, the sense used extensively in sexual encounters in other mammals, and they probably use behavioral means to determine the sexual status of potential mates. In humpbacks *Megaptera novaeangliae* a range of activities has been described that probably indicate sexual activity—for example, rolling,

Dean Lee

M. Osmond

ABOVE: Surface behaviors, such as the flipper slapping by this humpback whale, could have many different functions. In this case, it may be a greeting ritual, a displacement activity to ease tension, or even a way of determining sexual status.

LEFT AND BELOW: Lobtailing may be used by sexually active males as an aggressive display toward their competitors. Adult male humpbacks use ritualized displays as well as physical violence to fight for the prime position next to a female.

THE FEMALE REPRODUCTIVE ORGANS

The anatomy of whales' female reproductive organs is similar to that of many other mammalian species. The two ovaries lie in the abdominal cavity behind the kidneys, as do the testes in the male. The uterus consists of a body and two horns, which narrow at their ends to become the uterine tubes. The cervix, or neck of the uterus, opens into the vagina. On the vaginal walls are a series of folds projecting toward the vulva and resembling a series of funnels. Their function is unknown, but they may prevent the entrance of water into the reproductive tract or possibly the loss of semen after copulation.

The ovaries of toothed whales are shaped like elongated eggs, with a relatively smooth surface. Those of baleen whales are highly irregular in shape, and studded with numerous rounded protuberances. The mature ovary contains egg cells or oocytes surrounded by other cells to form follicles. Some of these follicles enlarge and develop a fluid-filled space. In baleen whales these enlarged follicles are responsible for some of the protuberances seen on the surface of the ovary.

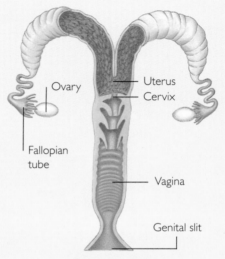

Ovary

Fallopian tube

Uterus

Cervix

Vagina

Genital slit

Female organs

As the breeding season approaches, one of the follicles enlarges further and, around the time of copulation, eventually bursts—ovulation—to release the oocyte, which is drawn into the end of the uterine tube. The cells remaining in the collapsed follicle after ovulation multiply and form a large grayish yellow structure, the corpus luteum. If the oocyte is not fertilized, the corpus luteum degenerates. If fertilization does occur, the corpus luteum persists to the end of the pregnancy. In either case, the degenerated corpus luteum is white and is called the corpus albicans.

A peculiarity of whales is that their corpora albicantia remain for the rest of the animal's life, providing a record of past ovulations and the reproductive history of individual whales: each corpus albicans represents one ovulation (though not necessarily a pregnancy). It is often possible for the biologist to use this information to estimate how many pregnancies a whale has had.

BELOW: A young male spotted dolphin (lower) mates with an older female.

THE MALE REPRODUCTIVE ORGANS

The penis is coiled or curved within the sheath (prepuce) except when erect; it is held in this position by a pair of straplike retractor muscles. In most mammals the body of the penis is made up largely of three columns of spongy tissue and erection results when these fill with blood. Although the whale's penis contains the three columns, they are not very spongy but instead contain a relatively large amount of tough, fibrous tissue. It has been suggested that erection results simply from the elasticity of this fibrous tissue when the retractor muscles relax. Probably, however, the mechanism is more complex than that, as it has been shown to be in the bull, whose penis resembles that of the whale in many anatomical features.

The testes are elongated and lie not in an external scrotum as they do in most mammalian species, but within the abdominal cavity just behind the kidneys. This arrangement is also found in the elephant and the hyrax. The testes increase dramatically in size at puberty—the testis of an immature dolphin is about half the size of a little finger and weighs about 20 grams, whereas in the adult it is as long as the forearm and considerably thicker, and weighs several kilograms.

Sperm are produced in the testes, then pass into the epididymis, which, as in all mammals, is a long, greatly convoluted tube. The sperm mature as they pass along this tube to be stored near its end, the tail of the epididymis, which in some species forms several masses. From here the short ductus deferens conducts the sperm to the urethra. Most of the fluid portion of mammalian semen is secreted by accessory sex glands of various kinds. The only accessory sex gland present in the whale is the prostate, which is quite small in immature whales but large in adults.

Male organs

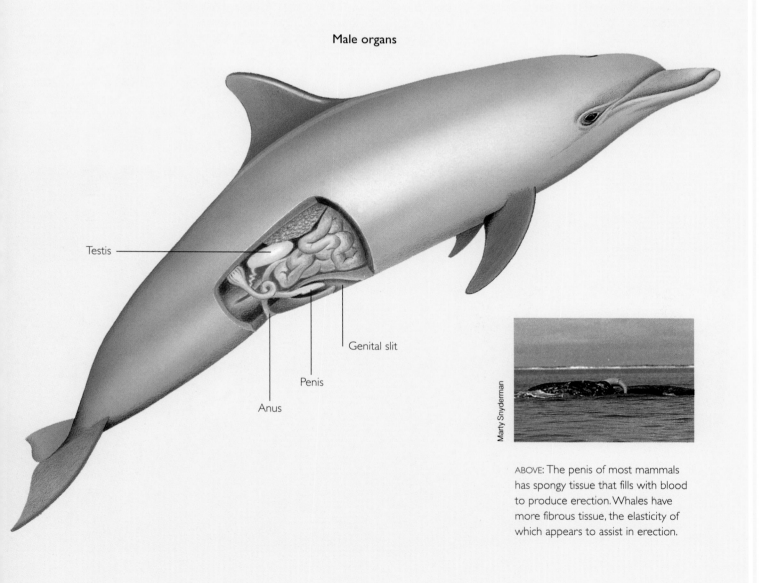

Testis

Genital slit

Penis

Anus

Marty Snyderman

ABOVE: The penis of most mammals has spongy tissue that fills with blood to produce erection. Whales have more fibrous tissue, the elasticity of which appears to assist in erection.

P. Amantho/Earthviews

ABOVE: Three stages in the birth of an Irrawaddy dolphin *Orcaella brevirostris* show the usual cetacean flukes-first or breech presentation. The newborn (often assisted by its mother or an "aunt") swims to the surface for its first breath.

RIGHT: Whales are assiduous mothers and will often support a calf at the surface, sometimes with another adult in attendance for protection.

slapping the water surface with the long flippers, fluke slapping and breaching. Some of these may also be used as threats by males toward competitors, along with more aggressive and direct actions at close quarters such as lunging with the head or sideswiping with the flukes and tail stock.

We have almost no information concerning the duration and frequency of copulation in whales. However, in captive bottlenose dolphins *Tursiops truncatus* intromission lasts 2–10 seconds. The male swims up from beneath its partner and they mate more or less at right angles to one another.

Male dolphins of several species in captivity will sometimes attempt to mate with other dolphins, male or female, of another species, genus or even family. Such cross-matings have sometimes resulted in offspring, even where the two parents were of different families. In the wild, however, it is unlikely that such matings, if they occur at all, result in viable offspring.

BIRTH AND MATERNAL CARE

The general principles of prenatal development of whales are similar to those of other mammals. In most baleen whales gestation lasts 10–12 months. It probably lasts about 12 months or a fraction less in the migrating species such as humpbacks, which coordinate birth and mating with annual migrations. The gestation length of toothed whales varies more, from about nine months in some species to 18 months in others.

The birth process of any mammal is stressful, but it must be particularly so in whales because the fetus is expelled from the uterus directly into the water, in which it can drown or lose body heat at an excessive rate. There have been observations of births in captivity but only rarely have births in the wild been reported. In most, if not all, births the calf is born flukes first rather than head first, in contrast with land mammals, in which such a presentation (breech birth) can cause severe birth difficulties. The spindlelike shape of the fetal whale probably means that flukes-first presentation causes no more difficulty than head-first presentation.

However there do seem to be exceptions: a gray whale calf in Baja California, Mexico, was recently observed emerging head-first. Birth occurs rapidly, which is necessary because the young must surface for its first breath very soon after the umbilical cord breaks, otherwise it would die of anoxia. Some unknown mechanisms must prevent the newborn whale from breathing in until its blowhole is above the water surface.

Multiple births may occur, but they are extremely rare. Twin, triplet and even quadruplet fetuses have been observed inside whales killed for commercial gain, but it is doubtful that they would have been born and reared successfully. In seals, which like whales produce large and advanced (usually single) young, multiple births are extremely rare and even twins are rarely raised successfully.

The mother will actively protect her calf and will attempt to drive off intruders. There are many accounts of the propensity in cetaceans, dolphins in particular, for other adults in the group to assist the mother. These animals, referred to as "aunts," have been seen to help the mother guide the newborn calf to the surface to take its first breath, to protect it from other whales in the group, and to assist a sick or even dead calf by supporting it at the surface. It has been claimed that human beings have been saved in this way. However, in captivity at least, these "aunts" have at times taken little interest in sick or stillborn calves, or have even mauled them. More than once, the mother or another dolphin has been seen to take a stillborn or weak newborn calf to the bottom of the pool and hold it there. Perhaps "aunts" can tell whether their potential charges are dead or alive, and even estimate their chances of survival.

Such maternal care in whales is to be expected because the mother has, in genetic terms, made a very significant investment in the calf, and we would expect behavior to evolve that will enhance survival. Probably the many stories of dolphins saving people are related to this behavior (cases of mistaken identity), rather than being the result of a special affinity that dolphins have for humans.

The calf is suckled underwater but close to the surface, so mother and calf can breathe intermittently. The milk is actively ejected into the calf's mouth by muscle action, increasing the speed of transfer—an obvious advantage underwater. A calf remains close to its mother for at least its first few days or weeks. Lactation lasts 4–11 months in rorquals (Balaenopteridae) although body size does not seem to factor—blue whales lactate for seven months whereas smaller humpbacks lactate for nearly 11 months. In most toothed whales it lasts considerably longer, about a year or more. There is evidence that older pilot whales and sperm whales continue to nurse calves 10–15 years old, although the youngsters are also taking solid food.

BREEDING CYCLES

Little is known about the relationship between the social structure of most freeranging whale schools and reproduction. The major obstacle to examining this in the past has been that we have had no idea of the age or sex structure of schools, or of relationships among individuals that made up a school. However, we now have some understanding of these issues in a few species.

In sperm whales, for example, we have a fairly good picture of social structure and migration. Older male sperm whales, the harem masters, migrate to high latitudes in search of food in the non-breeding season, but the "nursery schools" containing the mature females and calves remain in temperate or tropical waters throughout the year. Because there is no marked seasonal migration of

ABOVE: A sperm whale cow with her rare albino calf. Sperm whales (like many other species) have a low reproductive rate and females can therefore invest many years of care in each calf.

DEVELOPMENT RATES

SPECIES	GESTATION (MONTHS)	BODY LENGTH AT BIRTH (METERS)	WEIGHT AT BIRTH (TONNES)	WEIGHT OF ADULT (TONNES)
Blue whale	11–12	5.9–7.0	2.5	100–120
Fin whale	11–12	5.9–6.5	2.0	30–80
Humpback whale	11–12	4.0–5.0	1.0–2.0	25–30
Long-finned pilot whale (male)	16	1.8–2.0	0.075	1.8–3.5
Harbor porpoises	9	0.67–0.85	0.005	0.055–0.065

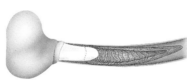

ABOVE: Advances in research techniques and measurements have enabled scientists to determine the age of individual whales by examining and counting the growth layers in the teeth of toothed whales (top) or in the waxy earplugs of baleen whales (below).

the breeding cows, the breeding pattern is not clear. Mating occurs in winter, gestation takes about 15–17 months, and lactation lasts about two years. An adult female has a calf about every fourth year.

Recently, the collaborating Australian and Japanese biologists, Drs. Helen Marsh and Toshio Kasuya, showed that the short-finned pilot whale *Globicephala macrorhynchus* has a most intriguing reproductive biology. Their research led to the conclusion that pregnancy rate decreases with age and reproduction ceases somewhere between the ages of 30 and 40 years. Lactation seems to be prolonged in older females, lasting up to 15 years, and a close cow–calf association may last at least until the calf is sexually mature. Females less than 20 years old, by contrast, suckle their calves for much shorter periods, 2–6 years at most. Prolonged lactation does not mean that a calf feeds only on the mother's milk; on the contrary, all calves begin to take solid food when less than a year old.

Baleen whales have a regular breeding pattern. Most spend the summer at feeding areas in high latitudes, and move to subtropical or tropical waters to breed in winter. Gestation takes about 11 months, lactation lasts less than 12 months, and an adult female produces a calf about every two to three years. However, it has been shown that some females may, on occasions, reproduce in successive years. Perhaps the incidence of having calves in successive years has increased in some species with the depletion in whale numbers.

ESTIMATING AGE

Our understanding of the biology of whales has been advanced significantly in recent years as a result of improvements in estimating the ages of individual animals. This has permitted biologists to determine the ages at which animals mature sexually and at which they die, how fast they grow and how old they are when they first calve. This information is important if we are to build an accurate picture of the animals' life history, and vital for management of threatened populations.

For determining the reproductive potential of an animal it is particularly important to know the age at which it becomes sexually mature. The earlier it matures, the greater its potential number of offspring. Because sexual maturity is associated closely with physical size, a young whale that grows faster will become sexually mature at a younger age. One reason for faster growth and earlier maturity might be the increased availability of food, which could result from reduction in the numbers of whales. This, coupled with increased frequency of pregnancy as discussed earlier, would accelerate the rate of increase in the population. There is good evidence that a reduction in age at first breeding observed in southern fin whales *Balaenoptera physalus* and sei whales *B. borealis* is the result of overexploitation of large baleen whales in antarctic waters. The mean age of sexual maturity of female fin whales declined from 10 years to six years between 1930 and 1950.

A method of age estimation developed in seals—counting growth layers in the teeth—has been applied successfully to toothed whales and has proved to be of considerable value. The details of the method vary among species, but the principle is similar. Layers can be seen in a thin lengthwise section of a tooth. Patterns of these layers, referred to as growth-layer groups, occur in cyclic fashion, somewhat like the growth rings in trees. There are some problems with the method, and the actual rates of deposition of layers are known for a limited number of species, so it is not always possible to put an absolute figure on age. However, the layered structure of teeth is essentially similar among species, varying only in detail, and sufficient is known at present for the method to be useful and widely applied.

In baleen whales, which lack teeth, a different method has been developed. When the peculiar horny plug that lies in the ear canal of these whales is cut lengthwise, it too shows a layered pattern. Layers of shed skin cells alternate with layers of ear wax, so that sections of the plug have alternating light (horny) and dark (waxy) layers. Again, these occur in cyclic fashion, but as in the case of the teeth there has been controversy about the rate of accumulation of the layers.

In recent years biologists have been using photographic identification of the natural markings on individual whales and dolphins to study their lives from birth to death, and have thus been able to obtain actual figures for their lifespans. Using all available evidence, it seems that cetaceans can live for less than 15 years (harbor porpoises) to more than 100 years (some large baleen whales). Wild bottlenose dolphins live for about 50 years.

RAPID GROWTH

The rate of growth of the fetus, as in all mammals, is greatest in the later part of pregnancy. Quite astonishing figures are recorded in large whales—in the last two months of pregnancy the fetal blue whale *Balaenoptera musculus*, for example, increases its weight by 2 tonnes, the daily weight increase being about 100 kilograms at the end of pregnancy. This growth is greater than in any other whale, at least 10 times that of any mammal other than a whale, and 500 to 1,000 times that of the human fetus. Whales differ from land mammals in that species' differences in birth size are achieved mainly by alternating the rate of fetal growth rather than the gestation period.

Now that we are able to estimate the age of individual whales, we can also determine the rate of growth after birth. Marine mammals grow very quickly in early postnatal life. Whales produce milk that is very rich in fat and, to a lesser extent, protein, so growth of the calf is rapid. Thus a newborn blue whale calf, measuring about 6 meters in length and 2.5 tonnes in weight, will grow so rapidly that at eight months old it will be about 15 meters long and weigh some 22 tonnes.

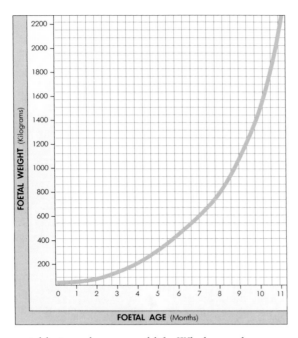

LEFT: The extraordinary growth of the blue whale is achieved mainly during its last two months in the uterus. While a human fetus increases in weight by 2 kilograms during the last two months of pregnancy, a blue whale fetus adds 2 tonnes to its weight in the same time.

BELOW: A blue whale, up to 8 meters long at birth, may be twice as long by the time it is weaned before the end of its first year. It increases in weight by 90 kilograms a day— roughly equivalent to the weight of a grown man.

CETACEAN INTELLIGENCE

M.M. Bryden and Peter Corkeron

The frequent newspaper and magazine articles about whales, dolphins and porpoises almost always refer to their "intelligence." It has become widely accepted that dolphins, at least, are highly intelligent. But is there evidence to support this?

Most people come into contact with whales and dolphins only when they are in captivity, and they form their opinions regarding intelligence based on performances developed especially for public entertainment. The "cleverness" of a trained dolphin is undeniably impressive, and it is tempting to equate this cleverness with intelligence. Add to this the dolphin's sophisticated ability to use sonar and to produce complex sounds, and it becomes even easier to assume a high degree of intelligence. But it does not necessarily follow that an animal capable of learning and executing complicated routines is intelligent. A skilled trainer can teach a wide variety of animals, from rats and pigeons to parrots and dogs, to perform complex routines, and we do not assume that these animals are particularly intelligent. Such performances often tell us more about the skill, patience and intelligence of the trainer than that of the animals they train.

BELOW: Trained dolphins are undoubtedly "clever," but are they intelligent? Despite the popular belief that cetaceans are intelligent creatures, there is no conclusive evidence for this assumption.

OPINION AND OBSERVATION

People who spend a great deal of time with whales and dolphins—whether in captivity or in the wild—are also often impressed by their gentleness and apparent friendliness toward humans. On many occasions, dolphins have even been known to rescue swimmers in distress or, sometimes at great personal risk to themselves, to fight off attacking sharks. Such observations have encouraged the belief that some kind of special understanding exists between cetaceans and people. In turn, of course, this also implies intelligence, but there is no evidence to support such an assumption.

The study of human intelligence is difficult enough, even with the help of a complex language and an ability to work with tools, such as pens or computers. The intelligence of animals other than humans is even more difficult to investigate, let alone to measure with any degree of accuracy. Consequently, any discussion of relative intelligence among different species or groups of animals usually has to be subjective. We tend to form opinions about whether a dog is more intelligent than a sheep, for example, or a horse more intelligent than a pig, yet such opinions vary enormously depending on the amount of time we have spent observing or interacting with a particular species.

BRAIN SIZE AND STRUCTURE

In the past, it was assumed that dolphins were intelligent simply because of their large brain size. In the seventeenth century, biologist John Ray was sufficiently impressed by the large size of the dolphin brain to state that "this largeness of brain, and correspondence of it to that of man, argue this creature to be of more than ordinary wit, and capacity." Much later, in the 1960s, John Lilly achieved considerable notoriety when he wrote about the large, complex cetacean brain and his belief that these animals possess a high level of "non-human intelligence." However, such assumptions were pure speculation, as was Lilly's belief that dolphins have a complex language that they use to exchange significant amounts of information. No research has lent direct support to such a belief.

Many cetaceans do have large brains, with toothed whales having proportionately larger brains than baleen whales, relative to their body size. In fact, the relative brain size of some dolphins approaches that of humans. This alone makes it tempting to speculate that they are highly intelligent. Size alone, however, reveals little about either the nature or the extent of the intelligence of dolphins. First, brain size tends to increase with body size and we know that large animals are not necessarily more intelligent than small ones. A more useful measurement is the size of the brain as a percentage of total body weight,

which in dolphins varies from 0.25 percent to 1.5 percent, depending on the species. This compares with a figure of 1.9 percent in humans. Second, the brain is not only used for intellectual functions, but also to control bodily functions from hearing to movement. Therefore, brain size may be more directly related to the development of other functions.

One possible explanation of the large brain in dolphins has been advanced by the Nobel laureate Francis Crick (who made major contributions toward the discovery of the double helix molecule of DNA). Crick has related brain size in mammals to whether or not they experience "dream sleep" or REM (rapid eye movement) sleep. He observed that those mammals in which dream sleep is absent or reduced (which includes dolphins and whales) have large brains, and proposes that their brains may be large because they require a much larger storage area for the unwanted information (called "parasitic modes"). In other mammals, this unwanted information can be eliminated during dreams. Like so many other discussions about brain function in whales and dolphins, this is only a theory, but it does provide an alternative and possibly viable explanation for the large size of many cetacean brains.

As well as relative size, another possible measure of intelligence is the development of the brain. This is measured by the number of convolutions and the complexity of the region known as the cerebral cortex or the gray matter. The surface of the cerebrum is intricately folded, and consists of an outer layer of nerve cell bodies (the gray matter) and an inner mass of nerve fibers (known as the white matter). The feature that sets the human brain apart from most other mammals is the advanced development of this region, which is where the conscious control of body functions occurs. It is also where complex functions such as correlation, association and learning are centered. The human cerebrum is bigger than all the other parts of the brain put together and the folding is extensive.

In order to measure the relative extent of gray matter development among other animals, the term "encephalization" has been used as a comparable index. Scientists believe that the degree of encephalization—the size of the cerebral cortex and the amount of folding—relates directly to the degree of intelligence. In this respect, studies of the dolphin brain show that it can be as developed as that of the human brain, and is usually more developed than other highly encephalized mammals, such as the chimpanzee *Pan troglodytes*. Evidence suggests that toothed whales appear to be more advanced than baleen whales, having a greater number of convolutions and a better developed cerebral cortex, although this may be because a

Human brain

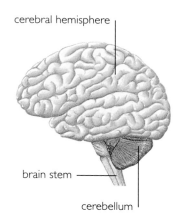

cerebral hemisphere

brain stem

cerebellum

Bottlenose dolphin brain

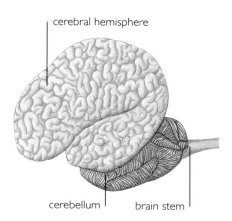

cerebral hemisphere

cerebellum   brain stem

ABOVE: Humans and cetaceans both have large and complex brains. Human brains are used for language and for manipulation of the environment. Cetaceans, however, do not use language in the human sense, nor do they manipulate their environment. We still have much to learn about the intelligence of cetaceans.

ABOVE: Responding to the artificial gesture "language" developed by researchers at the University of Hawaii, a bottlenose dolphin named Akeakamai obeys the instruction "get a hoop and carry it to the pipe."

Alan Levenson/Courtesy Kewalo Basin Marine Mammal Laboratory

ABOVE: A dolphin trainer communicates instructions to Akaekamai with stylized gestures for (from top) "pipe," "hoop" and "fetch." Reflective goggles eliminate eye-gaze cues.

major portion of the toothed whale brain is devoted to processing acoustic information for echolocation. However, the cetacean cortex is significantly thinner than the human cortex and, in other ways, the cetacean brain generally bears little resemblance to the human brain; indeed, the pattern of folding is much more like that found in the brains of hoofed animals, such as cattle, sheep and deer.

STUDYING CETACEAN INTELLIGENCE

Despite the difficulties involved in studying intelligence in whales and dolphins, several different avenues of research are being followed with the aid of an impressive range of skills, knowledge and high-tech equipment.

Current studies focus on two main themes. The first involves a detailed investigation into the size and structure of the brain, concentrating in particular on the parts responsible for learning. The second investigates the dolphin's ability to learn from experience, under both wild and captive conditions. In some studies, this has involved teaching the dolphins a simple form of "language."

We still do not understand how cetaceans communicate with each other, or if they have a true spoken language of their own. While the existence of a true language in the human sense is unlikely, there is no doubt that cetaceans do communicate. Using a combination of sound and body language, they can pass on basic information about everything from their emotional state to their own identity (in some dolphins, researchers have identified the existence of "signature whistles" that are unique to individuals—almost like human names). The big question is whether they discuss more abstract concepts, such as changes in the weather, or plans for the future.

A major stumbling block in language research has been that many species often "speak" in frequencies well beyond the range of human hearing, although the use of computers is helping to rectify this problem. It has even been suggested that cetaceans are telepathic and able to communicate without speech. If this were true, it would open up a baffling range of possibilities.

EVIDENCE FROM CAPTIVITY

It can be difficult—even impossible—to study dolphins and other small cetaceans at close range and for extended periods in the wild, but in captivity they can be observed around the clock. Observations can also be made under controlled conditions. Much of the early intelligence work on captive toothed whales had serious flaws in both design and execution, and so is of relatively little value. Even today, some critics of captive research argue that any discoveries made under such artificial conditions give a thoroughly inadequate picture of the wild situation.

More recent research on captive animals has provided a greater insight into the intelligence of the bottlenose dolphin *Tursiops truncatus* in particular, which is by far the most common and best studied dolphin in captivity.

Bottlenose dolphins process most of the information about their underwater world through their auditory (hearing) centers. In captivity, they perform quite badly in tests relying entirely on their visual memory. When they are given the opportunity to associate visual information with auditory information they perform much better. This is to be expected, since there are many problems associated with using sight underwater. Water does not absorb light uniformly because it is much less transparent to light than air is. Research projects must therefore take such variations into account, and compensate for them in measurements.

A remarkable study carried out by the University of Hawaii involved teaching captive bottlenose dolphins artificial languages using "words" produced by hand and arm signals, and by computer sounds. The aim was to test the dolphins for sentence comprehension, rather than language production. A variety of objects, including balls, pipes, frisbees and hoops, were placed in their pool, and the dolphins were taught to associate a sound or gesture with each object. They were then taught a variety of verbs, such as "touch" and "fetch." Gradually, they were trained to understand two words strung together in simple sentences, such as "touch ball" or "fetch hoop." From a total of

600 two-word sentence instructions, they gave correct responses 80 percent of the time, and were eventually taught to respond to sentences up to five words long.

This was impressive in itself, but more importantly, they could take account of both the meaning and grammatical arrangement of the words: they could distinguish, for example, between "ball–fetch–hoop" (which means "get the ball and take it to the hoop") and "hoop–fetch–ball" (which means "get the hoop and take it to the ball"). At the very least, these studies demonstrate that bottlenose dolphins can grasp the essentials of human language and seem to have the potential to develop a language of their own, even if they have not done so independently.

One difficulty with assessing intelligence is the assumption that, if an animal is shown to demonstrate a reasonable or poor level of intelligence in one field, it will show similar results in other fields. But this is not necessarily the case. Research by Dorothy Cheney and Robert Seyfarth on vervet monkeys *Cercopithecus aethiops*, for example, has shown them to be good primatologists (they understand the way their society is organized), but hopeless naturalists (they do not recognize subtle signs indicating the presence of predators). In a similar way, cetaceans may be good at interpreting their own acoustic and visual signals, but not so skilled at understanding ours.

Other studies on captive dolphins help to shed light on the way they perceive their environment, although they may not be specifically designed to do so. One captive bottlenose dolphin was taught to attack sharks. It would attack sandbar sharks *Carcharhinus plumbeus*, lemon sharks *Negaprion brevirostris* and nurse sharks *Ginglymostoma cirratum*, none of which is known to attack dolphins in the wild. However, the dolphin refused to attack a bull shark *C. leucas*, which is a known predator of dolphins in the wild. This suggests that bottlenose dolphins may be capable of classifying different shark species according to the threats they present.

One factor often overlooked is the differences between species of toothed whales. Many observations on the smaller toothed whales in captivity, combined with physiological research in the laboratory, suggest that there is a great deal of variation in intelligence between them. Harbor porpoises *Phocoena phocoena* and river dolphins, families Platanistidae, Iniidae and Pontoporiidae, for example, do not appear to be as intelligent as rough-toothed dolphins *Steno bredanensis* or bottlenose dolphins. However, ranking them among more familiar, terrestrial species is extremely difficult and fraught with problems.

EVIDENCE FROM THE WILD

The larger toothed whales and the baleen whales are generally too large to be maintained in captivity, so any information on their intelligence must come from the study of wild animals at sea. Similar studies have added to our knowledge of the intelligence of the smaller toothed whales.

There are several examples of toothed whales displaying what appears to be an understanding of cause and effect. Orcas *Orcinus orca* demonstrate this in some of the ways they catch their prey. In the Antarctic, small pods have been observed cooperating to create waves sufficient to tip seals off ice floes. In Argentina, they intentionally strand themselves on beaches along the coast of Patagonia to catch sea lion pups—and the females actively teach their pups this difficult and potentially dangerous hunting technique. Bottlenose dolphins also strand themselves intentionally to catch prey. In parts of South Carolina, USA, they drive fish toward mudbanks and then rush at them, creating small

ABOVE: Learning to jump through a blazing hoop is more a tribute to the trust that develops between a dolphin and its trainer than an example of intellectual ability.

BELOW: The bottlenose dolphin is the best studied of all captive cetaceans.

ABOVE: There are many long-term studies of wild bottlenose dolphins around the world and, consequently, more is known about them than almost any other cetacean species. But there is still a great deal to learn, and new discoveries about their biology, behavior and ecology are being made all the time.

Robert Pitman/Earthviews

RIGHT: False killer whales usually travel in groups of up to 50 animals, with both sexes and all ages mixed together. They are fast and acrobatic swimmers and behave more like playful dolphins than their close relatives pilot whales and orcas.

waves that wash the fish ashore. The dolphins then hurl themselves out of the water to catch the stranded fish.

But what do these examples tell us about the intelligence levels of toothed whales relative to other animals? The examples of orcas and bottlenose dolphins using topography to trap prey are similar in many respects to the way tools are used by other animals. While such behavior is often thought of as a characteristic of chimpanzees and other "higher" primates, birds and some other animals frequently use tools in a highly sophisticated manner. Such behavior is not necessarily indicative of higher intelligence.

There is plenty of circumstantial evidence to suggest that some cetacean species are able to learn from experience, and that they reason to solve problems. There are reports of bottlenose dolphins undoing the knots that fishermen tie in their nets, for example; even if they are pulling with no set pattern, this at least demonstrates that they understand how the nets are held together. In heavily fished areas of the eastern tropical Pacific, many of the local dolphins have become wise to the tuna-fishing operations and if they get trapped inside the nets, they wait patiently in the knowledge that they will eventually be released. During the height of modern whaling, sperm whales *Physeter macrocephalus* were hunted by whaling boats using depth-sounders. They would sometimes swim to a region of the ocean known as the deep scattering layer, where apparently they would hide behind midwater fish, essentially making themselves invisible to the whalers' sensing equipment. When sperm whales were hunted by sailing ships, they would frequently swim into the wind. It is possible they had learned that the whalers could not sail to windward.

HOW INTELLIGENT ARE WHALES AND DOLPHINS?

One major problem with studies in intelligence is the difficulty in defining the word itself. Because we have only a human perspective, we risk imposing our own ideas and measures of intelligence on other species. Yet we can scarcely begin to imagine what goes on inside another animal's mind.

In general terms, intelligence is the ability to understand. It is the ability to learn from experience and thus to analyze new situations rather than simply react to them. This is quite different from instinctive responses that get things right merely by trial and error. Intelligent animals are able to solve problems by making considered judgments about the possible consequences of their actions. Clearly, this cannot be achieved in the absence of a thinking process, but whether or not it requires self-awareness or subjective thinking is another matter altogether. We are a long way from drawing any definitive conclusions if, indeed, we will ever be able to draw them.

It has been shown that land animals that live in groups show the greatest potential for the development of intelligence when their food is either difficult to capture or hard to find. Not surprisingly, the most intelligent land mammals tend to be primates and dogs. Ecologically, the toothed whales show similarities to both these groups, whereas the baleen whales are closer to the large grazing herbivores such as cattle and giraffes—animals not renowned for their great intellectual abilities. For a variety of other reasons, many scientists believe that toothed whales are more intelligent than baleen whales. But the nature and degree of that intelligence is still hotly debated.

Perhaps the greatest mistake humans make is attempting to compare whale and dolphin intelligence with our own in the first place. After all, cetaceans have embarked upon an entirely different evolutionary path. No matter how they fare in human intelligence tests, the details of their own intelligence suit their needs. They could still be far more intelligent in their world than we are in ours.

BELOW: It is difficult to measure intelligence in humans—let alone in animals such as humpback whales. Their unearthly songs, ability to navigate across vast oceans and cooperative feeding have all been cited as important evidence. But even these extraordinary accomplishments are not in themselves enough to assume a high level of intelligence.

SOCIAL BEHAVIOR

PETER CORKERON

W*hy do some animals spend most of their time alone, while others prefer to live in groups? Why are minke whales normally loners, for example, while orcas live in extended family pods? These are questions that have been perplexing biologists for a long time.*

Since natural selection operates on the individual, not on groups, it must sometimes be in the long-term interests of the individual animal to remain in a group. But assessing the relative cost and benefits of group living is complicated by the fact that animal social systems are also adaptations to ecological conditions—and that the evolution of social behavior is influenced by how closely (or distantly) individuals are related. The ecological factors that appear to affect the social behavior of whales include habitat; rates and types of predation; the quality and spacing of food patches (and the ease with which they can be located); and the constraints placed on mammals in an aquatic environment.

BELOW: Pelagic or open-ocean dolphins hunt large patches of prey scattered over huge areas. Gatherings of a thousand or more animals can locate and herd prey more efficiently, leading to the formation of highly coordinated groups that appear to emphasize their coordination with leaps and sudden changes of direction.

Don Croll

INFLUENCES ON SOCIAL BEHAVIOR

Habitat can influence sociality. River dolphins, for example, live in shallow, structurally complex habitats that offer escape routes or hiding places from predators, with low apparent rates of predation, and with prey more or less evenly dispersed. These dolphins are normally found in small groups or are often solitary. Inshore dolphins, which live in bays or along ocean beaches, are normally found in slightly larger groups from about six to 20 animals. Their habitat is slightly more open, prey patches are somewhat larger and more clumped, and predation pressure is greater. By contrast, pelagic (open-ocean) dolphins are normally found in much larger groups—up to thousands of animals—in very open habitats where huge prey patches are distributed in clumps, separated by vast expanses of ocean, and predation pressures are assumed to be more substantial.

The way the individual animals are related to one another, and how this affects their social behavior, is somewhat harder to assess. It is assumed that individual animals attempt to maximize the proportion of their genes transmitted into the following generations. This is referred to as maximizing their "inclusive fitness." The most obvious way to achieve this is by producing sons or daughters. However, if an animal assists in the survival of its nieces and nephews, aunts, uncles, sisters, brothers or cousins, it is still helping at least part of its genetic complement to be carried on.

Assistance may come in the form of "altruistic" acts. The helping behaviors observed in many animal societies certainly do not appear to fit the concept of competition: mathematical modeling has demonstrated that it can sometimes be in an animal's best interests to assist another member of the group—but only if all animals in the group adopt this attitude and none "cheats." Altruism doesn't necessarily imply a conscious intent to carry out an act of kindness. Instead, the term refers to the evolutionary development

of a "suite" of behaviors involving the assistance of group members, with the assumption that they, in turn, will reciprocate such behavior should the need arise. This is known as "reciprocal altruism."

Examples of altruistic behavior among cetaceans are common, and while there are many examples of altruistic acts among terrestrial mammals, the fact that cetaceans live in an aquatic environment appears to provide a special impetus for such altruistic acts. An injured whale or dolphin incapable of swimming to the surface to breathe may rely on other members of its group to support it; whether cetaceans learn that assistance to group members is one of their social rules, or assist an injured animal instinctively is

not at issue here. The need (induced by living in an aquatic environment) to develop such behavior is what is important, and appears to be sufficient for acts of reciprocal altruism to form an integral part of cetaceans' social behavior. Such nepotism, as the assistance of kin is called, does not, of course, have the political connotations it attracts in human society.

To add to the complexity, the long-term interests of males and females differ. Males need to compete for access to breeding females, and need to "convince" females that they are the female's best choice of a mate. Females have to maximize their energy input, as the energy costs of reproduction (and especially of lactation) are great.

BELOW: More is probably known about the social behavior of humpbacks than of any other baleen whales.

To put all this simply, males invest in obtaining the greatest number of mating opportunities, while females invest in ensuring that their young survive and get a good start to life.

The basic unit of cetacean society appears to be the bond between mother and calf (rather than, for instance, the bond between a mated male and female). This develops, under suitable conditions, into female-bonded or matrilineal groups. Pilot whales, for example, seem to display this form of social system. There is good evidence that females of this species undergo menopause, a rare phenomenon in the animal kingdom. The "grandmothers" of a group may be the repositories of learned information—for example, where to find the best food patches in different seasons—and may act as group leaders in much the same way that tribal elders do in human society. The existence of menopause also suggests that as the females of some species age, they invest more in the rearing of an individual calf, while young females invest in producing many calves.

Regrettably, cetacean social behavior is far from completely understood. There have been many studies in captivity, and the observation of captive cetaceans (predominantly the smaller species) still continues, but most of the answers to so many perplexing questions lie in studies in the wild. Fortunately, such research has grown exponentially in recent years and, consequently, our knowledge of humpback whales, right whales, pilot whales, orcas, bottlenose dolphins, Atlantic spotted dolphins and many other species has also increased enormously. But it is a long, time-consuming process relying on tiny snippets of information that gradually build up a more complete picture.

While there is a great deal of overlap, observations on one species do not necessarily apply to other species, so it is necessary to take some broadly representative samples of different cetacean social systems, and examine them in more detail.

THE BOTTLENOSE DOLPHIN

Bottlenose dolphins *Tursiops truncatus* are found throughout the world in both coastal and offshore waters. As they were among the first cetaceans to be kept in captivity, and have proved remarkably adaptable to their life in oceanaria, a large body of data about their social interactions has been collected under controlled conditions. More

ABOVE: The study of social behavior involves recording the interactions between individual animals. The aquatic habitat of cetaceans poses difficulties for researchers. Natural markings such as distinctive pigmentation patterns, scarring and dorsal fin shape help to distinguish individuals.

importantly, there are also a number of long-term studies in the wild that are continually adding to our knowledge. There are current studies from as far afield as South Africa and Australia and from Scotland to South Carolina. Such a broad geographical spread has allowed differences in habitat and variation in social structure within the species to be taken into consideration and, consequently, has thrown light on the influence of external factors on social behavior.

Since social behavior is strongly influenced by ecological conditions, different living conditions should, in theory, result in different social structures. But the differences can be quite subtle. Indeed, one study in a restricted Florida bay looked at a community of about 100 dolphins, all

Bernd Würsig

ABOVE: The leaping of the bottlenose dolphin has probably been witnessed by more people than any other aspect of cetacean behavior. With its long history in captivity, its widespread distribution and its relative abundance inshore in the wild, it is one of the best studied of all cetaceans.

living within a range of about 85 square kilometers, and these showed no signs of interaction with dolphins in waters outside their range. Another study, in Queensland, Australia, looked at a community of more than 250 animals inhabiting a range of up to 250 square kilometers. Again, they were never seen to associate with the other bottlenose dolphins just outside the bay.

Bottlenose dolphins are found in groups ranging in size from two to more than a thousand animals. They also show a decidedly unsocial phenomenon—some individuals live solitary lives and are never seen in the company of other dolphins. Whether they have left voluntarily or have been driven out by other members of the group is unknown. Apart from the basic unit of a mother–calf pair, the social structure is fairly fluid and individuals constantly leave and rejoin groups. Subadults of either sex tend to group together, as do adult females with their calves, and adult males. Some female calves may accompany their mothers for life, others join subadult groups; adult females form loose, changing groups. Males leave their birth groups at puberty and join groups of subadults; these get smaller and smaller as the animals age, until fully mature males form alliances of just two or three animals. Such adult male alliances appear to be among the most lasting bonds in bottlenose society.

There is a great deal of touching within a group and the dolphins frequently stroke and caress each other. Sexual behavior, including copulation, is used casually—apparently indiscriminately—to reaffirm bonds. True mating opportunities, however, are relatively rare because females calve only every four to five years and so there are relatively few receptive females at any one time. In some areas, for example at Shark Bay, in Western Australia, male alliances have been seen to subdue and herd unwilling mature females, presumably as a prelude to mating; at other times, however, the males do not cooperate. Instead, they compete and even fight for females.

Within the groups, there appear to be dominance hierarchies, which tend to be dominated by the largest males. Female dominance patterns appear to be less rigid. A great deal of time is spent sorting out the pecking order and reaffirming bonds. Agonistic or aggressive behavior patterns include chasing, ramming, biting, and slapping subordinates with their flukes. Jaw clapping is also common—in which a dolphin shuts its jaws firmly to cause a sharp report in the water. Adult males display aggressive behavior toward calves as well as adults; in these instances, the mother will fight back or try to escape the source of aggression. Angry squawks, clicks and pops frequently accompany such aggressive behavior.

There is a good example of dominance hierarchies at work in a population of bottlenose dolphins in the waters off the coast of Queensland, Australia. The local dolphins feed on the bycatch behind shrimp trawling boats, which discard non-commercial fish that are caught incidentally in the nets. In some areas, a large proportion of their food is obtained in this manner. Interestingly, the most dominant individuals—generally adult males—have first choice of the bycatch and are very selective in what they eat. Lower-ranked animals—generally females and juveniles—have second choice and take the fish species and leftovers that the more dominant individuals ignore. Many of the animals show scars from encounters with large sharks, which also follow the same boats. The danger posed by the sharks does not seem to discourage the dolphins from feeding behind trawlers—yet bottlenose dolphins studied in other parts of the world, such as Florida, go to great lengths (for example, by moving into shallower and presumably safer waters) to avoid shark attack.

The range of feeding methods adopted by bottlenose dolphins is remarkable. At one extreme, in rocky reef areas, they feed individually; at the other extreme, in open water, they cooperate in herding large schools of fish. In one shallow, marshy habitat in South Carolina,

they cooperate to drive fish up onto a muddy riverbank, and then beach themselves temporarily to grasp the struggling prey. There are several places around the world where bottlenose dolphins even cooperate with humans by corralling and herding fish—a joint effort in which both parties benefit. Such a diversity of feeding techniques suggests that bottlenose dolphin groups act as teaching institutions, with young animals learning from their elders.

THE ORCA

Orcas or killer whales *Orcinus orca* are found in all the oceans, in both inshore and offshore

waters. One population in the waters of British Columbia, Canada and Washington State, in the United States, has been studied intensively since the early 1970s. As a result, we probably know more about the social structure of the orca than of any other cetacean. There are three separate communities in this particular population: a resident northern community, a resident southern community, and a transient community comprising whales seen only sporadically within the areas where the two resident communities are found.

There are many differences in ecology between residents and transients—in their pod

ABOVE: Like a cat toying with a mouse, the bottlenose dolphin will sometimes play with its prey, grasping it gently before releasing it, then darting forward to seize the hapless fish or squid again.

structure, feeding preferences and home ranges. There are also more subtle differences in appearance (transients tend to have more pointed, centrally positioned dorsal fins) and behavior (transients vocalize less frequently, make more abrupt changes in swimming direction and tend to stay underwater for longer). It is even quite possible that the two kinds are undergoing speciation, especially since they never associate with one another and often appear actively to avoid social contact. To confuse matters even more, a possible third kind of orca—dubbed

ABOVE: Orcas are extremely vocal animals and produce three different types of sound. Each pod appears to have its own "dialect" of clicks, whistles and pulsed calls.

RIGHT: Orcas are among the more obviously sexually dimorphic whales. Males grow to 9.8 meters in length and have a distinctive dorsal fin that is sharply triangular and may stand 1.8 meters high. Females are lighter in weight, shorter (a maximum length of 6.5 meters) and have a smaller, less robust dorsal fin.

"offshore"—has been discovered in waters far from the coast of British Columbia.

In residents, the basic social unit is a matrilineal group made up of between two and nine animals which are closely related—an older female and her direct descendants. This group is known as an intrapod and its members always remain together. Two to 12 intrapods together make up a subpod, whose members spend 95 percent of their time together and are more distantly related. One to three subpods together make up a pod, whose members spend about half their time together and are even more distantly related. All members of a pod share a common maternal descent. On average, a pod contains about a dozen whales, but there may be as many as 50 in some instances. Sometimes, as many as half the whales in a community gather together temporarily to form a superpod. It is possible that these mass meetings are orca orgies; in other words, mating occurs when different pods meet. But, despite a huge amount of research on orcas, and many thousands of hours spent observing them in the wild, mating has never been observed.

Transient pods are generally smaller than resident pods, perhaps as an adaption for hunting mammalian prey. They also appear to be

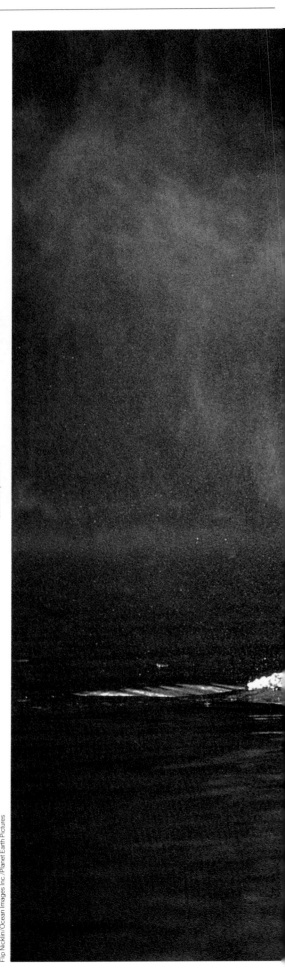

Corel Corporation

Flip Nicklin/Ocean Images Inc./Planet Earth Pictures

Jen and Des Bartlett/Bruce Coleman Ltd

ABOVE: In Patagonia, Argentina, a small number of orcas hunt sea lion pups and young elephant seals along the coast. They literally strand themselves on the beach, grab a young animal and then wriggle back into the water. It is an extraordinary hunting technique—most whales are in serious trouble if they strand—and requires several years of training from an early age.

FACING PAGE: There are records of orcas attacking whales as large as blue whales. They harass them and bite them until they are too weak to escape, and even drown them by forcing them underwater. This blue whale was attacked by a pod of orcas off Baja California, in Mexico, and eventually died of its wounds.

structured differently. While resident males or females never leave their mother's groups, there is some evidence that both sexes may leave transient groups on reaching sexual maturity (or, in the case of females, after the birth of their first calf).

In British Columbia and Washington State there are about 20 pods of residents, numbering about 280 individuals in total. Individual animals are identified by their distinctive dorsal fins and by the size, shape and position of the light "saddle patch" on their backs. Whales from the southern and northern communities have clearly defined home ranges and even seem to recognize an invisible boundary in northern Georgia Strait: each community stays on its own side. There are about 100 transients, which cruise in small pods from Washington State to Alaska.

Orcas are extremely vocal animals, and produce three different types of sound: rapid clicks, canary-like whistles and far more complex calls that can be heard as far as 15 kilometers away. The clicks are used for echolocation, to

build up a "sound picture" of their surroundings. The loud whistles and more complex calls seem to be a form of social signaling. Interestingly, the calls vary with the situation and it appears that no single call is used in a particular context— which makes it very difficult to interpret their meaning. But the whales do seem to be prompted by one another and, if one uses a particular call, another may respond with exactly the same call. Some of these calls are shared by other pods but, at the same time, each pod appears to have its own unique "dialect."

Intriguingly, the differences and similarities between dialects seem to be directly correlated with the degree of relatedness between the pods. The dialects of pods within a single community are similar, while those of pods from different communities share very few calls. Transients are generally quieter than residents and will often stop communicating altogether while they are hunting—probably to avoid warning seals or cetaceans of their approach.

Hunting behavior also varies significantly from region to region, although all orcas employ pack-hunting techniques much of the time. Broadly speaking, resident orcas feed on fish, while transients prey on marine mammals. But overall they are known to feed on anything from squid and seabirds to otters and caribou (caught by transients while attempting to cross rivers). Transients are even known to tackle blue whales and other large whale species, using techniques that demonstrate an impressive degree of social coordination. The target animal is "herded" by the orcas, which actively prevent it from diving and even seem to prevent it from breathing by throwing themselves over its blowhole.

The same kind of prey may be caught using different techniques in different parts of the world. One of the most extraordinary hunting methods is used along the coast of Patagonia, in Argentina, and around the Crozet Islands. The orcas there intentionally strand themselves on beaches to snatch sea lion pups and young

Bob Vile / Hubbs Sea World Research Institute / Harcourt Brace Jovanovich

Dean Lee

ABOVE: Explanations for orcas' fluke slapping or lobtailing vary from ritualized aggression to signals that alert other members of the pod to intruders or danger.

FACING PAGE: Orcas often spyhop, thrusting their heads and upper bodies above the surface to inspect their surroundings. They are believed to be able to see fairly well above the surface, as well as underwater, and learn to spyhop at an early age.

orcas lived in what were described as three "mobs" or "families" that, over the years, combined to form one group—a social pattern quite similar to that described for orcas off the west coast of North America.

Orcas also associate with human activities today. Herring seining in the waters off Norway and Iceland attracts hundreds of orcas to feed around the fishing boats as they work. This poses some interesting questions. How does the social organization of orcas allow for the development of such large aggregations? In such situations, do the divisions between pods and communities remain and, if so, how are they maintained? There are still many questions yet to be answered.

THE LONG-SNOUTED SPINNER DOLPHIN

Long-snouted spinner dolphins *Stenella longirostris* are found in tropical, subtropical and occasionally warm temperate waters worldwide. They are most common far out to sea, but are also found close to shore in some areas and around oceanic islands. They live in groups ranging in size from about half a dozen to as many as 1,000 individuals.

The population sizes and stock separation of spinner dolphins inhabiting the waters of the eastern tropical Pacific Ocean have been studied in some depth. Unfortunately for the dolphins, much of this information has come from animals killed in tuna-fishing operations. Literally millions of long-snouted spinner dolphins and their close relatives, pantropical spotted dolphins have been killed "incidentally" due to their association with tuna. There have also been long-term studies on their social behavior in other parts of the world.

From studies of Hawaiian animals, it is apparent that spinner dolphins make use of different habitats during the course of a 24-hour period. In daylight hours they rest inshore, while at night they move offshore to deeper waters where they feed on deepwater fish, which sink out of reach as the sun rises. As they move between habitats, their group size changes. During the day's rest they swim slowly in groups of 20 or so, probably because the available bays are small and therefore they are forced to split up until morning. But at night they congregate in feeding groups that may number several hundred individuals which comb large areas of ocean in a coordinated search for food. The transition from rest to active traveling and feeding is quite marked. As evening draws near, the aerial activity of the spinners increases—they were actually named in honor of their impressive acrobatic displays—and is followed by a period of zig-zag swimming. Once every member of the group is acting in a cohesive fashion, they move offshore to join similar groups.

This social structure and patterns of behavior appear to demonstrate how ecological factors can

elephant seals from the shore, then wriggle back into the water. The young orcas actually undergo an apprenticeship to learn how to strand safely and, indeed, there is good evidence that older orcas teach prey-hunting techniques to younger members of the pod elsewhere in the world. In the Antarctic, they cooperate by tipping seals from ice floes into the waiting mouths of other members of the pod. In other areas, transients work in shifts to catch seals that hide in underwater caves—by taking it in turns to rise to the surface to breathe, there are always some whales still submerged when the seals finally have to leave their hiding places and come up for air.

One of the most remarkable examples of working together concerns a cooperative fishery between humans and orcas from the last century. A pod of orcas at Twofold Bay, a small New South Wales town in Australia, actually alerted the local whalers to the presence of passing right whales—by lobtailing in the harbor. While the whalers prepared to kill the right whales, the orcas would herd them toward their boats and then keep them on the surface until they were dead. The whalers would usually leave the dead whales tethered for a couple of days to let their assistants feed on the lips and tongues as payment for their services. Interestingly, these Australian

R S Wells

ABOVE: Long-snouted spinner dolphins are among the most acrobatic of all cetaceans. Their aerial displays are most impressive and when they breach, they hurl themselves high into the air and then spin round up to seven times on the longitudinal axis.

BELOW: Spinner dolphins live alone, in pairs, in small groups or in enormous schools containing hundreds or even a thousand individuals.

bear directly on social behavior. Spinners move to inshore areas to rest in areas offering the greatest protection from predation by sharks—where group size is therefore related to the size limitations of the habitat. But because they feed on deepwater fish, which occur in large, dispersed clumps further out to sea, they have to move into more dangerous areas to feed. They form large groups at night to search vast areas of ocean more efficiently and, probably, to increase the likelihood of detecting dangerous sharks. In the oceanic waters of the Pacific, they are commonly seen in large schools with pantropical spotted dolphins—which could have considerable significance. While the spinner dolphins feed at night and rest during the day, the spotted dolphins rest at night and feed during the day, and it has been suggested that these alternating "shifts" work to the advantage of both species. While one part of the overall group is resting, the other remains alert and keeping an eye out for predators.

Analysis of dead spinner dolphins from the eastern tropical Pacific suggests that their groups are segregated according to sex and age. Research there and elsewhere suggests that groups are composed partly of familial units and more broadly of learned associations beyond the family group. Within this framework, social groupings

are very fluid and individuals move freely from one group to another over periods of minutes, hours, days or weeks. The small inshore groups, for example, tend to have different permutations of subgroups from day to day. It is only really the mother–calf bonds that appear to be persistent.

THE SPERM WHALE

Sperm whales *Physeter macrocephalus* are widely distributed in deep waters worldwide. They are difficult animals to study—not only do they live mainly far out to sea and spend a great deal of their time underwater but also, the males and females live separate lives for much of the year. Records from the whaling days provide some insights into their social behavior, but recent behavioral studies conducted from small sailing vessels have proved that it is possible to study them, alive and in the wild.

Sperm whales are the most sexually dimorphic of the cetaceans: when physically mature a male can be half as long again as a female, and may weigh up to three times as much. This great difference is associated with the different migration patterns shown by the two sexes. There is something of an evolutionary chicken-and-egg question here: are male sperm whales larger because they migrate to polar waters where there is more food, or do they migrate to

polar waters because they are larger? To answer this question, we need to return to the concept of males seeking to maximize their number of mating opportunities.

From whaling data, and from recent behavioral studies, it is known that the basic social unit of the sperm whale is the "nursery school." Adult females, calves and juveniles form groups of two to 50 individuals that seem to be fairly stable. Genetic analysis shows that these groups consist of related animals and, indeed, the adult females take turns in looking after the calves and even share the responsibility of providing milk for them. Nursery schools spend all year in warmer waters and do not normally undertake long migrations. But why should such groups exist? They may provide protection for calves and juveniles, which are preyed upon by orcas and large sharks. Certainly, there are reports of nursery schools keeping predators at bay, and it would appear that a group response can be a successful deterrent. At the

ABOVE: In some parts of the world, spotted dolphins have developed a mutually satisfactory social arrangement with spinner dolphins— while one species rests, the other species is alert and feeding.

LEFT: These sperm whales have arranged themselves in a protective circle around their calves as a pod of orcas approaches..

Al Giddings/Ocean Images, Inc. /Planet Earth Pictures

ABOVE: Although breaching is common in humpbacks, its purposes remain unclear.

same time, they may provide a valuable, concentrated resource of reproductively active females during the breeding season.

Males leave the nursery schools when they are about six years old. They migrate to high latitudes where, either alone or in small "bachelor" groups, they feed until they are old enough and big enough to compete with large males for females. The smallest males, which have only recently left their nursery schools, form groups of up to 50 animals. But, as they mature, the group size decreases to between three and 15 animals. It is not clear why such a decrease in size occurs, although there are several possible explanations. The distribution and abundance of their prey may play an important role. However, we do not know whether the young whales hunt cooperatively or even how they hunt (the fact that sperm whales can have mutilated jaws—yet still seem quite capable of feeding—is just one of many unsolved mysteries). Predation may also be a factor. The younger, smaller whales are probably

under threat from predators, whereas larger animals (which are reliably reported to have sunk wooden whaling ships) could out-swim, out-dive or out-fight large sharks and orcas. Alternatively, as they mature, aggression between members of a bachelor school may lead to its gradual break-up.

It is likely that the growing males are not ready to breed (or, more accurately, the females are not ready to accept them) until they are in their twenties. Then they migrate back to tropical waters during the breeding season, normally alone, to roam between female groups in search of sexually receptive females. Sometimes, two large bulls may form a "coalition" and work together to exclude other males from female groups. They probably do not remain "harem masters" for long—just a few hours or a few days at most. Sometimes, though, aggressive interactions are believed to occur between suitors. Accounts of battles between harem masters, mostly from the logs of old whaling boats, tell of mammoth contests between these magnificent adversaries. Many accounts suggest

that the whales attack each other with their jaws. But while a battle between harem masters must be an amazing spectacle, it is unlikely that bulls would regularly do themselves serious injury; most battles between animals tend to be ritualized affairs, with serious damage to either opponent a very rare occurrence. More likely, it seems that male sperm whales have evolved great size (up to 19 meters in length and as much as 50 tonnes in weight) to intimidate their rivals—a case of "honest advertisement" that enhances a larger animal's chances of mating.

THE HUMPBACK WHALE

The humpback whale *Megaptera novaeangliae* is one of the better known baleen whales and has been intensively studied in the wild for more than two decades. Found in all oceans, it divides its time between high-latitude summer feeding grounds and low-latitude winter breeding grounds, migrating long distances between the two twice every year. The migration itself is at least partially staggered: newly pregnant females are among the first to leave the breeding grounds, for example, but they are among the last to leave the feeding grounds. Certain individuals have been found to travel as much as 8,000 kilometers in a single journey.

Baleen whales rarely form stable associations, and humpback whales are no exception. They are usually found alone or in small groups and each individual spends time with many other individuals during the course of a day, a week, a month or a year. Occasionally, two animals have been observed together for extended periods, but this appears to be quite rare.

Despite this apparent lack of sociability, there are cooperative gatherings at the feeding grounds, where aggression is almost never observed. One of the best examples of this is in southeast Alaska, where large numbers of humpback whales gather every summer to feed on schooling fish. One particular group of apparently unrelated humpbacks has been observed together for long periods. While some members of the group come and go at intervals, the majority remain in the group all the time.

On the breeding grounds, where access to mature females is the main concern of all mature males, the situation is rather different. A mature female is normally accompanied by a male "escort" and he attempts to fend off challenges from other males intent on taking over his prime position. There may be as many as 20 other males—forming a "competitive group"—following the female for anything from a few minutes to several hours.

ABOVE: Humpbacks use a greater number of feeding strategies than other rorquals, including cooperative hunting in which schools of fish or shrimp-like krill are herded by up to 20 whales. The humpbacks then dive and lunge through their densely packed prey.

ABOVE: Herman Melville described the humpback as the most "gamesome and lighthearted" of whales. However, much of the humpback's apparently sociable behavior, including the head lunging shown here, has more to do with practical day-to-day survival than with cetacean high spirits.

These males often indulge in the most spectacular fights, slashing one another with their tails, head-butting and breaching on top of one another, until the group dissipates leaving whichever male has managed to win (or retain) the key position next to the female. These contests can leave rivals with raw and bleeding patches on their backs and fins, although they do not appear to be life-threatening. Unfortunately, no one has yet observed copulation between humpback whales, so we do not know what it is that leads to a successful mating attempt.

The famous song of the humpback whale is another strategy used by mature males. It is only the males that sing and they may do so for hours or even days at a time. Each song—which is incredibly complex—may last for a few minutes or up to half an hour and is repeated time and time again. The songs change progressively over time and, while the whales in one population sing the same song, those in other populations sing recognizably different songs. No one knows why they change or, indeed, which animals instigate the change. As with most animal species in which the males sing, such as songbirds, it is likely that the main function of the humpback's song is to attract females and, possibly, to maintain spacing between males. But the fact that singing also takes place on the feeding grounds, albeit rarely, adds to the mystery surrounding this remarkable behavior.

Another aspect of humpback whale behavior that has attracted much attention is breaching, or leaping clear of the water. This is common at all times of year and among whales of all ages. Various interpretations have been attached to breaching, including aggression, inspecting the environment, long-distance communication, play, or simply an "exclamation mark" at the end of some other behavior. Breaching clearly has many functions, according to the context in which it takes place, but exactly which functions is still unclear. Other spectacular aerial behaviors are also common, including flipper slapping and lobtailing.

STUDYING SOCIAL BEHAVIOR

These few examples of cetacean social behavior give some idea of the little we know, and show how much there is still to learn. The social behavior of many species remains a mystery and, even in the better-studied species, there are many gaps in our knowledge. But the use of innovative research techniques, such as photo-identification to recognize individual animals, radio and satellite telemetry to follow their movements, DNA "fingerprinting" to reveal special relationships, and high-tech hydrophones to eavesdrop on their underwater "conversations," is helping to increase our knowledge at an impressive rate.

Whale scientists identify individual whales, dolphins and porpoises in many different ways, depending on the species and the nature of the

project. Blue whales, for example, have an individual pattern of mottling on the body and the shape of the dorsal fin varies. Right whales can be recognized by the pattern of callosities on the head. Orcas are identified by a combination of the dorsal fin and gray saddle behind. Humpback whales are recognized by the unique black-and-white markings on the underside of their tails, which range from jet-black to pure white and include an endless number of

variations in between. Since no two humpbacks have identical tails, these markings are the equivalent of our own fingerprints.

In some whales, dolphins and porpoises, the differences among individuals can be quite subtle, and some animals are difficult to approach closely, or are so small and fast that it is hard to see details of any markings. At best, it takes a trained eye to tell them apart; at worst, it is almost impossible.

Since the risk of human error is so high, most whale biologists do not rely on sight and memory. They take photographs of each animal instead. These help to confirm their identity, as well as provide a record of their markings. They are particularly useful when researchers are discussing individual animals. This invaluable research technique, known as "photo-identification," has dramatically extended our knowledge of the behavior and habits of wild cetaceans.

ABOVE: In southeast Alaska, groups of humpback whales cooperate in the summer to feed on rich shoals of herring. They blow bubbles to form nets around their prey and then rise through the center with their mouths wide open. This group of more than a dozen humpbacks has just broken the surface—shoulder-to-shoulder—having gorged themselves on a school of fish.

Claire Leimbach

ABOVE: Bottlenose dolphins regularly
visit Monkey Mia in Western Australia,
where they delight humans of all ages.

WHALES AND PEOPLE

THE LORE AND LEGEND OF WHALES

RUTH THOMPSON

ABOVE: This coin from Syracuse (480–400 BC) shows the head of Arethusa, crowned with an olive wreath and surrounded by four dolphins. The dolphin motif appeared frequently on coins—dolphins held a special significance for travelers.

Michael Holford/British Museum (Natural History)

The earliest known portrayal of whales, dolphins and porpoises in art is a series of ancient drawings carved into rocks in northern Norway. One shows an orca whale with moose and other local wildlife and is estimated to be some 9,000 years old; another, more than 4,000 years old, shows a man in a boat apparently hunting a seal and two porpoises. Several thousand years later, early Greek and Roman artists—inspired by the dolphin's intelligence and kindness to humans—began to adopt dolphin motifs in sculpture, drawing, painting, on mosaic floors and on coins. This artistic tradition, based on the idea of the dolphin as a source of creation, survives to the present day.

RIGHT: A contemporary artist's depiction of a whale can be seen in this mural painted by Lou Silva in 1979 on a wall of the building that houses Berkeley University Press.

THE DOLPHIN RIDERS

The authors and poets of the Mediterranean regarded whales and dolphins as sacred creatures. Many believed that they were reincarnations of the human soul and represented the vital power of the sea. To some, like the Greek philosopher Aristotle (384–22 BC), they were objects of great curiosity and fascinating subjects for scientific observation. He observed that whales and dolphins were mammals, and recorded the fact in *Historia Animalium*:

The dolphin, the whale and all the cetaceans— that is, all that are provided with a blow-hole instead of gills—are viviparous ... All animals that are ... viviparous have breasts, as for instance all animals that have hair, such as man and the horse and the cetaceans.

Aristotle, like other writers of his time, embellished his factual descriptions with stories told to him first hand. In these stories, dolphins appeared as gentle creatures with an almost human-like intelligence. In one story, a school of dolphins entered a harbor and stopped there until

a fisherman, who had caught and wounded another dolphin off the coast of Karia, let his captive free. Only then did the school depart.

Like Aristotle, the Roman soldier-traveler Pliny the Elder (AD 23–79) collected stories for his *Naturalis Historia*, but unlike Aristotle, these were often second- or third-hand accounts, which led to inaccuracies in his writing. In *Naturalis Historia*, he wrote one of the most famous stories about dolphin and human relationships. It involved a boy who would go to the "pool Lucrinus" at noon, with bread to attract the dolphin he called "Simo." The dolphin would emerge, take the bread, and gently offer the boy his back to ride on to Puteoli, where the boy attended school. When the boy became sick and died, the dolphin mourned him deeply. Some time later, the dolphin, overcome with grief, was found dead on the shore.

"The Dolphin Rider at Iassos" is a similar tale of love between a boy and a dolphin. It is a powerful evocation of love and death, in which the beginning of the world, the sea's creative and

AELIAN: THE DOLPHIN OF IASSOS

Ronald Sheridan/Ancient Art and Architecture Collection

Here is a famous story about a dolphin's love for a beautiful boy at Iassos:

Iassos' gymnasium is near the sea
after running and wrestling all afternoon
the boys went down there and washed
a custom from way back when
one day a dolphin fell in love
with the loveliest boy of the time
at first when he paddled near the beach
the boy ran away in fear
but soon by staying close by and being kind
the dolphin taught the boy to love

they were inseparable
they played games
   swam side by side
      raced
         sometimes the boy would get up on top
            and ride the dolphin like a horse
he was so proud his lover carried him around on his back

so were the townspeople
visitors were amazed
the dolphin used to take his sweetheart out to sea
   far as he liked
      then turn around
         back to the beach
            say goodbye and return to the sea
the boy went home

when school was out
there'd be the dolphin waiting
   which made the boy so happy

everyone loved to look at him
he was so handsome
   men and women
      even (and that was the best part) the dumb animals
for he was the loveliest flower of boy ever was

but envy destroyed their love
one day the boy played too hard
tired he threw himself down belly first
   on the dolphin's back
      whose back spike happened to be pointing straight up
it stuck him in the navel
veins split blood spilled
   the boy died
the dolphin felt him riding heavier than usual
(the dead boy couldn't lighten himself by breathing)
saw the sea turning purple from blood
knowing what had happened
   he chose to throw himself on their beach by the gymnasium
      like a ship rushing through the waves
         carrying the boy's body with him

they both lay there in the sand
   one dead
      the other gasping out life's breath
Iassos built them both a tomb
   to requite their great love
they also set up a stele
which shows a boy riding a dolphin
and put out silver and bronze coins
stamped with the story of their love death

on the beach
they honor Eros the god who lead boy and dolphin here

destructive elements, and the ambiguities of human sexual relations are vividly depicted. The story may have had its basis in fact: it was written at a time when whales and dolphins were the familiar companions of fishermen, who considered it a bad omen to kill one, and when boys (and possibly girls) rode gentle dolphins in almost every bay and inlet of the Mediterranean Sea.

In the "dolphin rider" stories, the dolphin and the boy are clearly distinguishable as separate creatures. Other stories take the ancient view of creation flowing from the womb of a dolphin; *delphys*, the Greek work for dolphin, is related to

delphis, which means womb. In Greek mythology, the story of Apollo the Sun God and his defeat of Delphyne, the dolphin/womb monster, illustrates this aspect of the Mediterranean creation story. Apollo's triumph over Delphyne leads him to build a temple at Delphi (Dolphin Town) and take on the title of Delphinius or "dolphin-god." Apollo then becomes a giant dolphin, commandeers a boat of Cretan merchants, and at Delphi reveals himself as a god. Thus Apollo emerges victorious from the sea of creation (embodied by the dolphin) to rule and command the universe.

Michael Holford

LEFT: The dolphin fresco, a decorative panel on the wall of the Queen's Room at the Palace of Knossos, Crete, was painted by an unknown artist probably in the late Minoan II period, c.1450–1400 BC. It is one of the earliest known portrayals of dolphins in art. The dolphins compare favorably with medieval drawings of dolphins, which often depicted them with scales or gills.

Stories about friendships between dolphins and children are not limited to ancient Greek and Roman writings. In New Zealand in the mid 1950s, a long-term encounter between a child and a dolphin was remarkably similar to some of the encounters described in Roman times. A young female bottlenose dolphin suddenly turned up in 1955 after a storm near Opononi, Hokianga Harbor. She allowed children to pet her, play ball with her, and clamber onto her back—and was soon attracting as many as 2,000 people every day. Then, sadly, the day after a law had been passed by the local council to give her official protection, the dolphin was found dead. In recent times, one of the most famous friendly dolphins is Fungie, known to many simply as the "Dingle dolphin." Fungie appeared in Dingle Harbor, County Kerry, Ireland, in the mid 1980s, and has stayed ever since, becoming one of the country's best known tourist attractions.

THE ART OF DOLPHINS

Dolphin legends and motifs featured in a variety of art forms in pre-Biblical times. Cretan artists of the Minoan civilization, which flourished from the end of the fourth century to 1400 BC, used

BELOW: The Dionysus Cup (540 BC) illustrates the Greek legend of Dionysus, god of wine and frenzy. Dionysus learns of his crew's plot to sell him into slavery and plans his revenge—their oars become snakes and vines sprout from the loins of the god. The terrified sailors dive overboard and are rescued by the god of the sea, Poseidon, who turns them into dolphins.

realistic motifs based on floral and marine forms, including dolphins, in their decorative painting. The murals and frescoes that adorned Cretan palaces such as Knossos and Phaestos depicted dolphins as realistic, lively and playful creatures, unlike the paintings of later medieval artists that often portrayed whales and dolphins with scales and gills.

In Greek and Roman art, dolphins appeared on mosaics (the dolphin mosaic from "The House of Tridents" in Delos is an excellent example) and in sculptures, many of which were inspired by the tales of friendship between boys and dolphins.

The Greek genius for sculpture is most evident in the minting of their coinage and, interestingly, dolphins were a favorite motif on ancient coins as they were thought to provide safety for travelers.

BIBLICAL STORIES

Greek and Roman mythology underwent a rapid metamorphosis in the age of Christianity. Previously, dolphins had served pagan gods like Apollo and Poseidon, but now they became agents of the one deity. Dolphins saved St. Martian, St. Basil the Younger and Callistratus from martyrdom, and when the dead body of the

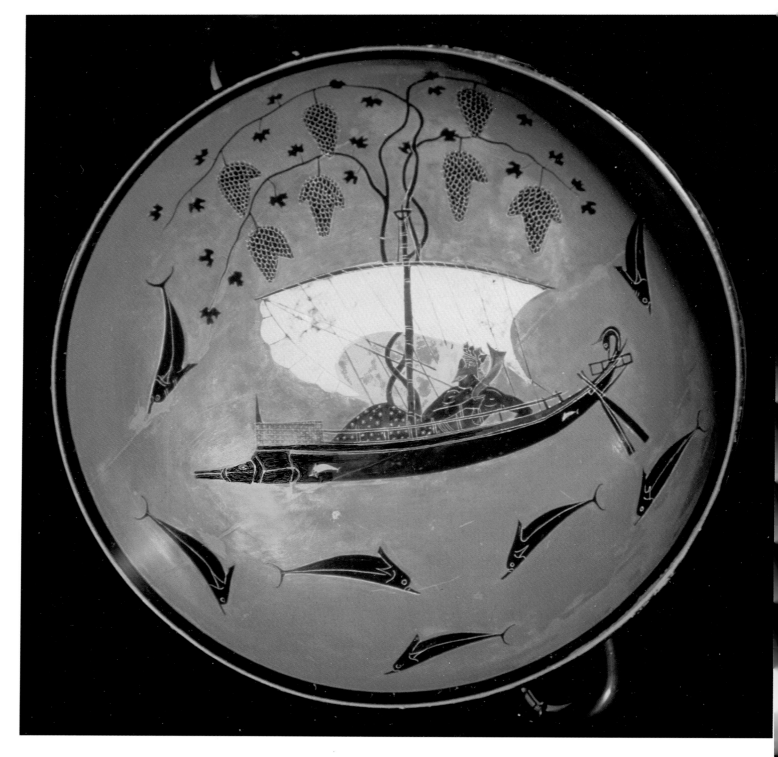

martyred St. Lucian of Antioch was thrown into the sea for predators large and small, a dolphin bore his body to Drepanum for a proper burial.

The affinity between human and beast is less apparent in stories about whales. While dolphins acquired mythic status as companions to—and sometimes saviors of—humans, whales elicited a response that was effectively the opposite. The sheer size of these animals instilled a sense of life on a huge scale. Their enormity suggested terrifying monsters, ready to prey on humans. This is apparent in many of the references that appear in the Bible. Job, for example, describes Leviathan:

Canst thou draw out leviathan with an hook? …
I will not conceal his parts, nor his power,
*   nor his comely proportion …*
Who can open the doors of his face?
*   his teeth are terrible round about.*
His scales are his pride, shut up together as with a
*   close seal.*
One is so near to another, that no air can come
*   between them.*
They are joined one to another, they stick
together,
*   that they cannot be sundered.*
By his neesings a light doth shine, and his eyes are
*   like the eyelids of the morning.*
Out of his mouth go burning lamps, and sparks of
*   fire leap out.*
Out of his nostrils goeth smoke, as out of a
*   seething pot or caldron.*
His breath kindleth coals, and a flame goeth out of
*   his mouth.*
In his neck remaineth strength, and sorrow is
*   turned to joy before him.*
The flakes of his flesh are joined together: they are
*   firm in themselves; they cannot be moved.*
His heart is as firm as a stone; yea, as hard as a
*   piece of the nether millstone.*
When he raiseth up himself, the mighty are afraid:
*   by reason of breakings they purify themselves.*
The sword of him that layeth at him cannot hold:
*   the spear, the dart, nor the habergeon.*
He esteemeth iron as straw, and brass as rotten
*   wood.*
The arrow cannot make him flee: slingstones are
*   turned with him into stubble. Darts are*
*   counted as stubble: he laugheth at the shaking*
*   of a spear…*
He maketh the deep to boil like a pot:
*   he maketh the sea like a pot of ointment.*
He maketh a path to shine after him; one would
*   think the deep to be hoary.*
Upon earth there is not his like, who is made
*   without fear.*
He beholdeth all high things:
*   he is king over all the children of pride.*

(Book of Job, Chapter 41, verses 1–34)

The best known whale story in the Bible is the story of Jonah. When Jonah disobeyed God's call for him to go to Nineveh to preach against the city's wickedness, a violent storm erupted, which prompted the sailors aboard Jonah's ship to throw him into the sea. A whale swallowed Jonah and he spent three days and nights in its belly. Finally, the whale spat Jonah on to land and he proceeded quickly to Nineveh as God had told him to do. The sinful Ninevites repented and God spared the city. Jonah, however, who had wanted to see the city ruined, felt angry at this turn of events. He prayed to be allowed to die if his enemies lived, but God chose to spare the once-sinful city and its newly repentant inhabitants. In the story of Jonah the image of the whale is an instrument of divine will that vividly conveys God's object lesson in true mercy.

Ronald Sheridan/Ancient Art and Architecture Collection

LEFT: This depiction of Jonah and the whale is from a woodcut, 1493. A naked Jonah is emerging from the whale's mouth, beseeching deliverance. The city of Nineveh is in the background but it is the huge whale, with its scaly skin, that dominates the scene. Medieval artists frequently portrayed dolphins and whales with scales.

BELOW: Another interpretation of the Jonah legend, showing the unfortunate Jonah being thrown overboard, with the whale waiting on the sidelines.

British Library, London/Bridgeman

BPCC/Aldus Archive

ABOVE: This Japanese print by Ichiyusai Kuniyoshi, c.1851, shows a stranded whale. The triptych is entitled *Diagyo kujita no nigiwai* ("Big fishing: crowding round the whale").

MYTHS AND LEGENDS

In Japanese folklore and mythology, the whale is depicted as the hare in Aesop's fable of the hare and the tortoise. The monster whale boasts that he is the greatest animal in the sea and challenges the slow sea slug to a race. They agree to begin the race in three days. The sea slug asks each of his sea slug friends to travel to a different beach and wait for the whale. The day of the race arrives. The whale surges forward, leaving the sea slug to follow slowly in his wake. At the appointed beach the whale calls out "Sea slug, sea slug where are you?" The waiting sea slug calls

back "What, whale? Have you only just arrived?" The sea slug suggests a second race to another beach. When the whale arrives he calls out "Sea slug, sea slug where are you?" The waiting sea slug responds "What, whale? Have you only just arrived?" The race continues with the same result until finally the whale admits defeat.

One of the few stories that depicts whales in a similar way to the dolphin myths of Greece is a tale from Polynesia about Putu (or Tinirau in a similar Maori legend), queen of the island of Nuku Hiva in the Marquesas. Putu rides on the back of the great sperm whale Tokama (or

Tutunui in the Maori tale), while her twin daughters travel astride Tokama's twin sons. The evil Kae arrives from Upolu, 2,400 kilometers away, intent on kidnapping and marrying the twin princesses, but he is held captive by the islanders. He begs to return to Upolu. Putu's daughters suggest that Tokama take Kae home, rather than risk a ship and crew. As Tokama bears Kae into the harbor of Upolu, the villagers attack the sperm whale viciously with spears and axes. Finally, Kae drives a spear into her skull and she dies, the first whale to do so by human hand. Tokama's sons return to Nuku Hiva to bear

witness to the treachery. Although Putu realizes that whales will no longer want to serve humans, she asks a final favor of Tokama's sons: to seek revenge for Tokama's death. Putu's twin daughters ride on the backs of Tokama's sons to Upolu and capture Kae. The priest of Nuku Hiva curses Kae and sacrifices him to the gods. Putu commands the sons of Tokama to take to the open water, away from humans, and the villages of Nuku Hiva bid the twin sons a sad farewell.

In this Polynesian story, the innocence of the animals, the sexual connotation of women on the bull whales, the treachery of man toward these

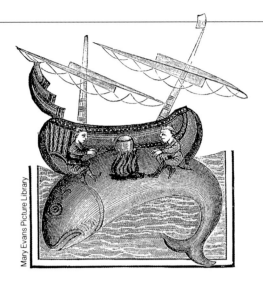

RIGHT: This etching by Richard Furnival, entitled *Bestiaire d'Armour*, shows medieval navigators mistaking a whale for an island. A number of such stories circulated in medieval times and usually the denouement came when the heat of the fire penetrated the skin of the whale and caused it to dive.

Mary Evans Picture Library

mammals, and the notion of whales and humans living in harmony reflect the Greek dolphin myths. The lack of Hawaiian whale myths suggests that the humpback whale may have migrated there only during the past 200 years.

CHANGING PERCEPTIONS

The middle ages heralded a significant shift in the mythology surrounding whales. For the first time they began to appear as animals that were not always what they seemed. A good example is the story of St. Brendan, the Benedictine monk, who left his native Ireland in 565 AD to find the Promised Land of the Saints. St. Brendan put ashore to say Mass on what he thought was an

MOBY DICK: A CLASSIC WHALING NOVEL

Herman Melville's *Moby Dick* is a classic nineteenth-century work. It is the story of Captain Ahab's revenge against the white whale that had brutally mutilated him, causing his severed leg to be replaced by a gleaming ivory jaw. The book is based on the author's personal experiences of whaling aboard the sperm-whaler *Acushnet*, which set sail for the Atlantic in 1841. Ten years later, New York-born Melville published *Moby Dick*. It was poorly received by the critics, and it was not until Melville's death in 1891 that interest in the book was renewed. It soon became the focus of considerable scholarly and literary criticism.

The story of Moby Dick opens with the now-famous words "Call me Ishmael," a Biblical reference (one of many that abound in the book) to Abraham's son by a slave woman. Ishmael becomes the unwanted wanderer when Abraham's wife Sarah produces a son and drives out Ishmael and his mother to prevent them from claiming the inheritance.

In *Moby Dick*, the young man Ishmael is attracted by "a portentous and mysterious monster"—the whale—and by a desire to see "the wild and distant seas where he rolled his island bulk." He decides to join the whaler *Pequod*, which on a cold Christmas Day "blindly plunged like fate into the lone Atlantic." On board the *Pequod* are Captain Boomer and three officers: Starbuck, the godfearing, prudent Quaker; Stubb; and Flask. The three harpooners on board are all pagans: Queequeg, a tattooed Maori; Tashtego, an American Indian; and Daggoo, an African. The rest of the crew consists of what Ishmael calls "isolatoes," who are loners and misfits like himself. They learn later that, as part of his plan for revenge, Ahab had secreted in his cabin an additional crew of pagans headed by Fedallah.

The novel reaches its climax when the white whale is finally sighted. Starbuck, the Christian among pagans, tries to dissuade Ahab from his quest for vengeance, but Ahab refuses. When the glow of St. Elmo's fire lights up the mast in a typhoon, a sign that death is near, Ahab ignores the omen. The chase begins. Armed with a specially fashioned harpoon edged with his own razors, Ahab battles with Moby Dick for three days. Moby Dick, his

huge body writhing from embedded harpoons, rams the lowered boats of the *Pequod* with his head. The foaming sea is a confused mass of half-drowned sailors, tangled lines and sinking boats. On the third day, the whale sounds, rises from the sea and smashes into the bow of the *Pequod* itself. Ahab, inflamed with vengeance, harpoons an iron into Moby Dick, but as the monster threshes to his death, Ahab becomes entangled in a line and is sucked into the sea and dies. Only Ishmael survives.

Moby Dick contains a plethora of allusions and symbols, conveyed superbly in eloquent language, ominous portents and brooding reflections. Critics have considered their significance at great length. One concludes that *Moby Dick* reflects the Nordic consciousness of the endless struggle against the elements. Others have argued that the whale is a symbol of vested privilege, which impedes the human spirit; or that Ahab is doomed because he is guilty of the Christian sin of pride. According to Freudian psychoanalysis, Ahab is the id, Moby Dick the ego, and the upright Starbuck the superego; when Ahab dies by the line attached to Moby Dick, it is a symbol of the umbilical cord, or of Melville's submission to parental conscience.

Yet Melville did not set out to write an allegorical novel as some might suggest. He described his work in a letter to his English publisher as "a romance of adventure based on certain wild legends of the Southern Sperm Whale Fisheries, and illustrated by the author's personal experiences of two years or more, as a harpooner." There is nothing to suggest that Melville had a symbolic plan in mind, rather, as Robert McNally sums it up in *So Remorseless a Havoc*, "he worked with his meanings and symbols as they revealed themselves in the course of the writing. Criticism assumes deductive art; Melville wrote *Moby Dick* inductively."

The writers D.H. Lawrence and E.M. Forster perhaps have come the closest to understanding what *Moby Dick* is about. Lawrence wrote an essay about Melville in his *Studies in Classic American Literature*. He notes that "of course [Moby Dick] is a symbol," but poses the question "Of What?" Lawrence doubts island, but in reality was a whale. God transformed the whale into a "real" island, named St. Brendan's Island. Such was the credibility and superstition of people at the time that explorers were still searching for the Atlantic "island" as late as the mid-eighteenth century.

Folktales about whales began to disappear around the fifteenth century, with the rise of commercial whaling. People began to perceive whales in terms of their income-producing capacity rather than as powerful creatures of the sea. Yet, it is remarkable that given the huge whaling industry that had developed by the nineteenth century, more writing about whales did not appear in contemporary novels by authors such

as Alexander Dumas and W.H.G. Kingston. One of the few novelists who did write about whales was London-born Frank Bullen. *The Cruise of the Cachalot* is an account of a voyage in which Bullen vividly recalls the customs and dangers of hunting sperm whales. In the 17 years before his death, Bullen wrote 36 books, mostly based on his experiences as a young man on a whaling vessel.

The lore, legend and literature of whales and dolphins has been rich and varied, and has reflected current social, religious and mythological beliefs. The tradition continues. In recent years whales and dolphins have been revered because of their perceived intelligence and their affinity, as mammals, with humans.

ABOVE: This eighteenth-century Chinese porcelain dish for the European export market shows an arctic whale hunt.

Sotheby's, London/The Bridgeman Art Library

---

that even Melville knew exactly, but goes on "That's the best of it. He is warm-blooded, he is lovable. He is lonely Leviathan, not a Hobbes sort. Or is he?" On Melville, Lawrence writes that he was:

> … a deep, great artist, even if he was rather a sententious man. He was a real American in that he always felt his audience in front of him. But when he ceases to be American, when he forgets all audience, and gives his sheer apprehension of the world, then he is wonderful, his book commands a stillness in the soul, an awe.

It was this "awe in the soul" that led Lawrence to conclude that Moby Dick is the "deepest blood-being of the white race, he is our deepest blood-nature." He writes:

> … And he is hunted, hunted, hunted by the maniacal fanaticism of our white mental consciousness. We want to hunt him down…And in this maniacal conscious hunt of ourselves we get dark races and pale to help us, red, yellow, and black, east and west, Quaker and fire-worshipper, we get them all to help us in this ghastly maniacal hunt which is our doom and our suicide.

In *Aspects of the Novel*, E.M. Forster argues that both Melville and Lawrence are what he calls "prophetic novelists." Their novels reach back to universal themes, which strike deep and often disturbing chords and give us "the sensation of a song or of sound." Thus, for Forster "the essential in *Moby Dick*, its prophetic song, flows athwart the action and the surface morality like an undercurrent."

The mystery of *Moby Dick* lies in its transcendent glory, the majesty of the sea at once hated and loved and, above all, in the mystery that lay within Moby Dick. As Melville movingly writes:

> … For that strange spectacle observable in all Sperm Whales dying—the turning sunwards of the head, and so expiring—that strange spectacle, beheld of such a placid evening, somehow to Ahab conveyed a wondrousness unknown before. He turns and turns him to it—how slowly, but how steadfastly, his homage-rendering and invoking brow, with his last dying motions. He too worships fire; most faithful, broad, baronial vassal of the sun!

Jonathan Cape Ltd/Mary Evans Picture Library

ABOVE: Rowland Hilder captured the terrible beauty of Melville's story in his illustrations, for many of the most moving scenes in *Moby Dick* are set on the sunlit ocean. Here, the *Pequod* sails to where Daggoo is about to harpoon a sperm whale.

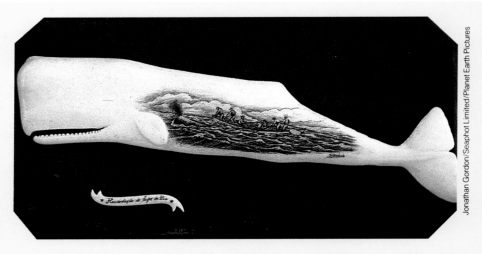

ABOVE: Using a jack-knife, or a box of "dentistical-looking implements", sailors created objects of startling beauty from sperm whale teeth and bones. This scene of open-boat whaling in the Azores would have been familiar to Herman Melville.

THE ART OF SCRIMSHAW

SIR RICHARD HARRISON F.R.S.

In *Moby Dick* (1851), Herman Melville described the "lively sketches of whales and whaling scenes, graven by the fishermen themselves on sperm whale teeth, or ladies' busks wrought out of the right whale-bone, and other skrimshander articles, as the whalemen call the numerous little ingenious contrivances they elaborately carve out of the rough material in their hours of ocean leisure."

Leisure is hardly the right word for the monotonous idleness and inactivity faced by the crews of whale ships. Whaling ships' crews were much larger than those of merchant ships of similar size; all four or five whale catchers needed to be manned and the mother ship had to be worked when the chase was on and the catchers were away. So there were many idle hands when the ship was cruising to the whaling grounds, when it was becalmed, or when it was halted by foggy weather. Days, weeks, even months could go by with nothing to do … and some trips could last four years!

Whalers turned to their own craft skills to occupy their minds and their fingers. Melville continued: "Some of them have little boxes of dentistical-looking implements specially intended for the skrimshandering business. But, in general, they toil with their jack-knives alone; and, with that almost omnipotent tool of the sailor, they will turn you out anything you please …"

It might have been a Mr. Scrimshaw who gave his name to the art; it would have been a fine name for a scrimping second mate, for it was he who usually doled out the raw material on board ship. Or the term might have been one of derision by the "real" sailors, who navigated whale ships far into the Southern Ocean (and often sailed them safely home) for the idle "scrimshankers" who did nothing until a whale was sighted. The Dutch word "skrimshander" means an idle or lazy man.

Scrimshaw products were decorative, sometimes artistic and often practical, and were made from whale teeth and bones distributed by the second mate as occupational therapy. Wood, shells and metal—even stones—were also worked, carved and etched. Designs tended to be nautical, patriotic or jingoistic; many represented the chase and the kill or the hazards and dangers of whaling. Also common were sea monsters, mermaids, seals, seahorses, whales, dolphins and porpoises. Some were complicated traceries depicting lace or intricate geometrical figures; others were sentimental, affectionate, poetic or, occasionally, mildly erotic.

Although some designs clearly had a particular person in mind and sent loving thoughts embellished with hearts and pretty flowers to a sweetheart, there was occasionally a slight doubt about her devotion …"This my love I do intend, for you to wear and not to lend." Few were initialed or signed by their makers; perhaps they were never too sure about their sweethearts' faithfulness, or of their own chances of a safe return home. Some sperm whale teeth bore a demure Victorian lady on one side and a grass-skirted maiden on the other, perhaps expressing the hope that wives and girlfriends might never meet. I have a tooth etched with a scene of a whaling disaster with the inscription "The Great Whaler Claims All."

The technique was fairly simple, but in a sailing ship with no lathes or electrical machinery, a lot of elbow grease was needed. The tooth or piece of bone had to be cleaned, prepared and polished to perfection. Every step of the polishing process had to be done slowly and laboriously because the smooth surface of the tooth was one of its qualities. It was then engraved, using a jack-knife, a sail needle or a carefully filed nail. The etchings were often freehand drawings, but could be made by pasting pictures from popular magazines on the tooth or bone, then cutting through the paper to obtain an outline. The engraved lines were then filled with lamp black, China ink or other coloring materials, and burnished with wood ashes or a substitute polish.

Hull Fisheries Museum

ABOVE: Scrimshaw for personal use or for gifts to wives and sweethearts was the result of patient work and skills born of whaling voyages that could last for as long as four years. Sometimes articles were made for sale back in port.

Other objects classified as scrimshaw were made from a whale's hard lower jawbone, such as a corrugated wheel set in a decorated handle, called a jagger, used for crimping the edges of pastries or pies. The most skilled workers (or the most patient) made whale jawbones into splendidly ornate snuffboxes for men and workboxes for women. Carved and decorated slats were made into front "busks" for ladies' corsets, and were often inscribed with dedications to the future wearer. Napkin-rings, bodkins, thimbles, knitting needles, buttons, brooches, walking-sticks, sword-sticks, handles for riding crops and toothbrushes were other popular products. Skilled men also made "swifts," which were adjustable frameworks on which silk or yarn could be wound; some were so well made that they were still in daily use many years after their maker had died.

Some scrimshaw dates from the late eighteenth century, but most was made between about 1830 and 1860. Craftsmen in many countries continued the tradition for years afterwards, and even today there are scrimshaw artists using teeth left over from the whaling industry or taken from dead animals washed ashore. Unfortunately, it is virtually impossible to ascribe any particular scrimshaw item to a known artist or date, and sometimes only an expert can tell whether the object is made from tooth or bone.

Most old scrimshaw now resides in museums, but should you find any in your attic, be careful. Recent scrimshaw is covered by the Convention on International Trade in Endangered Species of Wild Fauna and Flora (CITES) and cannot, since 1976, be imported or sold on the open market in the countries that are party to the Convention. The only exception is for scrimshaw made or obtained before the Convention came into force—a fact that would be very difficult, if not impossible, to prove. This embargo is not some meddlesome piece of bureaucracy; by restricting trade in endangered animals and plants, CITES has probably done more than any other legislation to protect species in danger.

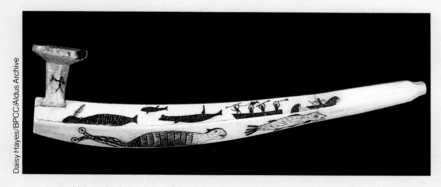

Daisy Hayes/BPCC/Aldus Archive

ABOVE: Although the origin of the word "scrimshaw" is uncertain, the art itself was probably learned from the Inuit whale hunters who first encountered European whalers in Greenland during the sixteenth and seventeenth centuries. This ivory pipe has a scrimshaw decoration of Inuit whaling scenes.

THE WHALING INDUSTRY

SIR RICHARD HARRISON

W*hales have probably been hunted since the beginning of human history. In earliest times, coastal communities would certainly have taken advantage of dead whales washed ashore, using the meat as a welcome source of food and other parts of the carcases for a variety of different products. Our Stone Age ancestors used whalebones as rafters for their dwellings, for example, while the Vikings made chairs from whale vertebrae. It is not hard to imagine how making use of these occasional finds might have developed into some kind of subsistence hunting.*

Pliny the Elder (AD 24–79), a famous collector of rumors and tall stories, witnessed the attack launched by Emperor Claudius and his Praetorian guards on an orca in the bay at Ostia, but the encounter was more of a sporting event than the start of commercial whaling. For many hundreds of years after this incident there is no written record of whaling activities.

BELOW: Many Stone Age inhabitants of northern Europe turned to the sea for food. This Neolithic rock carving from Skegerveien, Norway, demonstrates the importance of the occasional stranded whale as a source of protein.

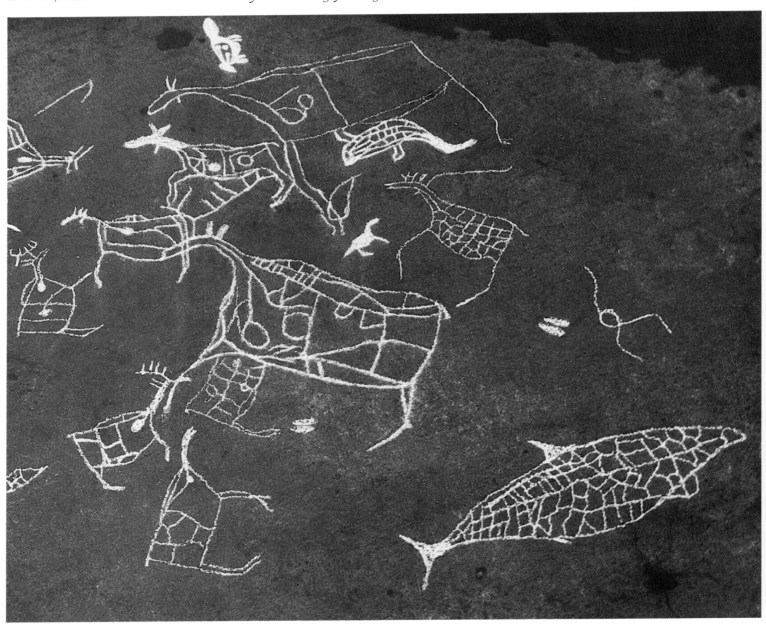

THE BEGINNINGS OF WHALING

The native people of Greenland and arctic Asia and America hunted large marine mammals as soon as they had learned how to make a harpoon that could be recovered if it missed its target. Single- and double-cockpit kayaks were used to hunt seals and narwhals, using harpoons fitted with floats and drogues. The hunting of bowhead whales was more hazardous and required a team effort with a larger, skin-covered whaleboat, the umiak, manned by a crew enlisted or bribed by an acknowledged leader. Temporary wife exchange between the leader and a crew member often helped to cement the hunting relationship.

Primitive whaling elsewhere involved men in rowing boats herding small whales, then driving them ashore. Long-finned pilot whales, in particular, were slaughtered in shallow waters or after being hauled ashore. This technique may have been practised in Japan, for example, as early as the tenth century; it was also used in Orkney and Shetland but has long since been abandoned. In the Faroes, long-finned pilot whales have been driven ashore and killed over many centuries; there are records dating from 1584. The average number taken during the past decade has been about 1,200 whales a year.

Catching large whales as a regular industry demands considerable skill, organization and equipment. It is thought to have been first practised by the Basques of northern Spain and France, who were catching northern right whales in the Bay of Biscay as early as the twelfth century. Watchtowers gave early warning of whales and the local men were ready to launch boats immediately. Many towns on the Basque coast have a whale in their coats of arms: royal personages of the thirteenth century gave grants to coastal villages to encourage whaling. In return, the king could claim a slice of meat or even the whole of the first whale caught—though he often gave most of his "perk" back to the people as a public relations gesture.

Around 1250, a Norwegian work called *Kongespeil*, which was an account of the whales off Iceland, gave the first description of the differences between local species. This work is of particular interest because it ascribed good and bad attributes to the various whale species. Some were thought to be ferocious monsters that hunted and sank ships. These were evil whales, and longed to consume human flesh: "never mention them by name when you are at sea, or … years later, when you sail again a whale will get you." There were good whales too: fin whales "will protect you but do not throw stones at them, or they will become evil." Some of these beliefs persisted late into the nineteenth century, and perhaps illustrate our deepest feelings about the "moral" qualities of animals, quite apart from their economic or commercial value.

Very little is known about whaling during the Middle Ages. The learned scholars of the time repeated what the ancients had claimed. Indeed, it was close to blasphemy to question Aristotle or Pliny, and almost anything that seemed new was entirely anecdotal. In illustrations, whales were given chimneys for nostrils, tusks and beards and bushy eyebrows, and were shown devouring ships and their crews.

The whales in Basque fishermen's home waters became scarcer as they were exploited. The population may never have been large, but by the middle of the seventeenth century Basque sailors had begun to venture much further afield in search of richer grounds. Their long whaling voyages to the other side of the North Atlantic, especially around Newfoundland, did not go unnoticed, however, and England, Holland and several other countries soon began commercial whaling as well.

INTO THE ARCTIC

Two new discoveries attracted the Basque whalers into the Arctic: Davis Strait, in 1585, which was discovered by English Captain John Davis in the

Rose Bierce, Centre for Environmental Education

ABOVE: This 1920s whaler of the Makah tribe, from an isolated corner of America's Pacific Northwest, holds two sealskin floats filled with air, which were tied to the harpoon's rope to keep the harpoon afloat after being thrust.

LEFT: Knowledge of whales languished for a thousand years after Aristotle and Pliny. This woodcut by Conrad Gesner, first published in 1551–58, shows a hazy appreciation of the size and power, if not the anatomy and behavior of the whale.

Shelburne Museum, courtesy American Heritage/BPCC/Aldus Archives

ABOVE: *Capture of a Sperm Whale*, an early nineteenth-century American painting, is alive with the drama and the immediate peril of open-boat whaling. An injured and enraged sperm whale could easily smash a small whaling boat to matchwood with a blow from its flukes.

Mary Evans Picture Library

ABOVE: This Dutch tryworks fouled the air, but shore-based tryworks were more efficient than the same operations carried out at sea.

barque *Sunshine*; and Bear Island and the Svalbard archipelago, in 1596, which were rediscovered by the Dutch explorer William Barents. The Basques were soon followed by Dutch and English sailors with the scent of whale oil in their nostrils.

Many other interested parties joined the hunt: French, Danish, Norwegian, German and Portuguese whalers. The Dutch, and some of the others, were joined by the Basques, who seemed prepared to help in return for a suitable fee. Rivalry for the spoils intensified. The English claimed sovereign rights and prepared to fight. Their well-armed Muscovy Company ships tried to drive away interlopers, even those from the English ports of Hull and Yarmouth. Quarrels over whaling rights resulted in divisions of the coast, and the English wasted much time in trying to exert their alleged authority. It was the Dutch who gained supremacy, simply by bringing in more ships and more men.

The cities of Amsterdam, Flushing, Middleburg and others in the Low Countries contributed to the establishment of a veritable whaling town on Spitzbergen, in Svalbard. They sent out a shipload of building materials in 1622 and called it Smeerenburg, or "Blubber Town." This coped with the housing problems of all those employed in the whaling business, namely men busy at the oil cookeries, shopkeepers, vintners, tobacconists, bakers and all kinds of artisans, as well as the shore crews. On one occasion, one particular Dutch "barn" (or "tent" as it was called in those days) provided winter protection for the crew of the Muscovy Company that had been separated from their ship.

At the height of activity at Spitzbergen the Dutch claimed to have 300 ships in the region and to have employed 18,000 men. The attraction for some kinds of men to go whaling was inevitable at the time—there was, potentially, a lot of money to be made. The work was hard, but only for short periods when catches were made and cutting-up took place. Originally, the cutting-up was done on shore at "Blubber Town," or at some other shore station, but later the raw blubber was taken back home and boiled down there.

The capture of northern right whales increased with such international activity, so attention moved to the Greenland right whale or bowhead whale. This little-known whale, by swimming in coastal waters, became vulnerable to hunting. Both species were reduced by Spitzbergen's whalers to a tiny remnant of their original populations, and seemed in danger of extinction.

New catching endeavors were established in the waters off Greenland and in Davis Strait. The Dutch appeared in 1719 and the English in 1725. The Dutch were dominant for much of the eighteenth century, but suffered from the predatory activities of French and English privateers. English whalers were encouraged by a government bounty, which was also paid to the colonists, and helped stimulate the development of American whaling.

Political events—namely the American War of Independence (1775–83) and then the French Revolution with the outbreak of a virtual world war from 1793—were now having an impact across the world. The seas increasingly became the possessions of the dominant warring nations. France and Britain forced the Dutch out of the whaling business and, by 1798, Dutch whaling interests in the North Atlantic had been destroyed.

INTEREST FROM AMERICA

Meanwhile, a new interest in whaling had been generated in Nantucket and Long Island from as early as 1640, when colonists became aware of the value of drift whales cast ashore. Around the same time, American whaling had its humble beginnings in shore-based boats. By 1700, the industry was well organized, with watchtowers erected along the shore from which lookouts could spot the numerous right whales in the vicinity. This practise continued until about 1712, when "an accident of the weather" caused a Mr. C. Hussey to be blown far from land and to encounter a school of sperm whales. He killed one, towed it back to port and so established a business that immediately brought wealth to the region. There were more sperm whales out there in the ocean, but some distance "to the southward," so larger ships and crews were needed to hunt them.

Trading jealousy and general disputation about whaling rights between the neighboring settlements were made worse by the imposition of taxes and regulations from England. But by 1715, six Nantucket sloops were busy whaling, away at sea for about six weeks at a time and returning with a valuable catch. Meanwhile, northern right whales had become too scarce near the shore—another reason for venturing farther out into the "deep." Whalers also turned their attentions to humpback whales, slow swimmers that appeared close to the eastern coast of North America at certain times of the year.

By the 1730s, many more Nantucket whalers were in operation, helped by the bounty from England. Vessels became larger and voyages much longer—to the equator and even beyond. Many ports on the east coast of America had become well known for their early whaling activities. Besides Nantucket, Bedford (later New Bedford) was a leading center, along with Martha's Vineyard, Cape Cod, Sag Harbor, Salem, New Haven and Providence. Many of these ports still retain evidence of their whaling past in churchyards and local museums.

TECHNOLOGICAL INNOVATION

A technological advance in the 1760s was the installation of tryworks—brick ovens in which blubber was rendered into oil—on the decks of the whaling ship. This was clearly a fire hazard, but few of the wooden ships seem to have been lost and it meant long voyages could be made southward into the deep. It also opened up whaling into warmer climates, since tryworks on board removed the need for the cooling of a dead whale which occurred quite naturally in cold northern waters.

Modern whaling is often said to have begun in 1868 when, after several seasons of

BELOW: Its dying breaths tinged with blood, a victim of the nineteenth-century South Seas whale fishery is shadowed by a whaleboat. In the background, the tryworks on an early version of the factory ship convert another whale into oil, corset stays and other products.

Coo-ee Historical Picture Library

RIGHT: *A Whale Brought Alongside a Ship*, published around 1813, illustrates the centuries-old techniques of flensing or cutting up a whale that has been lashed to the whaleship, but conveys nothing of the dangers and discomfort of a whaler's working life.

AFTER THE HARPOON HAD STRUCK

In the old whaling days a dead whale was towed back by a catcher to the whaleship and secured alongside at head and tail, with a line through a flipper to haul it up high in the water. A ship's boat or two then took up position beside the whale, and the harpooners and other crew members started to "flense" the corpse. They fitted metal spurs to their seaboots to grip the whale surface and, armed with long-handled, keenly sharpened "spades," cut the blubber into long strips. At the start of each strip a hole was cut for a rope, which was fastened in with a toggle and then led through a heavy tackle fixed to the mast. Men pulled on the ropes to peel away strips of blubber from the body. These "blanket" pieces were cut up into smaller chunks in a process called "making off." The skin was stripped from the outside and the unwanted fibrous "kreng" from the inside was removed. After more chopping the small pieces of blubber were sent down below deck to be put into casks under the supervisory eye of the "skee-man." Much stowing and restowing of empty and full casks made activity in the hold hard work, and if it was not done properly a cask might explode as the kreng decomposed and gave off gases.

When the head was reached, the whalebone was hacked out from each side and hauled on the deck. What was left of the carcase was abandoned to the sea as kreng, to be recycled by sharks and any other animals capable of taking a bite.

Later techniques differed somewhat according to the species taken and the use of a new modification—a cutting-in stage rigged over the side of the whaleship with a handrail to give support to those plying the cutting-in spades. In whaleships equipped with tryworks fitted up on deck, the blanket pieces of blubber were further reduced on a mincing-horse with wicked mincing knives and the pieces were forked into the trypots for rendering into oil. Much care was taken to ensure that the fires lit below the pots did not set the wooden ship alight, but occasionally such a disaster did occur. Alternative solutions to this fire problem were properly equipped modern factory ships and efficient shore stations.

The floating factory ships were popular for a while. They could take aboard the entire whale and process it completely, either at sea or at a good anchorage. They could arrive laden with supplies at the start of a season and return with a load of oil and other basic whale products. But quarters were cramped, welfare and cleanliness were difficult to maintain, and shelter from weather was essential for high efficiency.

Shore stations had obvious advantages—space; plenty of fresh water for making steam to work winches and saws, and for cleansing down; protection from storms; facilities that allowed the processing of a whale carcase to be undertaken at leisure with methodical precision. There was room for the flensing plan on to which the corpse was winched from the sea and secured by a chain. There was also room for boilers, cookers, meat stores, bone lofts, storage tanks, glue pots, workshops, staff houses and recreation huts. All of this made it easier to obtain as much as possible from the whale in the way of marketable products.

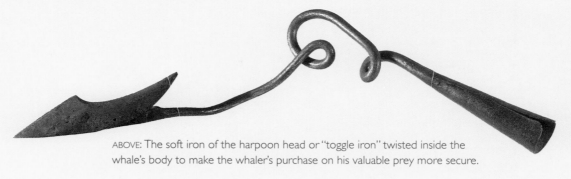

ABOVE: The soft iron of the harpoon head or "toggle iron" twisted inside the whale's body to make the whaler's purchase on his valuable prey more secure.

experimentation, the Norwegian whaler Svend Foyn developed a type of harpoon gun that could be fired from the bow of a small catcher. It was not just the gun that marked the beginning of modern whaling—after all, a harpoon gun mounted on a swivel had been in use since 1731 on boats that carried sails and oars. It was also the fact that the cannon was so solidly made that it could absorb the considerable recoil on firing, and was so well balanced that it could be aimed with great accuracy.

There were various other improvements, as well. The catcher boats became oil-fired, making them much faster, safer and more maneuverable. They were also redesigned so that the gunner could move quickly into position by running along a gangway. Machinery was installed to inflate the dead whales with air so that the carcases would float: some species, such as humpbacks, sink to the seabed very quickly after death and surface again only when decomposition is well advanced.

Even the traditional harpoon was improved. The harpoon lines became longer and stronger, and were wound on engine-driven winches and run over a block hung on springs, so that the struggles of the whale would not break the line. On the tip of the harpoon itself was a grenade, consisting of a detonator and a sack of black

Mary Evans Picture Library

gunpowder in a steel container equipped with barbs. The destructive power of this deadly weapon precipitated an enormous increase in whaling worldwide and is still in use today, albeit in modified form.

But the need to return to shore-based stations to process the whales limited the growth of the whaling industry. The next major development solved this problem, too: by the turn of the century, the mother ships had become floating oil cookeries and, by 1924, they were fitted with stern slipways to winch the entire whales on board for processing at sea.

LEFT: The cry of "Thar she blows!", though now a cliché, was real enough to the wind- and spray-lashed lookout, swaying wildly in his barrel crow's nest. First sight of a whale meant extra income for a vigilant lookout.

BELOW: Norwegian whaler Svend Foyn was probably responsible for the deaths of more whales than any other person. He transformed the whaling industry by building the first steam-driven catcher ship and inventing an explosive harpoon that could be fired from fixed cannon.

ABOVE AND RIGHT: The "slum of the Southern Ocean" was the name whalemen gave to the shore stations of South Georgia, a barren subantarctic island east of Cape Horn. Now abandoned, Grytviken was the focus of an appalling slaughter of whale populations for more than half a century.

Colin Monteath/Hedgehog House, New Zealand

EXPANSION TO THE SOUTH

At around the same time, the Southern Ocean was being opened to whaling—and this ultimately spelled disaster for many of the world's large whales. A land station on the subantarctic island of South Georgia had been established in 1904, but within 20 years the first factory ship had arrived on the antarctic whaling grounds. The catcher boats simply planted a radio beacon on each whale corpse—ready to be collected and processed by the factory ship—while they moved on to the next kill. During the next 50 years or so, some 2 million whales were killed in the Southern Ocean. Some years were particularly bad: for example, more than 28,000 blue whales were killed in the 1930–31 season alone. Pelagic whaling never entirely superseded shore-based methods, but it was the main factor responsible for the disastrous decline of southern whale stocks.

As early as 1912, it was noted that "Foyn's harpoon gun still pursues its march of death through the oceans … with so limited a power of reproduction the stocks of whales will inevitably be reduced." At around the same time, the British

Museum (Natural History) called for scientific research into the immense and unrestricted slaughter of antarctic whales, especially of humpback whales. Protective measures on an international scale were demanded from the Colonial Office: committees sat and reports were published soon after World War I. In 1924, the *Discovery* began research on whales in the Southern Ocean and, over many years, made important contributions to our knowledge of large cetaceans. However, as one expert wrote at the time, "As all the world knows, the immense expenditure of time, effort and money was futile, for the information that should have guided the whaling industry was constantly disregarded, the populations of whales were severely reduced and the whaling industry, once profitable in material and money, was ruined."

THE BEGINNINGS OF PROTECTION

In 1929, a Bureau of International Whaling Statistics was established in Norway in an attempt to record details of catches. Then, in 1931, the League of Nations drew up a Convention for the Regulation of Whaling, which came into force in 1935. Sadly, it was severely inadequate and few countries adhered to its regulations—but it was the first coordinated attempt to control whaling. In the years immediately before World War II, Norway and Britain were the largest pelagic whaling nations and their activities continued unabated (British participation declined after World War II and ceased in 1965). However, it was not long before the whaling industry's own survival was threatened by overexploitation.

Eventually, in 1946, the International Whaling Commission (IWC) was established. Its original aim was to make possible the orderly development of the whaling industry—in other words, to achieve the maximum sustainable utilization of whale stocks, and by definition to protect the future of the stocks as a resource. It has met annually since 1949 to assess statistics and to set limits and quotas on catches.

Agreement has been difficult and not always honored. Some countries refused to sign at all, while others signed with exceptions or left the Commission later. Meanwhile, the advice of scientists on the Scientific Committee (the IWC's advisory body) has frequently been ignored and, consequently, the quotas and regulations have generally been inadequate. There is no doubt that the IWC did much too little far too late—more than 2 million whales were killed during the organization's first 30 years. Yet it had a difficult role, because it was given no powers of enforcement.

After World War II, it was mainly the Japanese and Russian whaling industries that grew—and went on growing until well into the

LA CHASSE A LA BALEINE

Navire baleinier moderne, avec dispositif permettant le dépeçage à bord.

Ann Ronan Picture Library

1960s. Apart from antarctic whaling, fair-sized industries were built up in Peru, South Africa, Chile and Australia (much reduced after 1963). Smaller and less regular interests were stationed in Argentina, Brazil, Canada, Denmark, the Faroe Islands, France, Iceland, Newfoundland, New Zealand, Panama, Portugal, Scotland, Spain and the United States.

During the 10-year period 1956–65, the total reported world catch of baleen whales was 403,490, with a further 228,328 sperm whales taken during the same period. Annual catches were greatest for baleen whales in the 1960–61 season, with more than 40,000 being taken, and they were greatest for sperm whales in 1964, when more than 29,000 were taken.

The popularity of the different whale species changed with time, depending on the market value of their products, the whaling

ABOVE: Disturbingly similar to the snout of a bowhead whale, the hinged prow of this Norwegian-owned factory ship took the conversion of whales into margarine and soap to a new height of efficiency, and was suitably feted in this 1920s French magazine.

International Whaling Commission

ABOVE: Although it has been heavily criticized, the International Whaling Commission has long been the world's only means of supervizing whalers whose declining profits led them to pursue almost any whale of any species.

techniques available at the time, and the availability of the whales themselves. As one species became scarcer, the whalers simply moved on to another species.

PROBLEMS AND POSSIBILITIES

Unfortunately, official protection came much too late for most species and, besides, the killing often continued long after it was declared. As recently as the early 1990s, for example, it was discovered that Russia had been killing protected species, and grossly exceeding its IWC quotas for other species, for more than 30 years. Nevertheless, bowhead whales were protected in 1931, northern and southern right whales in 1935, gray whales in 1946, humpback and blue whales in 1966, sei

rules, allows it to take any number of whales "for purposes of scientific research." This is highly controversial, since little research is undertaken and the whale carcases are processed commercially in the normal way. Japan also concentrates on minke whales, taking approximately 500 every year in the North Pacific and around Antarctica. Meanwhile, untold numbers of whales of several species are killed every year by so-called pirate whalers, who avoid international regulations altogether by registering their vessels under the flags of non-IWC members.

Another breakthrough of sorts came in 1994, when IWC members voted for the Southern Ocean Whale Sanctuary around Antarctica. The sanctuary was established to protect this critically important feeding ground for seven species of great whales. But, sadly, the sanctuary exists on paper only, since Japan continues to hunt minke whales within the so-called protected area.

The future of the IWC—and the whales themselves—is still far from certain. Several countries have recently announced their opposition to whaling under any circumstances, which is a controversial position to take, while others have announced their determination to continue whaling. At every annual meeting there are proposals and counter-proposals, threats and counter-threats, and behind-the-scenes deals and politicking. Only time will tell whether the IWC can survive into the new millennium. Meanwhile, the whales are still being killed.

INDIGENOUS WHALING

The IWC rules currently allow indigenous or subsistence whaling in the Russian Federation, the United States, Greenland, and on the Caribbean island of Bequia, which forms part of St. Vincent and the Grenadines. Special quotas are agreed by the IWC, which allow certain communities to hunt a specified number of whales every year.

The numbers involved are quite small compared with the whales killed by commercial whalers and, ironically, some of the traditional communities have to live with the historical legacy of commercially decimated whale populations. Nonetheless, indigenous whaling can still have a significant impact on whale populations and, perhaps more importantly, it has much wider implications for whaling in other parts of the world.

A strong argument against indigenous whaling, at least in some parts of the world, is that many "traditional" communities are actually quite modern. They no longer rely on whales for their survival.

A good example is a town called Barrow, on the northern tip of Alaska. The local Inupiat and Yup'ik people have hunted bowhead whales

Smithsonian Institution

ABOVE: When the IWC was founded, in 1946, its objective was to make possible the orderly development of the whaling industry. However, more recently, it has been working toward better protection of whales—even though some of its 39 member countries are still strongly pro-whaling.

FACING PAGE: The weathered bones of an antarctic whale, neatly arranged by some forgotten visitor to King George Island, provide an eerie memorial to the hundreds of thousands of whales taken by the Southern Ocean whalers since the late nineteenth century.

whales (except in the Denmark Strait west of Iceland) in 1979 and sperm whales in 1984.

More recently, the IWC has been working toward better protection of whales. A major breakthrough eventually came in 1982, when its members voted for an indefinite moratorium on commercial whaling. In theory, the moratorium was excellent news for the whales. But, in practise, it has not really worked. There are so many loopholes that, since it actually came into effect, in the whaling season of 1985–86, more than 22,000 whales have been killed.

Even today, Norway and Japan continue to hunt whales in defiance of the IWC—and against world opinion. Norway officially objected to the moratorium decision and so, under IWC rules, is legally entitled to continue hunting whales. Every year, it takes several hundred minke whales in the northeast Atlantic and its annual quota, set by the Norwegian government itself, is steadily increasing. Japan took a rather different approach and renamed its whaling "scientific research" which, also under IWC

Q. Compton-Bishop/Seaphot Ltd/Planet Earth Pictures

ABOVE: When the IWC agreed to demands from scientists and conservationists to ban the commercial exploitation of whales, some small island communities and native arctic peoples were allowed to continue hunting small numbers of whales under a special permit system.

BELOW: It has been estimated from whaling records that more than half a million fin whales were killed by commercial whalers. They were still being hunted as recently as the late 1980s.

THE AFTERMATH OF WHALING

In just a few hundred years, countless millions of great whales were slaughtered. Two million whales were killed in the Southern Ocean alone. By the time whales were given official protection, it was almost too late and some species may never recover. The rarest whale in the world—the northern right whale—came so close to extinction that even after more than 60 years of protection there are only about 300 survivors. The bowhead whale has all but disappeared from much of its former range. But, against all the odds, some whales appear to be re-establishing themselves. The gray whale is the ultimate success story. Although the North Atlantic stock is now extinct and only a remnant population exists in the western North Pacific, it has made a dramatic recovery in the eastern North Pacific, and is believed to be now as abundant as the days before whaling. The figures below are very approximate minimum population estimates.

SPECIES	ORIGINAL	PRESENT
Sperm whale	2,500,000	1,500,000
Blue whale	350,000	6,000
Fin whale	600,000	120,000
Sei whale	250,000	40,000
Bryde's whale	90,000	90,000
Minke whale	850,000	750,000
Humpback whale	250,000	18,000
Gray whale	20,000	20,000
Northern right whale	200,000	300
Southern right whale	55,000	6,000
Bowhead whale	30,000	6,000

Jean-Paul Ferrero/Auscape International

in the region for more than 2,000 years and, even today, they are allowed an annual quota of more than 60 whales.

But the hunt is a sensitive issue. Not only is the bowhead an endangered species, but Barrow is no longer the primitive settlement it once was. Even the hunt has changed beyond all recognition, with no traditional hunting techniques being used. The whalers use motorized boats and rely on spotter planes to find the whales. They use heavy iron harpoons, including some that explode on impact, to do the killing. Then, since the modern local people do not rely on whale meat themselves, they generate a profit from their kills by selling carved baleen, or whalebone, to visiting tourists.

The Inuit are caught in the Catch-22 position of being swept up into an affluent, developed society while, at the same time, being expected to adopt the conservationist concerns of the outside world.

Perhaps inevitably, indigenous whaling has attracted the attentions of Japan and Norway. It is yet another possible loophole in the IWC rule book and, on many occasions, the two countries have attempted to expand their own whaling operations under this guise. In particular, they repeatedly propose "small-type community-based coastal whaling" for towns and villages with a "whaling tradition." But in their efforts to deflect attention away from the commercial nature of the hunt, they ignore the fact that most of these "whaling communities" have not hunted whales for many years or, worse still, they began whaling as recently as the 1930s or 1940s.

Ultimately, the challenge is to balance the nutritional needs and genuine long-established cultural rights of native people with the importance of protecting whales. Of course, each case has to be judged on its own merits but, even at its best, the balance will always be a delicate one.

ABOVE: As the number of whales declined, the whaling industry itself was threatened with extinction. These whale bones, left behind at Port Lockroy on the Antarctic Peninsula, are mute testimony to an industry of greed that nearly wiped out the world's large whales.

ABOVE: The layer of insulating blubber was rendered into oil for lighting and lubrication.

RIGHT: Shore-based whaling stations made the processing of whales more efficient. Protection from bad weather minimized wastage of the carcase.

A VARIETY OF WHALE PRODUCTS

Whales have provided an astonishing range of products over the years. Long before the Europeans and North Americans started commercial whaling, native peoples around the world took advantage of dead whales that had been washed ashore. Traditionally, meat was the most important product, but the whales were sometimes stripped bare in order to provide clothing, tools and a variety of other essential commodities as well.

In recent times, whale meat has not been in great demand in Europe or North America and it was really a secondary product during the height of the whaling industry. Whale oil—obtained by heating the thick layer of blubber around the whale—was the main product. Indeed, it was known as the "liquid gold" of the whaling industry: used mainly in lamps and

candles, it was also an important ingredient in everything from soap and shampoo to paints and machine lubricants. The baleen plates, or whalebones, were important as well, and were used for whip handles, fishing rods, umbrella ribs and even ladies' corsets.

Every other part of the whale's corpse, whether it be the teeth, skin, blood or tendons, was used in one way or another. The teeth and the bones were carved and decorated to make snuffboxes, jewel cases, buttons, chessmen, cufflinks, brooches and other fancy articles. Whale skin was turned into bootlaces, shoe leather, slippers and coverings for cases, radios, bicycle saddles, and so on. Tendons were used for stringing tennis racquets and even as "catgut" for surgical purposes. Skeletal remains were made into fertilizer and the connective

ABOVE AND RIGHT: Whalebone established fortunes and fashions. Trimmed of its fibers, the whalebone was softened and shaped to make corset stays, umbrella ribs and shoehorns.

tissue was rendered into glue or gelatin for use in the photographic and food industries. In addition to the use of byproducts in food manufacture, whale derivatives had a number of medicinal applications: vitamins were obtained from the whale's liver and hormone preparations were made from extracts of the endocrine organs. The sheer variety of uses for whale products was extraordinary and for a long time, whale products touched almost every aspect of life in Europe and North America.

The captains of whale boats made sizeable profits from their long and hazardous voyages, although the real whalers—the crew—did not do so well. One large right whale could provide nearly 2 tonnes of baleen and 25 tonnes of oil. On a good market, the yield would cover all costs and give, in today's money, a profit of many hundreds of thousands of dollars. Only one whale was needed to pay for the venture. It is not surprising, then, that the overexploited right whale soon became rare and the whalers turned their attentions to other species.

The really big business in whale products started with the hunting of sperm whales in the early nineteenth century. The oil from their blubber was used in the manufacture of margarine and soap. A byproduct of soap preparation was glycerine, an essential war material when turned into the explosive nitroglycerine. The oil was also used as a drying agent in the making of paints, and in tanning chamois leather.

There was also spermaceti, the oil from the head of the sperm whale. This was used initially for making candles—indeed, the definition of a "standard candle" (the first unit of light used in science) was a pound's weight of candles made from spermaceti that burned at a certain rate. Later, spermaceti oil was used in the manufacture of polishes, soaps, crayons and pencils, and in various food coatings. It has also been used as a wax base for a wide variety of cosmetics from lipstick, rouge and eyeshadow to cold and cleansing creams, shampoos and antiperspirants, as well as in some cleansing emulsions and preparations for protecting the skin.

A mixture of sperm whale oil and spermaceti was called sperm oil. At first, it was used to make candles. But it was later

ABOVE: A triumph of ingenuity if not of taste, this nineteenth-century love seat is constructed of whale ribs and carved vertebrae. Much "artistic" use of whale products was of similar questionable quality, though whalers often produced delicate chessmen or finely etched scrimshaw.

The Whaling Museum, New Bedford, Mass.

ABOVE: For much of commercial whaling's long history, sperm whale oil was the single most important product. Oil from sperm whales was used for lighting, and in soap and paint manufacture. It was without peer for candlemaking, lubricating machinery and as a base for cosmetics.

converted to produce germicides, detergents and antifoams. Sulfur could be attached to the oil components to make sulfurized sperm oil, which made an excellent antiwear additive for lubricants used under extreme pressure and temperature. It could also be used to make sulfated and sulfited oils (sulpfo oils), which were used to finish leathers and as lubricants in metal-cutting and wire-drawing processes.

Finally, there was one interesting sperm whale product that could be obtained without killing, or even encountering the animal. Ambergris (gray amber) is a waxlike, flexible substance with an ashy or brown color, found floating in the sea or sometimes washed ashore; it originates in the intestines of some sperm whales. Bits of the harder tissues from cuttlefish have been found in ambergris and experts think that it is formed in the intestine by a pathological process involving feces. It smells of musk—Alexander Pope observed that "a little whiff of it … is very agreeable." Ambergris was originally used as a medicine to treat indigestion and convulsions, among other ailments. It was used in love philters as an aphrodisiac, in cooking and then as a fixative in high-quality perfumes and soaps. Some huge lumps of ambergris have been found, a few looking more like large boulders than the product of a sperm whale. The largest recorded piece of ambergris weighed an incredible 635 kilograms. Ambergris was once worth its weight in gold, but there are now many synthetic substitutes, so it is no longer as valuable or as sought after.

In recent years, there has been a great decline in the use of whale products for three reasons—the moratorium on the hunting of whales and the general decline of the whaling industry; the development of acceptable substitutes for most whale oil products; and the prohibition of international trade in whale products. Yet some illegal trade does still exist. In April 1996, for example, 6 tonnes of Norwegian whale meat was confiscated by Japanese customs officials. Disguised as a mackerel shipment, it was the first instalment of a 60-tonne shipment of whale meat due to be smuggled into the country. Where profit can be made, it seems, international law is of small concern to the whaling industry.

WHALES AND DOLPHINS IN CAPTIVITY

MARK CARWARDINE

*W*ild *whales, dolphins and porpoises have been captured and kept in captivity since the mid-1800s. In the beginning, bottlenose dolphins were the main target species but, initially, capturing them without injury, minimizing the stress they inevitably suffer during transport, and encouraging them to adapt to their new confined homes proved to be more difficult than many people had anticipated. A great many dolphins died from shock in the first few hours or days after capture, and the others rarely survived more than a few months.*

After years of trial and error, and the unfortunate loss of many animals, the capture and holding techniques were gradually improved. Since those early days, at least 25 different species have been held in captivity—including orcas, belugas, Irrawaddy dolphins and Pacific white-sided dolphins—with varying degrees of success. Even today the transition from life in the wild to confinement in captivity can be most traumatic.

BELOW: Orcas are undoubtedly the most popular cetaceans in marine parks around the world. Although they draw huge crowds, many experts believe that it is cruel to keep such large and social animals in captivity.

Ian Beames/Ardea London Ltd

CHANGING PERCEPTIONS

In the 1870s, five belugas were on display to the public in England, and bottlenose dolphins and harbor porpoises were kept in the Battery Aquarium, New York, in 1913. However, the latter were not very popular due to a tendency to exhibit "overt sexual behavior" regardless of the age of the audience. In the 1930s the Aquarium of the Marine Biological Association of the United Kingdom at Plymouth periodically displayed animals rescued from live strandings, but did not begin to keep animals permanently until about 1962, when two female bottlenose dolphins were obtained.

In 1938, Marine Studios, a Hollywood film company, set up a marine tank in Florida, primarily to shoot underwater footage of dolphins. The dolphins became a tourist attraction, and a curator was appointed to train them. This was the first prolonged observation of dolphins' social life and behavior, and signaled the beginning of the development of marine mammal facilities all over the world.

The largest species ever captured and put on public display is the gray whale. The first time this happened, a female gray was captured in Scammon's Lagoon, Baja California, Mexico, on March 13, 1971, by a collecting expedition from Sea World. At the time, she was approximately 6–10 weeks old and 5.5 meters long. She arrived (by boat) in San Diego, southern California, USA, four days later, where she was named Gigi. By the time she was one year old, Gigi had grown to 8.2 meters in length and weighed an estimated 6.3 tonnes. She was seriously outgrowing her artificial home and, on March 13, 1972, was returned to the sea. Her release was timed to

Australian Picture Library/Volvox

coincide with the annual migration of gray whales traveling from their breeding grounds in Mexico to their feeding grounds in the Arctic. Gigi joined up with the herd and was observed for five days as she moved northward. Seven years later, in the autumn of 1979, she was sighted in San Ignacio Lagoon, Baja California, with a newborn calf.

During the 1970s, the number of captive facilities increased dramatically throughout North America, Europe, Japan and parts of Southeast Asia. Many of them still exist today, and new facilities continue to swell their ranks. They include a motley collection of netted pools, concrete tanks and even hotel swimming pools. The captive animals are often trained to "kiss" their trainers, fetch balls, jump through hoops, perform somersaults and make synchronized leaps in special shows for the fee-paying public. The vast majority are put on display purely for financial profit. The rest are kept for research purposes, or are used by the military.

LEFT: Belugas were being put on public display as early as the 1870s, when five individuals were shipped from their arctic home to England. At least 25 different cetacean species have been kept in captivity over the years.

LEFT: A child watches a beluga through the glass wall of an aquarium in Vancouver, Canada.

Marty Snyderman

ABOVE: Many orcas were taken from the Johnstone Strait area of British Columbia from the early 1960s until the mid 1970s. Today, whale watchers go to see the surviving members of the same pods in the wild.

Randy Wells

ABOVE: One argument for keeping whales and dolphins in captivity is that they are safe from the hazards of life in the wild—such as the boat propeller that severely damaged this animal's dorsal fin. But animal welfare groups argue that cetaceans are completely unsuited to life in captivity.

A few cetaceans are bred in captivity, but the vast majority are still being taken from the wild—and their plight has become a highly controversial issue in recent years. Can keeping a relatively small number of animals in captivity, albeit primarily for financial gain, be justified by the educational and research spinoffs that are sometimes claimed could benefit their wild relatives? Marine parks and zoos argue that captive whales and dolphins are immensely popular and act as "ambassadors" to encourage people to take an interest in the plight of their wild relatives. They say that captivity is a simple trade-off: the animals lose their freedom and natural companions in return for escaping the two biggest problems of life in the wild—going hungry and being eaten. But animal welfare groups maintain that it is immoral and cruel to keep cetaceans in small tanks and pools, because they are completely unsuited to life in captivity, and claim that the potential spinoffs have been greatly exaggerated.

THE PROBLEMS OF TANK LIFE

The transition from life in the open sea to confinement in a small tank can be extremely traumatic for any cetacean. The larger the species, the more difficult it must be for the animal to adjust.

Some marine parks and zoos have much better facilities than others. The best keep their animals in carefully structured family groups in large netted enclosures in the sea. Filled naturally with seawater, and flushed with every new tide, these are often several acres in size and are deep enough for a reasonable amount of diving and swimming. The animals are fed a varied selection

of fish, as well as vitamin and mineral supplements, and have regular checkups by experienced vets. The worst keep their animals in bare and featureless concrete tanks filled with filthy water—alone or mixed with several species that would seldom, if ever, live together in the wild. The captives can no longer hunt or hear the sounds of the sea, they are unable to dive or swim properly and they may even be deprived of natural sunlight.

Unfortunately, it is difficult to judge whether whales and dolphins can ever be "happy" in captivity. They are just as likely to suffer from psychological stress as other captive animals, though their permanent "smiles" tend to hide any inner suffering. A small number do seem to adjust to life in a tank and, with professional care and attention, may eventually come to accept their new homes. Indeed, a few have life expectancies comparable to those of their wild relatives. But the vast majority do not seem to cope so well. They repeatedly circle their small tanks, develop stereotyped behavior, stop vocalizing, become aggressive, get depressed and often die prematurely. Some inflict injury upon themselves and there are even reports of others committing suicide by banging their heads violently against the tank walls.

One of the most controversial aspects of keeping cetaceans in captivity is training them to perform special shows. The animals are often obliged to perform tricks for their human admirers several times every day. These tricks are usually based on natural behaviors—such as breaching—and the whales or dolphins are simply trained to perform them on command for suitable rewards.

RIGHT: A captive bottlenose dolphin is studied by biologists. As animals frequently behave abnormally in captivity, research findings from captive animals should be treated cautiously.

The trainers argue that, as well as keeping the animals mentally stimulated, such shows keep them physically and mentally fit. But animal welfare groups argue that they do little more than perpetuate the manipulative attitude we have toward nature. Without a doubt, some shows can be very demeaning—with trainers riding around on the animals' backs, for example— and onlookers inevitably leave with the wrong impression of cetacean behavior in the wild and their "natural" relationship with humans.

The shows are usually accompanied by a commentary by one of the trainers. The best of these commentaries provide both comprehensive and accurate information, ensuring that people leave enlightened and well-informed. But the worst—the vast majority—provide no relevant information at all or are so carefully worded (to avoid criticism from people concerned about keeping whales and dolphins in captivity) that they have become grossly inaccurate; in fact, it is hard to believe that some commentaries have not been prepared intentionally to mislead. If there is any educational element, it merely pays lip service to the concept of an informed commentary.

ABOVE: Their playfulness and apparently smiling faces, as well as their willingness to learn new tasks and tricks, have made bottlenose dolphins firm favorites with marine parks and zoos.

RIGHT: Captive cetaceans are frequently trained to perform shows for the fee-paying public. They "kiss" their trainers, fetch balls, jump through hoops, do somersaults and make synchronized leaps.

CONSERVATION AND RESEARCH

Sadly, it is a myth that marine parks and zoos help to protect endangered whales, dolphins and porpoises merely by keeping them in captivity. Despite many claims to the contrary, particularly during the commentaries accompanying public displays, this has no practical benefit. Holding endangered species in captivity is certainly not conservation and, in reality, the opposite is frequently true because taking the animals from the wild can be a significant drain on local populations.

There may be one exception, however. The baiji, or Yangtze river dolphin, is so rare that its only hope of survival may lie in semi-captivity. Fewer than 50 individuals are believed to survive in the wild and they face so many threats, from overfishing to dam construction, that they are already doomed in their natural home, in the Yangtze River, China. Establishing a small breeding colony in the relative safety of a semi-natural reserve may be their only hope of survival.

Studying whales and dolphins in the wild is extremely challenging. After all, these are animals that often live in remote areas far out to sea, spend much of their lives diving to great depths underwater, and then show little of themselves when they rise to the surface to breathe. Many are quite shy and elusive, and tend to avoid boats so, even at the surface, close encounters are frequently impossible.

FUTURE POSSIBILITIES

Ultimately, there is no easy answer to the controversy about captivity. It is a complex issue involving a bewildering range of establishments, from badly run zoos with poorly treated whales and dolphins in tiny concrete tanks to professional marine parks with large enclosures and the best care that money can buy. Every year, millions of people—possibly even hundreds of millions—encounter these awe-inspiring creatures for the first time in confined conditions. For many, it may be the only opportunity they will have to experience the animals in real life.

But these days there are some interesting alternatives to marine parks and zoos. With the enormous growth in whale and dolphin watching around the world, more and more people are now able to see them in the wild. Some species can even be observed from the shore, so cost is no longer the limiting factor that it undoubtedly once was. Furthermore, it is also possible to learn about whales and dolphins, and to appreciate their special beauty and mystery, without even seeing them. After all, it is possible to learn about the Moon, for example, without actually standing on it. In other words, with modern technology, it should be possible to introduce people to whales and dolphins without having

Australian Picture Library

RIGHT AND BELOW: As part of his rehabilitation program, Keiko spent nearly three years in a specially built tank in the United States. He was transferred to a netted enclosure off Iceland in 1998.

Mark Carwardine

Mark Carwardine

FREEING KEIKO

The freeing of Keiko indicates what can be achieved with international publicity and financial commitment. Keiko become the world's most famous whale when he appeared in the Hollywood film *Free Willy* and touched the hearts of millions of people around the world. There was a public outcry when cinemagoers realized that the star of the film—about a small boy's efforts to release a captive orca—was still living in a small concrete pool in an amusement park outside Mexico City.

Keiko began life as a wild orca in the freezing waters around Iceland. He was captured in the late 1970s, probably at the age of two, then went on public display in Iceland, Canada and Mexico. The public outcry prompted the formation of the Free Willy Keiko Foundation and a massive worldwide fundraising effort. In 1996 Keiko was transferred to a purpose-built tank in Newport, Oregon, on the west coast of the United States of America. He then began a rehabilitation program, basically designed for orcas that have forgotten how to be orcas. It was the first rehabilitation program of its kind anywhere in the world, and the first three years cost nearly 12 million United States dollars.

Having been nursed back to health by an expert team from the Foundation, and having undergone daily exercises to build up his strength, Keiko was then taught to catch live fish. It was a long, time-consuming process. After spending most of his life in captivity, he needed as much help as a human hostage to be able to adjust to normal life in the wild.

Finally, in September 1998, Keiko was moved from his temporary home in Oregon to his original home in Iceland. Watched on television by nearly a billion people, the world spotlight was on him once again. A special netted enclosure has been built in a sheltered bay in the Weltman Islands, off the south coast of Iceland, where Keiko still lives. He continues his rehabilitation program in the hope that he can be released into the open ocean by the end of the century. After nearly 20 years in captivity, he deserves freedom.

Sadly, while millions of dollars continue to be lavished on Keiko, conservationists are still fighting to stop the capture of more orcas for display in marine parks and aquariums around the world. As recently as February 1997, a family pod of orcas was captured by Japanese fishermen. Ten of the animals were herded into shallow water near Taiji, in Wakayama prefecture on the main island of Honshu. Five were released and the remaining five were transported to marine parks in other parts of Japan. Since capture, two of the orcas are known to have died and there are rumours that a third has died, too. The sad fact is that unless the continuing capture of wild orcas can be banned worldwide, Keiko's story will merely repeat itself.

to keep them in captivity. IMAX films are one exciting possibility, bringing the animals to life with enormous screens and exceptional picture and sound quality. The challenge now is to find more inspirational and imaginative alternatives to taking animals from the wild. In years to come, it may even be possible to use computer technology to simulate virtual-reality encounters with whales and dolphins.

Meanwhile, animal welfare groups on several continents are undaunted in their campaign for the capture of wild whales and dolphins to be banned and, in some cases, for existing captives to be released.

IN THE FIELD

An increasingly popular way of observing whales, dolphins and porpoises is to view them in their natural, wild environment. Responsible whale watching provides opportunities for photography, study and enjoyment of a wide range of cetaceans. The growing popularity of whale watching—from the shore, from small boats or through organized commercial trips— has encouraged some countries to introduce guidelines that seek to protect the whales from intrusion, harassment and exploitation. Quietly observing the natural behavior of cetaceans without disturbing their activities is surely greater value than watching them perform tricks in a theme park.

ABOVE: An orca and a Pacific white-sided dolphin may well be predator and prey in the wild—but in captivity they live together in the same tank.

Don Croll

ABOVE: Gray whales were the first to be watched commercially and are still an immensely popular tourist attraction.

EYEBALL TO EYEBALL WITH A 40-TONNE WHALE

MARTY SNYDERMAN

I am not sure that anyone fully understands the affinity that humans feel for whales. Perhaps we feel some sense of kinship with creatures that, like ourselves, are mammals, or maybe we feel some sense of guilt for the cruelties we have imposed on many whale species. There are other reasons, too, that help explain the intense interest: the fascinating natural history of whales, their sheer size, and our admiration of their ability to survive in the harsh conditions imposed by life in the sea. For divers and professional underwater filmmakers like myself, this intense interest is dramatically increased.

I have had a lifelong dream of swimming with a whale—not just catching a fleeting glimpse, but spending some time with the animal. I have always wanted to know what it would be like to look directly into the eye of a whale, and I have fantasized about capturing the moment on film. To me, swimming with a whale would be the ultimate diving experience.

In my dreams, I swim next to the whale in the clear, calm waters of some tropical paradise; I can swim as fast as it can, hold my breath for as long, and dive as deep. In my dreams, the whale is as curious about me as I am about it, so I am able to swim eyeball to eyeball with my photographic subject for hours on end.

But my first extended encounter in the water with a real whale differed considerably from my dreams. The water was cold and rough, the wind was howling, the current was ripping, and visibility was less than 3 meters—common conditions in Magdalena Bay where I was attempting to film a gray whale *Eschrichtius robustus*. Magdalena Bay, a remote but well-known breeding and calving ground for gray whales, is located about halfway down the Pacific side of Mexico's Baja peninsula. Howard Hall and I were not on assignment, but in Magdalena Bay specifically to chase our dreams and swim with a whale.

On any winter day, a visitor to Magdalena Bay is likely to see a dozen gray whales, but getting close to one underwater is difficult. Conditions are extremely demanding. Other film teams had spent a season in the series of Pacific lagoons used by gray whales and all they had to show for their efforts were a few barely useable sequences of film.

Spotting the whales was easy, but chasing them in the water would be impossible. Howard and I realized that we must either find a whale "resting" at the surface or wait for an unusually curious whale to approach us. We waited patiently. One afternoon I spotted a lone gray whale that appeared to be frolicking at the surface rolling over and over.

We had been taking it in turn to film the whale while free-diving or snorkeling. It was my turn to swim with the whale and, as I entered the water, I remember seeing the animal roll over on the surface, and although it appeared to change direction, I could not be sure. Howard pointed toward the whale, and I thought how ridiculous it was that he should have to point out a 15-meter-long whale that was less than 14 meters from the boat. I could not see over the waves, and underwater I was hampered by limited visibility.

I swam, head down, in the direction Howard pointed and suddenly found myself at a wall of whale, round and mottled gray. The whale was enormous. I had no idea where I was along its body since every part looked the same.

When fully grown, gray whales attain a length of almost 15 meters, and at that length they weigh approximately 40–50 tonnes. This whale was obviously an adult. I had anticipated some problems in filming a whale, but had never considered the possibility that I could not recognize where I was in relation to the whale's body. To understand what I was looking at, I had to try to create the whale in my mind's eye to orientate myself. I did the best I could, made a decision, and swam down the body looking for that large eye and massive head. The whale disappeared and then, just as suddenly, reappeared in the cloudy water as the 4-meter-wide tail stopped right in front of my face mask. I had traveled in the wrong direction.

The whale moved as though aware of my presence, repeatedly bringing its powerful flukes within centimeters of me, but never making contact. I, on the other hand, could not resist the urge to reach out and touch the animal's rubbery skin. After a few moments, I swam back up the body toward the head. The great creature rolled as I reached its pectoral flippers and I suddenly realized what the dimensions "15 meters long and 40 tonnes" meant. The pectoral flipper, like the tail, was only a body part, but it was larger than my whole body. Yet it was not the whale's size that impressed me so much as its body control and grace. There was no question in my mind that the whale was aware of me. The flippers, too, came within a few centimeters of my body, but did not touch me.

I moved along the whale's body and finally found myself at the surface of the water looking at a tennis-ball-size eye. I did not

ABOVE AND LEFT: Despite their reputation for aggression during the old whaling days, gray whales are careful not to injure fellow swimmers with their fins or flukes.

feel any sense of impending danger—instead I felt a sense of elation. Upon reflection, I find it strange that I was eyeball to eyeball with a creature that weighed almost 500 times as much as I did, and yet I was afraid I was going to frighten it. I did not want the moment to end too soon. I remember trying to look for a clue—a facial expression, a movement—that would give me some idea about what the whale was thinking, but I did not perceive anything I could understand. I decided that as long as the whale saw me, which it obviously did, and did not swim away, it was not disturbed by my presence. This gave me a sense of relief, for I often fear that those of us who profess to love and respect wildlife, create situations that annoy the very creatures we so admire when we attempt to film them. Perhaps, in this case, the great creature was as curious about me as I was about it.

The whale suddenly rose above the surface of the water and, as I looked up, I realized that the horizon was changing shape. We were so close to each other that the whale blocked a portion of the sky from my view. Then it dropped down below the surface and I quickly followed. We were only 2 meters deep when the whale rolled over and eyed me for a final time. After a few seconds it descended and disappeared into the murky waters.

I do not know how long I had been able to swim with the whale, but I estimated it to be around three minutes. Although I had always dreamed of filming a whale at close range I had taken only a few pictures. I had tried to enjoy the moment and not allow my camera to rob me of that pleasure.

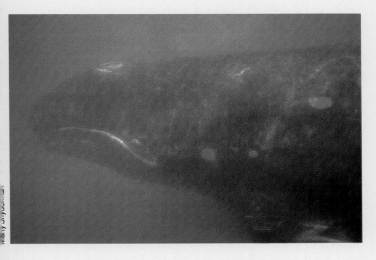

LEFT: The natural inquisitiveness of gray whales—even toward people in the water—has endeared them to whale watchers for a great many years.

Al Giddings/Ocean Images Inc./Planet Earth Pictures

ABOVE: With the growing popularity of scuba diving, more and more people are encountering dolphins in their underwater home.

ENCOUNTERS WITH WHALES

ROBERT J. MORRIS AND PETER GILL

O ur preoccupation with cetaceans goes back many thousands of years. They have featured in folklore, myths and legends since the earliest period of recorded history. Many of the larger whales live predominantly in the offshore regions of the oceans, and our ancestors had only infrequent contact with them. Some species of dolphins, however, live almost entirely in coastal waters and it is these animals that humans were first able to observe closely. Since first contact with dolphins, humans have held them in high esteem and there have been many accounts of intimate relationships between humans and these creatures of the sea.

A SALUTARY TALE

One account of this is given in a letter from Pliny the Younger written around 109 AD. It concerns the friendship between a local peasant boy and a dolphin called Simo. The boy lived in the small town of Hippo, on the North African coast of Tunisia, and he had befriended the dolphin after it had saved him from drowning. The two would regularly play together in the bay, the dolphin often giving the boy rides on its back. The local townsfolk got to hear of the dolphin and would gather to watch Simo and the boy at their games.

Gradually, Simo's fame spread until people from miles around started coming to see the dolphin. The town became very crowded and many of the local tradespeople realized that they could make a lot of money from the new visitors. As the number of visitors grew, the facilities of the town could no longer cope with the crowds and there were serious shortages of accommodation, toilets, water and food. Arguments broke out among the locals, causing unpleasant divisions in the community. Eventually, the town elders realized that something had to be done in order to save the stability of their community: they killed the dolphin.

This tale may sound fanciful, but it is more than plausible; there have been many other accounts during the intervening centuries of similar friendships. The sad tale of Simo graphically illustrates the danger faced by dolphins when they entrust their friendship to sometimes fickle humans.

Dolphins are normally found living with others of their kind in social groups but, occasionally, they live as solitary individuals having only occasional contact with their own species. These solitary animals, or "friendlies" as they are commonly called, sometimes actively seek to make contact with humans.

While social groups of dolphins often follow in the wake of vessels or ride their bow waves,

friendlies take the level of contact a stage further. They spend long periods in the water with swimmers and allow direct touching. Sometimes, they restrict intimate contact to certain selected people, apparently being able to tell one person from another by signals, such as voice, appearance or mannerisms. In addition, their sophisticated sonar system enables them to obtain detailed, three-dimensional anatomical pictures of swimmers, which may be used for identification purposes.

Although contact between humans and dolphins might appear commonplace to anyone who has visited a marine park, it must be remembered that captive dolphins have a limited choice and their "sociability" is continually being encouraged by careful attention, and regular training and feeding. But in the wild, dolphins have the freedom to swim away from anyone with whom they do not wish to make contact. The intimate relationships that have developed between humans and friendly dolphins in the wild are, therefore, of the dolphin's own choosing and are all the more remarkable.

PERCY: A DOLPHIN FROM CORNWALL

Percy was a very large, fully mature male bottlenose dolphin *Tursiops truncatus*, first seen off the north coast of Cornwall, England, in January 1981. For four years he occupied one small coastal area that included about 25 kilometers of coast.

Initially, Percy was quite aloof. He showed a clear interest in diving activities and often followed local boats, but he did not make close contact with people for two years. In 1983, he built up a close relationship with a local diver and spent long periods in his company, allowing a good deal of close contact. But in September 1983 he became extremely wary of any close encounter. Then someone noticed that he had a large fish hook embedded in his head, near his right eye, and there were fears that he might have been blinded. During the

FACING PAGE: Despite their name, orcas or killer whales do not deserve their killer reputation. They are supremely efficient predators, just like lions, tigers and polar bears, but unlike their terrestrial counterparts they are not aggressive toward people.

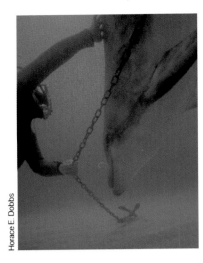

Horace E. Dobbs

ABOVE: Percy, an adult male bottlenose dolphin, made friends with many different people when he frequented the inshore waters of Cornwall, England, between 1981 and 1984.

BELOW: It soon became apparent that Percy demanded control of his relationships with humans: he would accept food or stroking only from his favorites. Unwelcome attention was rebuffed with sharp butting or with light warning bites.

winter nobody managed to get close to him. By the following spring, however, the hook had disappeared, with apparently no harm done, and he renewed contact.

Percy had one major fishing site in his territory—a narrow channel between Godrevy Point and Godrevy Island where the tidal currents were fierce. He would occupy this site at mid-tide for periods of an hour or more. He had little competition from people or other animals here, but on one occasion a local fisherman rigged a gillnet across the channel. The fisherman had possibly heard that the dolphin regularly fished in the area and decided that what was good for the dolphin was also good for him. But Percy had other ideas. Deprived of his favorite fishing site, he began biting and tearing the net until he had managed to separate one of the mooring buoys from it.

The local fishing boats were regularly accompanied by Percy as keep-pots were tended and lobster pots rebaited. Percy was apparently able to associate particular fishing buoys with particular boats and he was sometimes observed moving from one buoy to another ahead of the fishing boat concerned. When he was alone he would frequently play with the moored keep-pots on the seafloor, entangling their lines. Many people saw him doing this as they watched from nearby cliffs. On one occasion he had managed to get a set of pots into such a mess that the fisherman was unable to raise or disentangle the lines. The fisherman called upon a local diver for help. The diver happened to be Percy's special "friend," and while he was struggling to sort the lines out, Percy appeared to indicate individual lines with his jaws,

apparently in the reverse order in which he had initially tangled them up. The diver was then able to disentangle the lines without having to sever a single one.

On another occasion, the same diver was in the water with Percy when the dolphin suddenly started to push him back to his moored boat. When he attempted to resist, the dolphin grasped his hand roughly in his jaws, drawing blood, and forcibly propeled him to the boat where he waited until the diver climbed out of the water. The diver was shaken because in all the years of their acquaintance Percy had never behaved like this. After 20 minutes, the diver re-entered the water. Percy immediately made contact, but this time his mood was extremely gentle and friendly. It was assumed that for some reason the dolphin had not wanted his "friend" in the water. We can only speculate as to why, but sharks had been seen in the vicinity shortly before.

Percy spent many hours in the water with his human friends or alongside their boats, and always tried to get involved in any tasks being carried out. He particularly liked watching the anchor of one particular boat being paid out or raised. Being a powerful animal, he soon learnt how to dive down, pick up the anchor and bring it back to the people at the surface. With the anchor retrieved, he frequently treated everyone to a free ride as he towed the large heavy inflatable around at speed.

During the spring and early summer of 1984 Percy was generally placid and friendly. He would allow his body to be touched and stroked and would regularly give individuals rides while they hung onto his dorsal fin. Now that his body marks and scars could be inspected closely, it was possible to see that he had had recent, regular contact with other bottlenose dolphins, other whales and possibly even otters. Therefore, he was not a truly solitary animal.

As the summer passed, more and more people came to the coast of Cornwall to see Percy. Local and national newspapers published articles on his activities and television film crews appeared. On one occasion his photograph was published in a daily national paper apparently drinking a cup of tea with some of his admirers. Percy had become a celebrity and during the day he was surrounded by large numbers of people.

During this period his mood changed dramatically. What can only be described as aggressive or "warning-off" behavior was commonplace, often involving a firm butt with his snout in the chest or on the arm. The cause of this behavior could have been either over-excitement or, with so many people in the water around him, fear, leading to attempts to exercise dominance. He became

Horace E. Dobbs

very possessive of certain individuals in the water and on occasions other people seemed to be regarded as intruders who threatened to disrupt his play or even to remove his "playmate." Biting became quite a frequent occurrence and sometimes Percy would attempt to stop his "favorites" from leaving the water by pushing them out to sea. Luckily his chosen companions were strong swimmers and those on the receiving end of his displeasure suffered at worst some bruises.

Percy also started to exhibit quite indiscriminate sexual behavior. In one incident witnessed by the crew of a fishing vessel, Percy was reported to have attempted to insert his erect penis into a hosepipe 5 centimeters in diameter that was hanging over the side of the vessel. At least five separate approaches were made. Another curious incident was reported by the crew of another fishing boat. Percy was swimming with the boat when he suddenly veered away, swam some 12 meters, turned and rushed at the boat. As he closed with the boat he rolled onto his back and from his extended penis directed a stream of urine into the stern of the boat and onto the rather startled helmsman.

Other aspects of his behavior became violent. One incident involved a windsurfer on holiday in the area who had not heard of the dolphin. Percy often chased windsurfers and on this occasion the windsurfer was in full sail, well out to sea, when Percy arrived and attempted to jump over the sailboard. Either by accident or design, he landed right across the front of the board. Not surprisingly, with Percy weighing approximately 400 kilograms, the fiberglass hull broke up and the terrified surfer was thrown into the sea. The surfer, obviously in panic, released an emergency flare and the local lifeboat was called out to rescue him. The story received national coverage on radio and television and further increased Percy's fame.

At this stage, conflicts started to erupt between groups of locals as to how the dolphin should be treated. Percy was the cause of a number of acrimonious encounters that took place at sea and to most it was a relief when that particular summer came to an end.

As the summer ended, and the number of tourists declined, Percy gradually reverted to his gentle, placid and friendly nature. But he disappeared from the area later that winter and was not seen again.

ABOVE: Scientists attempt to distance themselves from too much emotional attachment to their subjects, but many admit to being seduced by their charm, good humor and curiosity, as well as by the deep level of trust they appear to place in their human "friends."

WATCHING WHALES

Whale watching has become a global industry, but it can be enjoyed by any individual who has an elementary knowledge of whales and knows where to look. One way to observe whales is to go on one of the whale-watching cruises, near places such as Monterey or Cape Cod in the United States, and entrust yourself to the experts on board. Alternatively, you could find a good vantage spot on land. Indeed, some of the best whale watching can be done from the shore.

Successful whale watching requires patience, a good pair of binoculars and an awareness of the prevailing weather conditions. You also need to know what species of whales are likely to occur in a particular area. To some extent this is predictable, because the migratory patterns of many species are well documented. Gray whales and humpbacks, for example, are known to migrate seasonally along coastlines, and to congregate in breeding and feeding areas. These include Maui, in the Hawaiian Islands, the fiords of Alaska in the United States, and Baja California, in Mexico.

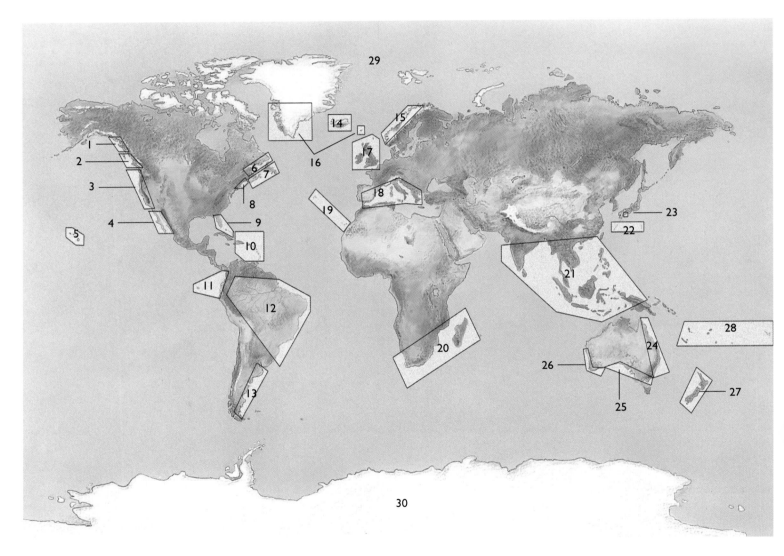

MAJOR WHALE WATCHING REGIONS OF THE WORLD

1.	Southeast Alaska	11.	Ecuador and Colombia	21.	South Asia
2.	British Columbia and Puget Sound	12.	Brazil and the Amazon River	22.	Japan: Ogasawara and Okinawa
3.	California, Oregon and Washington	13.	Argentina	23.	Japan: Kochi Prefecture
4.	Baja California	14.	Iceland	24.	East Coast Australia
5.	Hawaii	15.	Norway	25.	Southern Australia
6.	St. Lawrence River and the Gulf	16.	Greenland and the Faeroe Islands	26.	Western Australia
7.	The Maritimes and Newfoundland	17.	Britain and Ireland	27.	New Zealand
8.	New England	18.	The Mediterranean	28.	Tonga and other Pacific Islands
9.	Florida and the Bahamas	19.	Canaries and Azores	29.	The Arctic
10.	The Caribbean	20.	South Africa and Madagascar	30.	Antarctica

The best vantage points are usually those that are the highest. Find a spot that offers good views along the coastline as well as of the open ocean. Whales can often be seen well out to sea, and can even be visible underwater if they are close inshore.

Early morning and late afternoon are the best viewing times. Not only do whales seem more active then, but the low, slanting light highlights their blows and splashings. Very calm, glary conditions in the middle of the day make sightings difficult. Overcast days, on the other hand, are good for viewing, because they rest the eyes and blows show up well against a gray sea and sky. Spotting is almost impossible when winds are strong—to the excited imagination, the white cap of every wave can look like a whale.

Unless the whales are close, you will need binoculars in order to identify the species and observe details of their appearance and behavior. Serious whale watching is time consuming; it may take a whale an hour or more to pass a particular spot, and during this interval there will probably be a number of excellent photographic opportunities. Remember that, between breathing sequences, whales may dive for 10 minutes or more. Because they are unlikely to surface in the same place, you may lose sight of them for considerable periods of time.

When you begin a whale-watching session, scan around in a slow, methodical way, using binoculars if necessary. Focus on the direction from which migrating whales are likely to come. Look for anything out of the ordinary: a movement, a dark shape, a splash of white, or the cotton-wool puff of a blow. Your first sighting might be of a full breach, or merely a dorsal fin barely protruding above the surface.

When you sight a whale, use a field guide to identify its species. Make notes of your observations, especially anything out of the ordinary, such as the sighting of an unexpected species. Try to discuss what you see with local wildlife officers. Ask if there are any whale research programs nearby; you may even be accepted as a volunteer whale-spotter.

Commercial whale watching, which began as recently as 1975 off New England in the USA, is now well established throughout the world. In many former whaling communities and nations, it has proved to be a lucrative alternative to whaling—a benign form of whale exploitation that gives thousands of people an opportunity to experience living whales in their natural environment. Its introduction in Japan's Bonin Islands, for example, may be a sign that attitudes toward whaling in that country are starting to change.

Most operators are responsible, and display a genuine concern for the animals' welfare. Many cruises have qualified naturalists on

board to provide background information and interpret whale behavior. But in this highly competitive industry, there are some who are insensitive to whales' needs. It is not unusual for boats to pursue whales that are trying to avoid them—even though this practise is illegal in some countries. It may be that those operating the boats simply do not recognize a whale's avoidance behavior, such as frequent changes of direction, an increased breathing rate or more spectacular displays, such as breaching. The fact that whales remain in areas where they are subjected to regular harassment does not mean that they are undisturbed by such behavior; there may be no alternative habitat available. When treated with respect, whales will often approach boats out of curiosity, providing some close and very rewarding encounters.

If you have your own boat, study the local whale-watching limits carefully; they are as much for your protection as for the whales' welfare. Whales are usually incredibly gentle when they approach small boats, but if your actions seem to threaten them, or if you position yourself in an inappropriate place, such as in the middle of an actively feeding or mating group, or between a mother and her calf, you may provoke aggressive behavior. As soon as you sight whales nearby, you should slow down, then stop and watch. The whales may well come to investigate you.

Simply being near whales on the water is a memorable experience, which can easily be recorded in photographs or on videotape. If you wish to extend your observations by listening in to their calls and songs, you could use a hydrophone kit, available from many scientific equipment suppliers. A hydrophone will allow you to "tune in" to this fascinating aspect of whale behavior, even when the whales are not visible or are at a distance.

ABOVE: The bottlenose dolphins at Monkey Mia in Western Australia "strand" themselves willingly, vocalizing and accepting pieces of fish from tourists before using their flukes to wriggle back into deeper water. Observing whales and dolphins in their natural habitat is an increasingly popular activity.

Jean-Paul Ferrero/Auscape International

British Museum (Natural History)

A GUIDE TO WHALE WATCHING

These pages provide details of 30 special areas, from the Arctic to Antarctica, which provide opportunities for observing and studying cetaceans in their natural habitat. Tours range from easy half-day trips to full-scale expeditions. The guide indicates what you can expect to see at different times of the year, and the likely weather and sea conditions.

SOUTHEAST ALASKA

When to visit June–early Sept humpbacks, minke whales, orcas, Pacific white-sided dolphins, Dall's and harbor porpoises. Bubblenetting humpbacks best in June–early July
Weather June–Sept cool to cold on water and subject to extreme changes, including fog and rain; Aug prime month for weather, seas and whales
Types of tours Multi-day cruises on small and large cruise ships and kayak expeditions; day trips on fishing, sail, inflatable and whale-watch boats
Tours available Gustavus, Pt. Adolphus, Glacier Bay, Ketchikan, Juneau, Petersburg, Elfin Cove, Wrangell Island and Sitka; also long-range cruise ships from Seattle, Vancouver, Prince Rupert and San Francisco

BRITISH COLUMBIA AND PUGET SOUND

When to visit Mar–Apr gray whales (west Vancouver Island); May–Sept orcas, Pacific white-sided dolphins, Dall's porpoises (nth Vancouver Island), harbor porpoises (sth Vancouver Island), gray whales (west Vancouver Island)
Weather Mar–June, often rainy and cold on water; July–Aug, cool on water but usually dry, fog especially mornings on west coast Vancouver Island
Types of tours Half- and full-day tours, multi-day expeditions; inflatables, sailboats and large whale-watch boats; some whale watching from ferries
Tours available British Columbia: Alert Bay, Telegraph Cove, Port McNeill, Sointula, Tofino, Ucluelet, Victoria, Nanaimo; Puget Sound area: Anacortes, Bellingham, Friday Harbor, Seattle

CALIFORNIA, OREGON AND WASHINGTON

When to visit Dec–May migrating gray whales; June–Sept summering gray whales, north California to Washington; Aug–Oct blue, humpback, and other whales and dolphins off the coast of central California
Weather June–Sept cool to cold on water, even when hot on land; Oct–May, California to Washington, cold, rainy
Types of tours Half- and full-day tours, multi-day expeditions; inflatables, fishing, sail and large whale-watch boats
Tours available California: Avila Beach, Balboa, Dana Point, El Granada, Fort Bragg, Hollister, La Mesa, Long Beach, Monterey, Morro Bay, Oceanside, Oxnard, Point Arena, Redondo Beach, San Diego, San Pedro, Santa Barbara, Santa Cruz, Ventura; Oregon: Charleston, Depoe Bay, Garibaldi, Newport; Washington (west coast only): La Push, Neah Bay, Westport

BAJA CALIFORNIA

When to visit Jan–Apr, gray whales live in the lagoons of Baja California, blue, Bryde's, humpback, fin and minke whales move into the Gulf of California; year-round, Pacific white-sided, common and various tropical dolphins, bottlenose dolphins (in gray whale lagoons and in the Gulf of California)
Weather Dry, clear, warm winters; wind, especially on the Pacific side, can make it cool at sea
Types of tours Multi-day expeditions, some day trips; inflatables, pangas, sailboats and medium-size cruise ships
Tours available La Paz, Ensenada, Tijuana, Rosarito, San Diego

HAWAII

When to visit Late Dec–Apr for humpback whales, largest concentrations in Feb and Mar; year-round: spinner, bottlenose, and pantropical spotted dolphins, false killer whales, short-finned

pilot whales and many others
Weather Warm to hot; sometimes strong Kona winds bring rain and high seas
Types of tours Half- and full-day tours, some extended multi-day expeditions; inflatables, sailboats and large whale-watch boats
Tours available Maui: Lahaina, Kihei, Maalaea; Hawaii (big island): Keauhou, Kailua-Kona, Kohala Coast, Honokoha; Oahu: Honolulu, Kaneohe. Kauai: Hanalei

ST. LAWRENCE RIVER AND THE GULF
When to visit St. Lawrence at Saguenay River: June–Nov fin, minke whales, belugas, harbor porpoises; Les Escoumins to Pointe-des-Monts, river and north shore of gulf, especially Mingan Islands: June–Nov fin, minke, humpback whales, occasional orcas, Atlantic white-sided dolphins, harbor porpoises and blue whales in Aug–Nov
Weather July–Sept cool to cold on the water, fog common, some heavy summer rains, snow by mid-Oct or Nov
Types of tours Half- and full-day tours, some extended multi-day expeditions; inflatables, sailboats and large whale-watch boats; good land-based whale watching
Tours available St. Lawrence River, Quebec: Tadoussac, Baie-Ste-Catherine, Grandes-Bergeronnes, Les Escoumins, Godbout, Baie-Comeau, Baie-Trinité, Pointe-des-Monts; Gulf of St. Lawrence, Quebec: Longue-Pointe-de-Mingan, Havre-Saint-Pierre; Gaspé Peninsula: Rivière-du-Renard, Gaspé

THE MARITIMES AND NEWFOUNDLAND
When to visit June–Oct fin, humpback, minke whales, various dolphins and harbor porpoises; Aug–early Nov northern right whales, Bay of Fundy and off Nova Scotia
Weather June–Aug cool to cold; fog especially in Bay of Fundy; Sept–Oct colder but often clearer
Types of tours Half- and full-day tours, extended multi-day expeditions; inflatables, sailboats, whale-watch boats; some whale watching from ferries
Tours available New Brunswick: Grand Manan, Leonardville, Fredericton; Nova Scotia: Halifax, Tiverton, Westport (Brier Island), Cheticamp, Capstick; Newfoundland: St. John's, Bay Bulls, Trinity, Twillingate

NEW ENGLAND
When to visit Apr–May humpback, right, minke, fin and small cetaceans; June–Oct all whales are common, except right whales, which are seen only occasionally; Aug–Oct northern right whales off northeast Maine from Lubec
Weather Warm to hot especially from Massachusetts ports May–Aug, it can be cool out on the sea; rain is most likely in Apr–early May
Types of tours Half- and full-day boat trips; some extended multi-day trips; large whale-watch boats
Tours available Massachusetts: Provincetown, Nantucket, Barnstable, Plymouth, Boston, Gloucester, Newburyport; New Hampshire: Rye, Hampton Beach, Portsmouth; Maine: Bar Harbor, Kennebunkport, Lubec, Northeast Harbor, Ogunquit, Portland, Boothbay Harbor

FLORIDA AND THE BAHAMAS
When to visit For Atlantic spotted and bottlenose dolphins year-round; May–Sept best for Bahamas, although some tours at other times of year. Check hurricane reports June–Oct
Weather Warm to hot, generally calm during May–Sept
Types of tours Mainly 3-11 day expeditions to Bahamas (book in advance); some day tours in Florida waters; inflatables, sailboats, motor cruisers and dive boats
Tours available Florida: Key West; Florida to Bahamas: Jupiter, Dania, Fort Lauderdale, Indialantic, Miami Beach; Bahamas: West End, Port Lucaya, Freeport (Grand Bahama Island)

THE CARIBBEAN
When to visit Jan–Apr humpback whales; year-round sperm whales and various dolphins; inquire locally as tour operating seasons vary (for example, St. Vincent, dolphins, Apr–Sept)
Weather Warm to hot, seas sometimes rough; tours often confine activities to the lee side of islands. Storms sometimes Aug–Oct; rainy season varies, but seasonal daily rain may last for only part of a day
Types of tours Half- and full-day tours, some extended multi-day expeditions in Dominican Republic; inflatables, sailboats and large whale-watch boats
Tours available Dominican Republic: Samaná, Puerto Plata, Santo Domingo; Puerto Rico: Rincon; US Virgin Islands: Long Bay, St. Thomas; British Virgin Islands: Road Town, Tortola; Guadeloupe: Le Moule; Dominica: Roseau; Martinique: Carbet; St. Vincent: Arnos Vale; Grenada: St. George's, Carriacou (Grenadines)

ECUADOR AND COLOMBIA
When to visit Year-round: bottlenose, pantropical spotted and other dolphins Ecuador and Galápagos; offshore Ecuador: spinner dolphins, orcas, sperm and Bryde's whales; June–Sept humpback whales Ecuador, and Aug–Oct Colombia
Weather Coastal Ecuador and Colombia hot, humid year-round, sometimes rainy during humpback whale season; the Galápagos are drier, best months for sea conditions Mar–Aug, although year-round possible
Types of tours Half- and full-day tours, extended multi-day expeditions; inflatables, sailboats, small motorboats and small cruise ships
Tours available Ecuador: Guayaquil, Quito, Machalilla National Park, Puerto López, Salango; Colombia: Cali, Buenaventura, Bahía, Juanchaco, Ladrilleros, Bahía Solano, El Valle, Chocó

BRAZIL AND THE AMAZON RIVER
When to visit Year-round: river dolphins in Amazon–Orinoco but best during low-water seasons as dolphins are more confined, and you avoid rainy season; tucuxi dolphins at Santa Catarina Island, spinner dolphins at Fernando de Noronha archipelago, both in Brazil. June–Sept/Oct: southern right whales southern Santa Catarina Island. June–Dec humpbacks in National Marine Park of Abrolhos in Brazil
Weather Amazon–Orinoco hot, humid conditions; in southern Brazil, whale season is cold, windy, even from lookouts, often rough on the water
Types of tours Half- and full-day tours, some extended multi-day expeditions; inflatables, sailboats, motorboats, canoes and river ferries; some watching from land
Tours available Brazil: Florianópolis, Caravelas, Manaus;

Colombian Amazon: Bogotá, Leticia, and Puerto Nariño; Peru: Iquitos

ARGENTINA
When to visit Mid-July–Nov southern right whales at Península Valdés, Patagonia, best Sept–Oct; orcas year-round but catch sea lions on beaches mid-Feb to mid-Apr; Dec–Mar Commerson's dolphins and Peale's dolphins near Puerto Deseado
Weather Mid-July–Nov cold during right whale season, cool at sea even on best days for dolphin watching in Dec–Mar
Types of tours Mainly extended multi-day expeditions, some day tours locally; inflatables, fishing boats, sport-fishing boats, sailboats, kayaks
Tours available Buenos Aires; Chubut province: Puerto Pirámide, Puerto Madryn, Rawson, Trelew; Santa Cruz province: Puerto San Julian, Puerto Deseado

ICELAND
When to visit May–Sept several cetacean species (humpback whales more in early summer, orcas in late summer); best period June–Aug
Weather Cold on the water; rain and rough seas intermittent; snow is possible early and late in whale-watch season
Types of tours Half- and full-day tours, some extended multi-day expeditions; fishing boats and large tour boats
Tours available Húsavík, Höfn, Dalvík, Hauganes, Stykkishólmur, Keflavík, Grindavík, Arnarstapi, Ólafsvík

NORWAY
When to visit Late May–Sept in the Andenes area for sperm and other whales and dolphins; Oct-mid–Nov around Tysfjord for orcas
Weather Cold on the water late May–Sept in Andenes and Oct–Nov in Tysfjord; Tysfjord has very short days (few hours daylight by mid-Nov)
Types of tours Half- and full-day tours, some extended multi-day expeditions; inflatables, sailboats and large boats
Tours available Andenes, Nyksund, Myre, Stø, Storjord

GREENLAND AND THE FAEROE ISLANDS
When to visit June–Aug Greenland; Sept–Oct whales common but weather can be poor; May–Oct Faeroes
Weather Cold on the sea, rain and snow a possibility
Types of tours Half- and full-day tours, some extended multi-day expeditions; kayaks, fishing boats, large touring boats
Tours available Greenland: Paamiut (Frederikshåb), Aasiaat, and Ilulissat (Jakobshavn) in Disko Bay, Ammassalik; the Faeroe Islands: Tórshavn, Sandur

BRITAIN AND IRELAND
When to visit Year-round dolphins but best seen May–Oct; Apr–Oct minke whales in western and northern Scotland; June–Aug prime whale- and dolphin-watching season
Weather Cool to cold on the water; rain possible, even in summer, especially in western parts of Britain and in Ireland
Types of tours Half- and full-day tours, extended multi-day expeditions; inflatables, sailboats and large whale-watch boats; some whale watching from ferries; land-based whale watching
Tours available Britain: (England) Cornwall; (Wales) New Quay, Milford Haven; (Scotland) Dervaig (on the Isle of Mull), Mallaig,

Oban, Gairloch, Cromarty, Inverness; Republic of Ireland: Carrigaholt, Dingle, Schull, Castlehaven, Kilbrittain, Clifden

THE MEDITERRANEAN
When to visit June–Sept best for most cetaceans, although they are present year-round; May–Oct best for dolphins around Gibraltar, but tours also Nov–Jan
Weather Sept hot, dry, although sea breezes keep temperatures comfortable; May–Oct can be cool with occasional rough seas; Nov–Apr cool, sometimes cold at sea with rainstorms
Types of tours Half- and full-day tours, extended multi-day expeditions; inflatables, sailboats, fishing boats
Tours available Italy: Porto Sole, San Remo, Imperia; France: Toulon; Gibraltar; Spain: Almería, Barcelona; Greece: Kalamos Island; Croatia: Veli Losinj

CANARIES AND AZORES
When to visit Year-round Canaries: short-finned pilot whales, bottlenose, common and many other tropical dolphins, along with small, toothed whales. May–Oct Azores: sperm, other whales, but whales may also be seen before and after this period
Weather Canaries: subtropical year-round with cool, refreshing winds; sometimes hot, sandy desert winds from Africa make whale sighting difficult, but there are usually 300 good whale-watching days per year; May–Oct Azores: seas windy, cool to cold
Types of tours Half- and full-day tours, some extended multi-day expeditions; sailboats and large whale-watch boats
Tours available Canary Islands: Los Cristianos and Puerto Colón, near Playa de las Americas, on Tenerife, Gomera, Lanzarote, Gran Canaria; Azores: Horta on Faial; Lajes on Pico

SOUTH AFRICA AND MADAGASCAR
When to visit July–Nov southern right whales in South Africa; July–Sept humpback whales, and a chance to see mating behavior and calves in Madagascar; year-round bottlenose, Heaviside's and Indo-Pacific humpback dolphins
Weather July–Nov in South Africa weather mixed with rain and strong winds alternating with warm-to-hot temperatures; July–Sept, humpback season in Madagascar, warm weather even at sea
Types of tours Mainly land-based lookouts and tours; boat tours for dolphin watching in South Africa; small-boat and fishing-boat tours in Madagascar
Tours available South Africa: Hermanus, Plettenberg Bay (various), Lambert's Bay; Madagascar: Andampanangoy

SOUTH ASIA
When to visit Year-round, dolphins throughout region, sperm whales off Sri Lanka; Feb–Apr, blue whales off Sri Lanka; Apr–June, best for Philippines
Weather Hot, even at sea, but weather conditions vary across this vast region; main obstacles are prevailing winds that make whale watching in exposed areas difficult when the surf starts to build
Types of tours Half- and full-day tours, some extended multi-day expeditions; small boats, sailboats, canoes, outrigger boats and motor cruisers; some land-based whale watching. Visitors arriving during storm and monsoon seasons should pay attention to local weather advisories
Tours available Hong Kong; India: Goa; Thailand: Phuket; Indonesia: Lovina Beach on Bali; Philippines: Tagbilaran on Bohol

JAPAN: OGASAWARA AND OKINAWA

When to visit Feb–Apr, humpback whales winter on the mating and calving grounds around Ogasawara and Okinawa and the Kerama Islands; year-round, various dolphins

Weather Warm to hot during the season, but often windy and cool at sea

Types of tours Half-day tours; inflatables, diving and fishing boats; some whale watching from ferries

Tours available Chichi-jima and Haha-jima in the Ogasawara Islands; Zamami and Tokashiki in the Kerama Islands; Naha on Okinawa

JAPAN: KOCHI PREFECTURE

When to visit Mar–Oct (best May–Sept), Bryde's whales off Ogata, Saga, and other communities in Kochi Prefecture (some sightings through other months, but infrequent); year-round, dolphins in most locales, plus short-finned pilot whales and sperm whales off Cape Muroto, near Muroto, but best Mar–Dec

Weather Oct, varies from cool to warm at sea, depending on local currents and weather patterns; Nov–Feb, cool to cold at sea; typhoon season Aug to early Oct

Types of tours Half- and full-day tours; fishing boats; some watching from ferries

Tours available Ogata, Saga, Shimonokae, Tosa-shimizu, Kochi City, Cape Muroto

EAST COAST AUSTRALIA

When to visit Humpback whales: Queensland, including Hervey Bay, Aug–Nov; New South Wales, including Wollongong, late May–mid-July, late Sept–Nov, and Eden, June–July, Oct–Nov. Dolphins: year-round

Weather Queensland coast, warm to hot on humpback breeding grounds; New South Wales, cool to cold on water

Types of tours Half- and full-day tours, some extended multi-day expeditions; inflatables, sailboats, diving boats and large whale-watch boats; land-based whale watching also good

Tours available Queensland: Airlie Beach, Bundaberg, Hervey Bay, Tangalooma; New South Wales: Byron Bay, Coffs Harbour, Eden, Fairy Meadow, Wollongong

SOUTHERN AUSTRALIA

When to visit Year-round bottlenose dolphins at the Head of Bight, South Australia, and Port Phillip Bay, Victoria (summer best at south end of bay); May–Oct southern right whales at the Head of Bight and other bays along the South Australia coast; mid-June–Oct southern right whales at Head of Bight and Victor Harbor, SA, and Logan's Beach, Vic.

Weather Cool to cold on the water, but can be warm from sheltered lookouts

Types of tours Largely land-based whale watching, some organized as multi-day expeditions, but most are informal day trips; some half- and full-day boat tours, inflatables and small boats out of Port Phillip Bay

Tours available South Australia: Ceduna, Victor Harbor; Victoria: Moorabbin, Logan's Beach

WESTERN AUSTRALIA

When to visit Year-round bottlenose dolphins at Monkey Mia (Apr–Oct, dolphins approach swimmers most often, with less frequent sightings Nov–Mar); May–Oct southern right whales (Aug–Nov is prime for Albany area); Sept–Nov humpbacks in Perth area (July–Sept in northern part of Western Australia)

Weather Generally cool on the sea for boat-based whale watching; shore-based dolphin and whale watching can be warm or even hot in summer months, particularly at Monkey Mia

Types of tours Half- and full-day tours, some extended multi-day expeditions; inflatables, sailboats and large boats; land-based whale watching

Tours available Perth, South Perth, Hillary's Harbour, Fremantle, Geraldton, Exmouth, Carnarvon, Albany, Denham, Monkey Mia (land-based watching)

NEW ZEALAND

When to visit Year-round sperm whales, Hector's, common and bottlenose dolphins; Oct–May dusky dolphins close to shore (esp. Kaikoura)

Weather Cool (summer) to cold (winter) on the sea, Kaikoura, South Island and southern North Island; cool (winter) to warm (summer) on the sea from Bay of Plenty to Bay of Islands, North Island

Types of tours Half- and full-day tours, extended multi-day expeditions; inflatables, sailboats, motorboats, large whale-watch boats; some whale watching from ferries, helicopter and fixed-wing aircraft

Tours available South Island: Kaikoura, Akaroa, Picton, and Te Anau; North Island: Paihia, Tauranga, and Whakatane

TONGA AND OTHER PACIFIC ISLANDS

When to visit July–Nov humpback whales in Tonga; year-round, tropical dolphins in all locations, but Apr–Oct best for weather

Weather Hot during dry season Apr–Oct; sun averages 6–8 hours a day, even in wet season

Types of tours Half- and full-day tours, some extended multi-day expeditions; inflatables, sailboats, kayaks and diving boats

Tours available Tonga: Vava'u; Fiji: Nadi; French Polynesia: Moorea; New Caledonia: Noumea

THE ARCTIC

When to visit June–Aug for most of the Arctic; Aug best for belugas and polar bears in Churchill

Weather Cold on water throughout the Arctic, snow possible; Churchill, warm temperatures by day, often dipping to freezing at night

Types of tours Half- and full-day tours, some extended multi-day expeditions; inflatables, sailboats and large whale-watch boats

Tours available Canada: Churchill; Greenland: Uummannaq; Norway: Sveagruva on Svalbard

ANTARCTICA

When to visit Late Nov–Mar: baleen whales–humpback, minke, fin–feed around Antarctica, along with orcas and hourglass dolphins. The window for sailing to Antarctica is only 3-4 months

Weather Cold, take winter gear even in Antarctic summer; cruise ships offer shelter from rain and cold, but dress warmly to see whales close up from deck or inflatable boats launched from the ship

Types of tours Extended multi-day expeditions

Tours available Check local travel agent. Some cruise ships carry inflatables for close viewing

ABOVE: Despite its relative isolation Monkey Mia is one of the most frequented dolphin-watching sites in the Southern Hemisphere, and attracts more than 100,000 visitors a year.

THE MONKEY MIA DOLPHINS

HUGH EDWARDS

On a hot summer's night in 1964, Ninny Watts was on a boat anchored off the jetty at Monkey Mia, Shark Bay, Western Australia. "It was a hot, still night, and a full moon," she recalls. "I couldn't sleep, and this porpoise (as fishermen call dolphins) was splashing and blowing around the boat. I took a fish out of the ice-box and threw it to him."

Soon the dolphin was taking fish right out of Ninny's hand. She called him Charlie and he became a celebrity and a favorite at the jetty. Charlie brought other dolphins into the bay and a bond with the locals was established. In the 1970s, after Charlie had died, his friends continued to visit the locals.

Every year since, fascinated tourists have flocked to Monkey Mia to see these wild bottlenose dolphins *Tursiops truncatus* in their natural environment. The dolphins are, of course, free to come and go as they please—there are no constraints. They do not jump through hoops or perform tricks to amuse their human audiences. They swim between people's legs, wait to be scratched or tickled, and play "catch" with pieces of seaweed or fish.

In 1986, because of increasing crowd pressure, rangers were permanently stationed at Monkey Mia to ensure the safety and welfare of the dolphins. In the same year, an information center was completed by the Western Australian government in conjunction with the Shark Bay Shire. When the then Western Australian Premier opened the center, he described the dolphins' unusual choice of human friends as a "miracle."

After nearly four decades, Monkey Mia has become the longest running human–dolphin encounter site on record. From quiet beginnings, the site itself has changed beyond all recognition. The ramshackle caravan park has grown into a modern facility, with an assortment of buildings, a store, an information center, and hundreds of cars and tourist buses in the car park. It now has more than 100,000 visitors every year, including many international tourists.

In the past, individual dolphins have usually had a special affinity for one human friend, just as captive dolphins relate to their trainers. Most recorded dolphin–human relationships have been brief and all too often they have ended sadly, with the dolphins disappearing, or in tragedy, when they are accidentally or intentionally killed.

There is no doubt that some dolphins seem to enjoy human company. They readily come up alongside boats, often accompany fishermen, and seem to enjoy jumping and showing-off when people are around. But the Monkey Mia dolphins are exceptional. They have even evolved their own technique of stranding themselves, lying half-in and half-out of the water to enable closer contact with people. To get back into their natural domain, they have developed a kind of "reverse gear," which involves arching their tails as they pull backward to ease themselves back into the water.

Bottlenose dolphins abound in Australian seas, from the kelp water fringes of Victoria and South Australia to the warm, coffee-colored tidal reaches of the Gulf of Carpentaria. The herd at Monkey Mia, however, are the only ones to have established regular contact with humans over such a long period of time. About 20 different individuals have come onto the beach at various times, with about half a dozen coming in most days. Not only do they choose to come, but they also bring their calves with them—as if to carry on the tradition. Some of the animals are third or fourth generation.

During the period from the 1970s to when rangers were first introduced, the dolphins' unofficial guardians were Wilf and Hazel Mason, who ran the caravan park. Hazel named most of the dolphins and her initial favorite was "Speckledy Betty," a very tame old dolphin who was almost toothless. "She was so tame," Hazel recalls, "that once she got a fish-hook in her mouth and she came in to the beach for Wilf to get it out. It was deeply embedded and must have really hurt when he got it out with a pair of pliers. But she just lay there trusting him, with her mouth open, until he got it free."

Some caravan park proprietors, with an apparent dolphin bonanza in their front yard, would have sought to exploit the situation by turning it into a dolphin show with hoops and balls and, inevitably, captive dolphins. But Wilf and Hazel Mason discouraged tourists' attempts to teach the dolphins games. They instituted a number of regulations, requesting visitors not to sit children on the dolphins' backs, because their ribs are delicate and easily broken; not to pull their fins, which can also be damaged easily; and not to allow dogs into the water, since they may nip or bite the dolphins.

ABOVE: Caravan park proprietors Wilf and Hazel Mason were unofficial guardians of the Monkey Mia dolphins.

Strict regulations were also needed concerning the touching of dolphins. I have photographed dolphins at length underwater and have observed that they do not seem to like rapid or staccato movement. They are also particularly averse to being patted on the "melon," or forehead, which shields their sensitive echolocation center. All the visiting dolphins, however, are different. Some are placid and unruffled by almost anything; others have been known to get a little aggressive with anyone who frightens or provokes them.

The most important requests are connected with food. Dolphins have a small gullet, and swallow their fish headfirst. The wrong kind of food could kill them. They should be fed small fish. Amazingly, though, people have offered them a mind-boggling range of inappropriate food, such as chicken bones and even bones from steaks off the barbecue! Other objects, including bottle tops, have also been thrown to them. So far, the dolphins have resisted taking them.

Since Charlie's first contact with Ninny Watts, fish has always been a link between the dolphins and humans at Monkey Mia. Unfortunately, in recent years, this has been cause for considerable concern. Since the dolphins are being fed (a practise which is illegal in many other parts of the world) it seems that females with calves are spending too much time at the beach and not enough time teaching their calves how to catch prey, or defending them from sharks. As a result, there appears to be a higher juvenile mortality rate than in other bottlenose dolphin populations.

The tourist supplement of fish is appreciated, but by no means essential. Often, the dolphins cruise among people even when they are not hungry, and take the fish simply to flick it playfully in the air. "It is more like a courtesy, a lot of the time," says Wilf. "You've made the effort to bring a fish. They make the effort to be sociable in return. Like humans shaking hands, it's an introduction."

Sometimes the dolphins reciprocate by bringing fish in for the tourists. On several occasions, they have herded in snapper—a fish dolphins never eat, but tourists value—to the shallows. They shepherded them like marine sheepdogs to the feet of the visitors.

The Monkey Mia dolphins fascinate the crowds that line the water's edge to see them, and television cameras and crews often come to film this phenomenon.

WHALE STRANDINGS

Margaret Klinowska

There is no mystery surrounding the vast majority of whale, dolphin and porpoise strandings—they are simply the bodies of dead animals washed ashore by tides and currents. These animals have died as a result of the hazards they encounter in the wild, which may include entanglement in fishing nets, as well as disease, old age and other more "natural" causes. Many whales die at sea and go unrecorded, since only a proportion of them are ever washed ashore. Even those that do wash ashore often go unnoticed or unrecorded by humans. Therefore, it is not possible to relate changes in the numbers of dead animals reported on beaches directly to changes in the live population at sea.

ABOVE: Whales and dolphins have probably been stranding on beaches around the world for thousands or even millions of years. Strandings are rare but dramatic events that have always attracted public interest, as shown by this group in Cornwall, United Kingdom.

FACING PAGE: Offshore toothed whales tend to strand in large numbers more often than inshore species, and their social nature may encourage "rescue" or support behavior that only exacerbates the problem by leading more group members onto the shore.

LIVE STRANDINGS

The cause of live strandings, where individuals or groups of animals seem to swim ashore deliberately, has been the subject of much speculation over the years. Live strandings are very rare: for example, in the first 70 years of the United Kingdom's strandings recording system only 137 records (out of a total of almost 3,000 records, not all of which refer to animals found on beaches) could be identified as live strandings. These included 28 group strandings (with three or more animals involved) and 96 single and pair strandings. In about half the cases where people intervened to help single stranded animals, the rescue attempts seem to have been successful (that is, the animals did not appear to re-strand, alive or dead, in the weeks afterwards).

In the same United Kingdom sample, there were also near-strandings by another 13 groups, with all the preliminary features of live strandings; these ended in the escape of all or

most animals. Such events demonstrate that although some groups of cetaceans appear to be stranding, they often do not end up doing so; nor is it necessarily true that if one animal is beached the rest of the group will follow.

The low proportion of live strandings is not unique to the United Kingdom. Similar ratios are observed elsewhere in the world, wherever suitable systematic records are kept. All species (except, perhaps, some river dolphins) live strand, but, proportionally, offshore species do so more frequently than inshore species. The number of animals involved depends on the social habits of the species—those that live in groups tend to strand in groups, and those that live in large groups tend to strand in large groups (so-called "mass strandings"). This explains why baleen whales, which normally live in small social groups, tend to strand alone or in small groups.

WHY STRAND?

So why do these animals, which normally spend all their lives in water, come ashore? Aristotle, who was probably one of the first to record this aspect of cetacean behavior, simply said that he did not know the answer. Others, however, have put forward a variety of explanations, including the following: suicide; entering shallow water to rest or rub the skin; reversion to a primitive instinct to seek safety on land; confusion of sonar echoes by shallow water; inner ear parasites preventing proper reception of sonar echoes; brain infections leading to disorientation; attempts to use ancient migration paths now closed by geological changes; population pressure; noise from modern shipping and other activities; pollution; radar; television and radio transmissions; earthquakes; storms; and phases of the moon.

The recent increase in interest in these events may give the impression that live strandings, especially mass strandings, have increased. But

British Museum (Natural History)

records over the last few hundred years do not bear this out. Modern human activities, therefore, probably have not affected the live stranding rate, which immediately rules out some of the proposed causes. Some of the other possible causes can also be eliminated. Only about two-thirds of live strandings in the United Kingdom are on the sloping, sandy shores thought to confuse sonar echoes; the remaining third are on exactly the steep shores that should give good echoes. Furthermore, baleen whales do live strand, but they do not have high-frequency sonar like some toothed whales. Some live-stranded animals do have parasites or brain lesions, but others seem to be perfectly healthy. Some live strandings occur at places that were never seaways at any relevant point in geological time, so it seems unlikely that an ancient memory of previous routes is to blame.

The theory that population pressure results in live strandings is based on the observation

Dave Watts/Australasian Nature Transparencies

ABOVE: There are probably different reasons for strandings according to the species, the time of year, the location and many other factors. It is possible that, in some parts of the world, sloping, sandy coastlines may confuse animals that are used to echolocating in deeper water.

that group strandings of long-finned pilot whales *Globicephala melas* in Canada increased after catching ceased. Similarly, an analysis of sightings, live strandings and catches of long-finned pilot whales in the United Kingdom and Ireland since 1602 suggests that sightings and live strandings have also increased after catching ceased around 1900. However, this is not surprising, because before the turn of the century, schools near the coast were hunted and consequently provided a "catch" record. After the turn of the century, when catching ceased, observations were recorded as "sightings" or "strandings." Population pressure, then, is not a plausible cause for live strandings.

The ideas of suicide or reversion to a primitive behavior are not testable, but seem unlikely. Resting in shallow water is not normal

cetacean behavior and, although some groups of orcas *Orcinus orca* do strand themselves intentionally when hunting sea lion pups, this has never been observed to result in permanent strandings. In fact, as scientists in the former USSR have shown, cetaceans have evolved a very interesting way of "sleeping" in the water, without any danger of drowning. The animals only "sleep" with one side of the brain at a time—the other side is awake, and controls movement and breathing.

Craig Matkin/Earthviews

If earthquakes were the cause, we would expect more live strandings in areas particularly prone to earthquakes, but this is not the case. Weather patterns around the time of live strandings do not seem to show any common factor, either. It might be argued that all this demonstrates is that no single explanation is enough to account for the variety of live strandings we see among cetaceans. However, there is an explanation that does seem to account for many live strandings. This explanation emerged from investigations of another longstanding mystery—how cetaceans find their way around.

FINDING THEIR WAY AROUND

Whales are believed to use the total geomagnetic field (flux density) of the earth to supply them with both a simple map and a timer that allows them to monitor their position and progress on the map. They are not using the directional information of the earth's

ABOVE: Most baleen whale strandings involve single animals, primarily because they tend to be more solitary than most toothed whales.

field, as we do with our magnetic compasses, but small relative differences in total local field.

The total magnetic field of the earth is not uniform. It is locally distorted by the magnetic characteristics of the underlying geology, forming a topography that may be thought of as "hills and valleys." Cetaceans appear to move parallel to the contours, keeping higher field to the left and lower field to the right, or vice versa (rather like walking across the slope of a hill, with one foot up the slope and one foot down). In the oceans, the movements of the continents have produced series of almost parallel magnetic hills and valleys, which could be used as "highways."

Unfortunately, problems may arise near shore because the magnetic formations do not end at the beach, but continue on to the land—and sometimes so do the whales. All the live strandings analyzed in the United Kingdom have occurred at places where the magnetic contours are perpendicular to the coast. Dead cetaceans, on the other hand, wash up with equal frequency in places with parallel and perpendicular geomagnetic contours. This theory is supported by evidence from the United States. However, there appears to be no relationship between live strandings and the earth's magnetic field in the Southern Hemisphere, possibly because of differences in methodology used by researchers, or perhaps because cetaceans behave differently there.

Live strandings, therefore, could be the result of mistakes in map-reading. This explains why offshore species, which would not be familiar with the problems of using their system close to

BELOW: Care must be taken when attempting to rescue stranded whales. Follow the advice of trained and experienced cetacean scientists.

Steven French

Jin Lochman/Auscape International

LEFT: Disorientation, exhaustion, social concern, panic and shock may combine to cause re-stranding behavior, where animals already pushed back to sea return to the shore and to other members of the group still trapped. Patience and careful supervision are needed to reduce the incidence of repeated strandings.

shore, live strand more frequently than inshore species, which would be more familiar with the problems. The young, the old, the sick, the healthy, individuals or entire schools may be involved—accidents can happen to any sex, age or grouping. If they are accidents, this would explain why live-stranded animals appear to be shocked and may require assistance to leave the beach. An accident in their map-reading would explain why whales sometimes try to return to the same beach, or strand again at the next "magnetic trap" along the coast; they are traveling in what seems to them to be an appropriate direction and the fact that there is another beach in the way comes as an unwelcome surprise.

How Mistakes Are Made

Where and why do the animals make the mistake, or take the wrong turn, that leads them into unfamiliar waters?

The total geomagnetic field fluctuates in a fairly regular manner each day, providing a time cue each morning and evening, rather like dawn and dusk. There are also irregular fluctuations, caused by solar activity, which tend to occur more often at night than during the day. These irregular night-time fluctuations usually obscure the evening cue, but the morning cue is normally available and cetaceans can use it to reset their biological travel "clock." This "clock" may be used to tell them how long they have been traveling. So, in theory, if they have some idea of how fast they have been moving, they can then work out where they are.

These field fluctuations do not affect the basic shape of the geomagnetic topography, but are local distortions of the total field through the magnetic characteristics of the local geology. The situation is rather like that of a boat in tidal waters—the depth of water under the keel varies regularly with the tide, and the wave height will change irregularly with the weather, but the boat still floats at the surface.

The fluctuations in the geomagnetic field do reflect lunar, seasonal and sunspot cycles. Therefore, in theory, live strandings should be related to these events, but unfortunately the United Kingdom data set is too small to demonstrate long-term changes. Records from elsewhere are also insufficient, being too short, not sufficiently detailed or not systematically collected. However, with more worldwide interest in recording these events, this problem should be overcome in the future.

This picture of the cetacean travel strategy emerged from a series of calculations based on the behavior of the geomagnetic field around the dates of United Kingdom live strandings, using the dates of dead strandings as a control. Days when the morning travel cue is obscured by irregular fluctuations are associated with live strandings. However, it is only on the Irish and North Sea coasts that the strandings tend to occur on the day the cue was lost. Along the south coast, the strandings tend to occur about two days later, while in the north they occur about a day and a half later. A closer look at

RIGHT: No matter how great the commitment of human rescuers, there will inevitably be occasions when it is impossible to return every whale to the sea.

geomagnetic topography maps reveals that there are two major "crossroads" in the system—one about two days' steady swimming time from the south coast and another about a day and a half's swimming time from the Scottish coast. The North and Irish seas are too narrow for animals to be more than about a day's travel from the coast.

This suggests that the primary mistake may be made some distance from land. The animals simply continue the wrong way until they encounter the shore. Of course, we do not know how many times such mistakes are made, or how many are corrected before serious problems arise. (The near-strandings may represent "last minute" error corrections.) However, we do know that uncorrected mistakes resulting in live strandings are very rare—of all the hundreds of thousands of cetaceans in seas around the world, very few end up alive on the shore. This shows that the animals are usually very good at finding their way about. Their simple travel system, involving only a map and a timer, with information supplied by a single source, is applicable to journeys of any length anywhere on the earth at any time. No compass is involved, so no compensation is needed for magnetic pole wanderings, or even for reversals of the entire geomagnetic field. The

animals do need to be familiar with the geomagnetic area they use, but this learning could begin while the young whale accompanies its mother during lactation. As it grows older, this familiar area could be extended through individual exploration or travel with more experienced animals.

THE MAGNETIC SENSE

Almost nothing is known about how cetaceans "read" geomagnetic information, but they must have an extremely sensitive receptor system to be able to detect these tiny changes in the local geomagnetic field. Many animals, from birds and reptiles to bees and bacteria, are believed to have this sixth sense, and there is even some evidence that it exists to a limited degree in humans. But few geomagnetic receptor systems have been fully documented—and none has been documented in cetaceans. The main evidence for its existence in cetaceans lies in recent anatomical studies involving several different species. These have revealed tiny crystals of a magnetic material, a form of iron oxide known as magnetite, in the soft tissues covering the brain. It is believed that these crystals continually orientate themselves in line

PROJECT JONAH: HELPING STRANDED WHALES

Project Jonah is a non-profit organization concerned with education, research and conservation issues relevant to marine mammals. The organization has been active since 1971 and is run by a team of volunteers, with funds raised by membership subscriptions, donations and fundraising.

As the prime participants at New Zealand's many whale and dolphin strandings, Project Jonah calls upon a large database of trained "marine mammal medics." These "medics" undertake a Project Jonah-designed Marine Mammal Medic Course that teaches basic theory about whales and dolphins and how to assist at a stranding. The practical session of the course teaches rescue techniques using a life-size pilot whale replica and the Project Jonah-designed rescue pontoon system.

The "whale" is filled with water to create the effect of actually handling such large animals when they are out of the water.

The pontoon system has rescued more than 2,000 individual animals since its invention in 1973. Designed to function efficiently in water up to knee deep and on land, it uses the technique of rolling a mat under the animal, similar to the methods employed in first-aid training when moving injured persons. The mat is then attached onto two pontoons by a series of specialized clips. This enables animals to be either moved into more comfortable and life-saving positions, or transported into deeper water by vessel.

Project Jonah is involved in many issues concerning cetaceans, both in New Zealand and overseas. Committed to the overall welfare of marine mammals, the organization actively supports an end to capturing whales and dolphins, and encourages observation of these animals in their natural habitat. Community service is high on its agenda, with regular school talks, whale rescue demonstrations and other educational events.

The worst stranding on record was a herd of more than 400 long-finned pilot whales in New Zealand in 1985, but the country has also seen a large number of other whale strandings. Initiatives such as Project Jonah and the training that is provided have been significant in saving the lives of many thousands of whales.

Ingrid Visser/Focus New Zealand

LEFT: A specially designed sling is rolled under a stranded whale to make transport easier for the rescuers and more comfortable for the whale.

RIGHT: Project Jonah volunteers assist in the rescue of a group of stranded pilot whales, using pontoons to guide them out to sea.

Ingrid Visser/Focus New Zealand

RIGHT: It is virtually impossible to refloat very large stranded whales. The necessary equipment is rarely available, and damage from overheating and pressure on the lungs is almost inevitable. Painless destruction by someone with an expert knowledge of cetacean anatomy is usually the best that can be done to relieve an animal's distress in such cases.

with natural magnetic force fields, rather like tiny compasses. By sensing any change in the alignment of the crystals, cetaceans may be able to work out the direction in which they themselves are traveling.

However, although the small magnetite crystals are, in theory, capable of detecting these tiny fields, it is not clear that such a system would be sufficient to sustain the features we see in the cetacean travel strategy. Here, a total field detector is needed, but the magnetite system has so far only been shown to be capable of detecting the directional information—magnetite can work like a compass, but can it "read" the map? Also, loss of geomagnetic time information on one day is enough to upset the travel "clock." This means that cetaceans must be able to store the time information for 24 hours, but then need an external cue to reset the system. We do not yet know whether a magnetite-based system would be capable of this. In theory, larger magnetite crystals could do such a job, but the animals would need to encounter huge electromagnetic forces (for example, being struck by lightning) to reset these large crystals. It might even be that magnetite is not the answer where more complex animals are concerned.

Evidence is accumulating that the retina (the light-sensitive area of the eye), which contains no magnetite, is sensitive to these small magnetic fields. It is extremely difficult to study cetaceans for this kind of detailed anatomical and physiological research, so we may have to wait for information from other species before we can fully understand the mechanism of the magnetic sense of cetaceans.

CAN WE PREVENT LIVE STRANDINGS?
Unfortunately, possible explanations of live strandings do not provide any hope of actually preventing them. But a better understanding of why cetaceans strand may help to deal with live strandings after they have occurred.

The loss of individuals or groups in this way is not a threat to the survival of the species (except, perhaps, for a few with low populations) and therefore is not a conservation issue. But the rescue of live stranded cetaceans is a question of the welfare of the individual animals concerned.

With imaginative techniques developed in New Zealand and elsewhere, it is possible to refloat porpoises, dolphins and small whales—sometimes even entire schools containing hundreds of individuals—without risk of injury either to the cetaceans or to their human helpers. But rescuing stranded cetaceans is extremely difficult and time-consuming. Sometimes, in cases where the animals are very large, or are ill or injured, humane destruction by an expert is the only solution to prevent further suffering.

Jonathan Plaver/Ardea London Ltd

HOW TO HELP A STRANDED CETACEAN

If you come across a stranded cetacean, you should first find out whether the animal is alive or dead. In most cases this is obvious—the animal is either moving about or already decaying. However, if the animal is not moving, but seems in good condition, it should be approached cautiously from the front— keep away from the tail at this stage, as it may move suddenly and hit you. Listen for any breathing—this may take 10 minutes or more with some species. In the meantime, look at the eyes (without touching them). If they are open, and the animal is alive, they may follow a finger moved gently across the line of sight. However, take care that the animal cannot roll onto you or be washed onto you by waves.

DEALING WITH A DEAD CETACEAN

If you have examined the stranded whale and are sure the animal is dead, take a careful note of its position and report it as soon as possible to the local recording scheme. If in doubt about where to report, try local police, coastguards, lifeguards, school teachers, museum staff or even the tourist information office. In many areas, it is forbidden by law to damage any stranded animals, or to remove them or any parts from the site, without permission. Souvenirs of the occasion should, therefore, be confined to photographs or drawings.

If there is no prospect of contacting a recorder, if the tide is about to wash the body away, or there are other circumstances that clearly mean that nobody else will be able to arrive in time to make observation, you should do your best to make a record of the animal. Photographs are ideal because they provide enough information to identify the animal and the site. Photographs should not be "artistic," but carefully planned shots with some kind of scale included (a person, an object, or even a shoe of known size). One photograph must be at right angles to the body, showing the full length (one of each side is better), then photograph the head, the dorsal fin (is there is one), the tail, and the flippers. Close-ups of any marks, scars or parasites can also be useful. Do not forget a frame or two including some local landmarks so that the place can be identified. If there is no camera, record the same things using a notebook and some means of measurement (your pace, a piece of string).

If possible, bury the body (or at least the head) well above the high tide line, marking the place (bearings on landmarks are best for this; other people tend to move or take away things like sticks and piles of stones) so that it can be found again. If this is not practical, the whole head is the most useful part to remove for identification by an expert, but the lower jaw (or half the jaw), a tooth or a plate of baleen is almost as good. If you can see the

ABOVE: Volunteers care for stranded false killer whales on a beach in Western Australia. The whales must be kept cool and damp, with their blowholes free of water and sand to ensure that they do not become blocked.

LEFT: A stranded whale will overheat quickly and can suffer sunburn if it is not kept moist and cool. Protect it, if possible, using beach towels moistened regularly with seawater. Be careful not to cover the blowhole or to let water enter the blowhole.

belly, try to find out the sex of the animal—in males, the urogenital slit is some distance from the anal opening; in females it appears to be continuous with the anal opening. (If in doubt, take a photograph or make a drawing.)

Report your find promptly to the appropriate people, giving your name and address in case they need to contact you for more information.

WAITING FOR THE EXPERTS

If the animal is alive, or you are not quite sure whether it is dead, get help quickly, after taking a careful note of the rough size and shape of the animal and of the place. The more time the animal has to spend on the beach, the more difficult it will be to help it. If you have to leave the animal alone while you get help, do what you can to make it comfortable before you leave. For example, prop it up so that its blowhole is in no danger of filling with water; remove any objects, such as stones, which may damage the skin; try to find something cool and wet with which to cover the animal, for example, a wet sheet or seaweed. Be careful not to get water or sand in the blowhole (usually on top of the head). Water in the blowhole can drown the animal, while sand will damage the lungs. Also, do not let anything get in the eyes.

While waiting for help to arrive, keep the animal cool, calm and comfortable. Cetaceans are built for life in water and quickly begin to overheat on land, even if the weather is cool. They use a heat exchange system in their flippers, fin and tail for cooling, so these parts are the most important to keep cool. Keep the flippers as free as possible by scooping out the sand beneath them and letting them hang in a hole filled with water—this helps with cooling too. Also, their delicate skin soon begins to dry out in the air, so all parts need to be kept damp. An animal that is upset and rolling about is likely to damage both itself and any people in the way. Everyone involved should try to keep calm, behaving quietly and soothing the animal as best they can. It is a good idea to organize helpers into teams, with one person acting as "beachmaster." For example, one team fetches water for cooling the animal, another team deals with bystanders to keep them out of the way, others soothe the animal or take records. Teams should be changed around, so that everyone who wishes to help gets a chance to, and no one gets overly tired. The beachmaster then hands over to the experts when they arrive. If experienced

help is on the way, resist the temptation to try to get the animal back to the water—you may accidentally harm it.

ACTING INDEPENDENTLY

If it is clear that you are on your own without expert help, you will need to make a careful assessment of the situation.

- If you are completely alone, with no prospect of getting any help and the animal is too large for you to lift easily, there is nothing you can do except make the animal as comfortable as possible, record as much information about it as you can and report it promptly, so that at least the record is not lost.
- If the animal is so large that there is no prospect of moving it with the help available, again there is nothing more to be done than to keep it comfortable, record details and report promptly.
- If there is enough help available to lift the animal, and the sea

ABOVE: It may be possible to get help from a nearby farm or town. A tractor or front-end loader can increase the speed and efficiency of a rescue operation—but it is important to get expert help before attempting to move the animals.

The West Australian

ABOVE: Wherever possible, stranded animals should be moved using stretchers or slings. Great care is needed if they have to be moved, and they must never be lifted by their fins or flukes.

ABOVE: Whales that have been stranded for some time will probably be disorientated and confused, and must be supported until they have regained their balance and can swim freely by themselves.

conditions will allow people to support the animal in the water without undue risk to themselves, start planning the move, in particular working out who is to do what. You will also need to consider whether the tide will be able to help you with the maneuver and whether there is enough daylight left to complete the job. In cool conditions, an overnight wait may be possible and preferable.

- Before returning any animal to the sea, take photographs and records in the same way as for dead strandings. In particular, note any marks that could identify it again at sea or on shore.
- The greatest care is needed when returning an animal to the water. The flippers must never be pushed or pulled—they are easily injured or dislocated. The skin is also easily damaged, so some kind of sling is needed that will support the bulk of the body without cutting it. The animal is lifted onto the sling, or the sling is worked carefully under the body. Then the animal is carried into water deep enough to support its own weight. The sling is released once it is clear that the animal can keep itself upright and swim. Take great care that it does not fall on its side and that water does not enter the blowhole. The animal may be stiff after lying on the beach and need support for a while in the water. Sometimes gentle rocking helps overcome this stiffness. Never grab at the flippers or tail, but push on the sides or at the base of the dorsal fin.
- If the animal insists on returning to the beach and seems unable to swim properly even after your best efforts, it is not worth continuing to try to push it out to sea. Just make it as comfortable as possible on the shore.
- Never make any attempt to kill a cetacean humanely, even if it is in great distress. Only an expert can do this. Cetacean anatomy and physiology are significantly different from those of land mammals and such attempts may only cause further suffering. In particular, resist any temptation to try to shoot the animal—the bullet may be deflected by the shape of the skull and emerge to damage onlookers. However, do try to accept the situation if an expert decides that humane destruction is the best option for the animal. It is simply not

possible to save every animal and in this case the suffering should not be prolonged.

GROUP STRANDINGS

While single live animals are often too ill to swim, it is likely that the vast majority of the members of a group stranding will be in good health and can be successfully returned to the water (if they are not too large to handle). One difficulty, however, is that the group social bonds are very strong and it can be difficult to get one or two animals to swim away while the rest are alive ashore.

The other major difficulty is that there are simply a number of animals to deal with. If anything useful is to be done, many well-organized helpers are needed, as well as the guidance (even by telephone) of experts familiar with the social structure of the species. Lifting equipment, and people experienced in its safe use, can be invaluable if you can make slings strong enough to take the strain and rigid enough not to squash the animals during transport.

The most successful strategy for dealing with group strandings seems to be:

- Assess the resources in terms of helpers and equipment available. Deploy equipment and organize helpers into teams, with well-defined tasks and good leaders. Arrange for communications between each team and the beachmaster, for relief teams, and for the deployment of new helpers and equipment.
- Try to prevent any animals still in the water from getting onto the beach—by using boats and/or people to keep this group quietly bunched together in sheltered, shallow water.
- Get the beached animals back into the water with the others.
- Guide the entire group back to sea together. This is all obviously easier said than done! However, large groups often contain smaller subgroups with strong social bonds. If these can be identified, each subgroup can be treated in turn, starting with the group containing the least damaged and easiest to handle animals. If the group leader can be identified (if in doubt, try the largest animal) and moved a little way

out, the others sometimes follow. It may be necessary to secure these "leaders" carefully to a boat to prevent them returning to shore, taking care that their blowholes are above water at all times. Never tow an animal behind a boat by the tail—the blowhole will be forced underwater and the animal will drown. Many of the sounds that cetaceans make are highly directional, so in order for the animals near shore to hear the leaders, the leaders need to be held with their heads toward the shore.

- Animals that are awaiting refloating and any that clearly cannot be refloated need care also, with priority given to those that can be rescued. It is often said that humane killing of the beached animals that cannot be rescued facilitates the return of the rest to the water. However, unless there is an expert present this not an option, for the reasons already stated above.

- Even with all the difficulties in helping a group of stranded animals, recording should not be forgotten. If possible, record all the details as for any other stranding, but do try to get a note of the numbers and position of each animal. Also, try to get a clear account of the sequence of events leading to the stranding, and in particular, of the order in which the animals arrived on the beach. This information can help to identify subgroups and group leaders, as well as providing a valuable record of the event. (Very few good accounts of groups strandings are available, probably because everyone is too busy trying to help the animals. However, if we knew more about how strandings begin, we could probably get some valuable clues about how to reverse the situation.) Press and media people are often most helpful here, if you explain the kind of information required. This is also a good job for bystanders who are unable to help with the heavy work.

- In trying to help the animals, do not forget the people involved. They may be tired, cold and hungry—there may even be injuries. Appoint someone to organize this aspect as soon as you can; everyone will appreciate it. This is particularly important if you are returning to a stranding alone after calling for help. Arrange for someone to visit you every few hours, to carry messages and food, and to check there have been no accidents.

Simon Cowling/Horizon

ABOVE: The ideal refloating situation is one where human rescuers outnumber stranded whales—but coordination and definition of tasks by a "beachmaster" are essential if rescue efforts are to be successful. The safety and care of rescue personnel should be regarded as being more important than the welfare of the stranded animals.

GREENLAND WHALE.

British Museum (Natural History)

CHECKLIST OF LIVING CETACEANS

Whales, dolphins and porpoises—the order Cetacea—are elusive creatures and can be extremely difficult to study. Consequently, our understanding of their classification is changing all the time, especially with recent advances in genetic research. There is some contention as to how many species exist: new ones are still being discovered and there are constant discussions about whether others should be split into two or three different species. Therefore, while the classification and scientific names used here are accepted by the majority of cetologists (biologists who study cetaceans), some remain controversial, and future studies will, almost inevitably, lead to changes.

SUBORDER MYSTICETI
BALEEN WHALES

FAMILY BALAENIDAE—RIGHT WHALES

Balaena mysticetus . . . . .bowhead whale (Greenland right whale)
Eubalaena glacialis . . . . .northern right whale (black right whale, Biscayan right whale, North Atlantic right whale)
Eubalaena australis . . . . .southern right whale (black right whale)

FAMILY NEOBALAENIDAE —PYGMY RIGHT WHALE

Caperea marginata . . . . .pygmy right whale

FAMILY ESCHRICHTIIDAE—GRAY WHALE

Eschrichtius robustus . . .gray whale (Pacific gray whale, California gray whale)

FAMILY BALAENOPTERIDAE—RORQUALS

Balaenoptera musculus . . . . .blue whale
Balaenoptera physalus .fin whale (finback, finner)
Balaenoptera borealis . . . . .sei whale
Balaenoptera edeni . . . . .Bryde's whale (tropical whale)
Balaenoptera acutorostrata . . . . .minke whale (little piked whale)
Megaptera novaeangliae . . . . .humpback whale

SUBORDER ODONTOCETI
TOOTHED WHALES

FAMILY PHYSETERIDAE—SPERM WHALE

Physeter macrocephalus . . . . .sperm whale (cachalot)

FAMILY KOGIIDAE —PYGMY AND DWARF SPERM WHALES

Kogia breviceps . . . . .pygmy sperm whale
Kogia simus . . . . .dwarf sperm whale

FAMILY MONODONTIDAE—WHITE WHALES

Monodon monoceros . . . . .narwhal
Delphinapterus leucas . . . . .beluga (belukha, white whale, sea canary)

FAMILY ZIPHIIDAE—BEAKED WHALES

Tasmacetus shepherdi . . . .Shepherd's beaked whale (Tasman beaked whale)
Berardius arnuxii . . . . .Arnoux's beaked whale (southern four-toothed whale)
Berardius bairdii . . . . .Baird's beaked whale (northern four-toothed whale)
Mesoplodon pacificus. . . . . Longman's beaked whale (Indo-Pacific beaked whale)

Mesoplodon bidens . . . . Sowerby's beaked whale
(North Sea beaked whale)
Mesoplodon densirostris . . . . Blainville's beaked whale
(dense-beaked whale)
Mesoplodon europaeus . . . . Gervais' beaked whale
(Antillean beaked whale)
Mesoplodon layardii . . . . strap-toothed whale
Mesoplodon hectori . . . . Hector's beaked whale
Mesoplodon grayi . . . . Gray's beaked whale
(scamperdown whale)
Mesoplodon stejnegeri . . . . Stejneger's beaked whale
(Bering Sea beaked whale)
Mesoplodon bowdoini . . . . Andrew's beaked whale
(splay-toothed beaked whale)
Mesoplodon mirus . . . . True's beaked whale
(wonderful beaked whale)
Mesoplodon ginkgodens . . . . ginkgo-toothed beaked whale
Mesoplodon carlhubbsi . . . . Hubb's beaked whale
Mesoplodon peruvianus . . . . Peruvian beaked whale
(lesser beaked whale,
pygmy beaked whale)
Mesoplodon bahamondi . . . . Bahamonde's beaked whale
Mesoplodon species "A" . . . . Unidentified beaked whale
Ziphius cavirostris . . . . Cuvier's beaked whale
(goose-beaked whale)
Hyperoodon ampullatus . . . . northern bottlenose whale
Hyperoodon planifrons . . . . southern bottlenose whale

FAMILY DELPHINIDAE—DOLPHINS AND OTHER SMALL, TOOTHED WHALES

Peponocephala electra . . . . melon-headed whale
Feresa attenuata . . . . pygmy killer whale
Pseudorca crassidens . . . . false killer whale (pseudorca)
Orcinus orca . . . . orca (killer whale)
Globicephala melas . . . . long-finned pilot whale
(pothead, blackfish)
Globicephala macrorhynchus . . . . short-finned pilot whale
Orcaella brevirostris . . . . Irrawaddy dolphin
Steno bredanensis . . . . rough-toothed dolphin
Sotalia fluviatilis . . . . tucuxi (estuarine dolphin)
Sousa chinensis . . . . Indo-Pacific humpback dolphin
(Chinese white dolphin)
Sousa teuszii . . . . Atlantic humpback dolphin
Lagenorhynchus albirostris . . . . white-beaked dolphin (squidhound)
Lagenorhynchus acutus . . . . Atlantic white-sided dolphin
Lagenorhynchus obscurus . . . . dusky dolphin
Lagenorhynchus obliquidens . . . . Pacific white-sided dolphin
Lagenorhynchus cruciger . . . . hourglass dolphin

Lagenorhynchus australis . . . . Peale's dolphin
Lagenodelphis hosei . . . . Fraser's dolphin
Delphinus delphis . . . . short-beaked common dolphin
(saddleback dolphin, common porpoise)
Delphinus capensis . . . . long-beaked common dolphin
(saddleback dolphin, common porpoise)
Tursiops truncatus . . . . bottlenose dolphin
Grampus griseus . . . . Risso's dolphin (grampus)
Stenella attenuata . . . . pantropical spotted dolphin
Stenella clymene . . . . short-snouted spinner dolphin
(clymene dolphin)
Stenella frontalis . . . . Atlantic spotted dolphin
Stenella longirostris . . . . long-snouted spinner dolphin (spinner)
Stenella coeruleoalba . . . . striped dolphin (streaker)
Lissodelphis peronii . . . . southern right whale dolphin
Lissodelphis borealis . . . . northern right whale dolphin
Cephalorhynchus heavisidii . . . . Heaviside's dolphin
Cephalorhynchus eutropia . . . . black dolphin (Chilean dolphin)
Cephalorhynchus hectori . . . . Hector's dolphin (New Zealand dolphin)
Cephalorhynchus commersonii . . . . Commerson's dolphin

FAMILY PHOCOENIDAE—PORPOISES

Phocoena phocoena . . . . harbor porpoise (common porpoise)
Phocoena spinipinnis . . . . Burmeister's porpoise
Phocoena sinus . . . . vaquita (cochito, Gulf of California porpoise)
Australophaena dioptrica . . . . spectacled porpoise
Phocoenoides dalli . . . . Dall's porpoise (spray porpoise)
Neophocaena phocaenoides . . . . finless porpoise
(black finless porpoise, black porpoise)

FAMILY PLATANISTIDAE—GANGES AND INDUS RIVER DOLPHINS

Platanista gangetica . . . . Ganges river dolphin (Ganges susu,
gangetic dolphin, blind dolphin)
Platanista minor . . . . Indus river dolphin (Indus susu, bhulan)

FAMILY INIIDAE—AMAZON RIVER DOLPHIN

Inia geoffrensis . . . . Amazon river dolphin (bouto, boto, pink dolphin)

FAMILY PONTOPORIIDAE—BAIJI AND FRANCISCANA

Lipotes vexillifer . . . . baiji (Yangtze river dolphin, Chinese river dolphin,
beiji, whitefin dolphin, whiteflag dolphin)
Pontoporia blainvillei . . . . franciscana (La Plata dolphin)

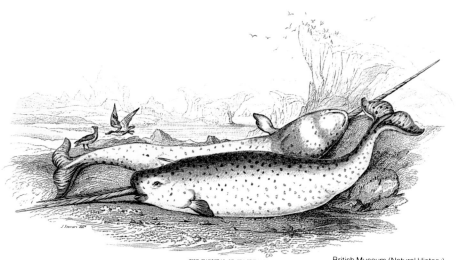

THE NARWHAL OR SEA UNICORN
F. Cuvier

British Museum (Natural History)

RESOURCE GUIDE

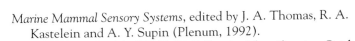

BOOKS

Among Whales, by Roger Payne (Scribner, 1995).

Arctic Whales, by Stefani Payne (Greystoke Books, 1995).

The Book of Dolphins, by Mark Carwardine (Dragon's World, 1996). A valuable reference source on dolphins, with the latest scientific research, up-to-date information, anecdotes and first-hand encounters.

Cetacean Behavior: Mechanisms and Functions, edited by L. M. Herman (Wiley, 1980).

The Conservation of Whales and Dolphins: Science and Practice, edited by Mark P. Simmonds and Judith D. Hutchinson (Wiley, 1996).

Dolphin Days, by Kenneth S. Norris (Norton, 1991).

Dolphin Societies, by Karen Pryor and Kenneth S. Norris (University of California Press, 1991).

Dolphins, by Chris Cotton (Boxtree, 1995).

Dolphins, Porpoises and Whales of the World, The IUCN Red Data Book, by Margaret Klinowska (IUCN, 1991). Detailed conservation reports and general species information on all cetaceans.

The Ecology of Whales and Dolphins, by D. E. Gaskin (Heinemann, 1982).

A Field Guide to Whales, Porpoises and Seals from Cape Cod to Newfoundland, 4th edition (revised), by Steven K. Katona, Valerie Rough and David T. Richardson, (Smithsonian Institution, 1993).

The Greenpeace Book of Dolphins, edited by John May (Sterling, 1990).

Guardians of the Whales: The Quest to Study Whales in the Wild, by Bruce Obee and Graeme Ellis (Whitecap Books, 1992).

A Guide to the Photographic Identification of Individual Whales, by Jon Lien and Steven Katona (American Cetacean Society, 1990). A species-by-species guide to identifying individual cetaceans based on their natural and acquired markings.

Handbook of Marine Mammals: Vol. III, 1985; Vol. IV, 1989; Vol. V, edited by Sam H. Ridgway and Sir Richard Harrison (Academic Press, 1994). Detailed accounts of cetacean species, along with literature surveys.

A History of World Whaling, by Daniel Francis (Viking, 1990).

Marine Mammal Sensory Systems, edited by J. A. Thomas, R. A. Kastelein and A. Y. Supin (Plenum, 1992).

Marine Mammals of the World, FAO Species Identification Guide, by Thomas A. Jefferson, Stephen Leatherwood and Marc A. Webber (UNEP, FAO, 1993). A good overall guide to marine mammals, including cetaceans, with identifying external views as well as skull and diagnostic jaw illustrations.

The Natural History of Whales and Dolphins, by P. G. H. Evans (Christopher Helm, 1987).

On the Trail of the Whale, by Mark Carwardine (Thunder Bay Publishing Co., 1994). Covers an adventurous year crisscrossing the globe in search of whales, from the North Atlantic to the South Pacific.

Orca: The Whale Called Killer, by Erich Hoyt (Firefly, 1990). A thorough book outlining the social behavior and biology of orcas; based on a narrative covering seven summer expeditions spent living with orcas around Vancouver Island, Canada.

Sealife: A Complete Guide to the Marine Environment, edited by Geoffrey Waller (Pica Press, 1996).

Seasons of the Whale: Riding the Currents of the North Atlantic, by Erich Hoyt (WDCS/Humane Society, 1998). An illustrated account of an eventful year in the lives of several humpback, right and blue whales known to both whale watchers and researchers.

The Sierra Club Handbook of Whales and Dolphins, by Stephen Leatherwood and Randall R. Reeves (Sierra Club Books, 1983).

Voyage to the Whales, by Hal Whitehead (Robert Hale, 1989).

The Whale Watcher's Guide, by Patricia Corrigan (NorthWord Press, 1994).

The Whale Watcher's Handbook, by Erich Hoyt (Doubleday, 1984). A definitive guide to worldwide whale and dolphin watching.

Whales, by W. Nigel Bonner (Blandford, 1980).

Whales, by Jacques-Yves Cousteau and Yves Paccalet (Harry N. Abrams, 1986).

Whales and Dolphins, by Anthony R. Martin (Salamander Books, 1990).

Whales, Dolphins and Porpoises, by James D. Darling, C. Nicklin, K. S. Norris, H. Whitehead, and B. Wursig (National Geographic, 1995).

Whales, Dolphins and Porpoises, by Mark Carwardine (Dorling Kindersley, 1995). A definitive field guide to all the world's

cetaceans; packed with comprehensive information on identification and behavior.

Whales, Dolphins and Porpoises, by Peter Gill and Linda Gibson (Reader's Digest, 1997).
A well-illustrated popular book.

Whales, Dolphins and Porpoises, edited by Mark Carwardine and Erich Hoyt (Nature Company/Time Life, 1998). Well-illustrated survey of biology, behavior and conservation, with a field guide to species and whale-watching sites.

Whales, Whaling and Whale Research: A Selected Bibliography, by L. R. Magnolia (The Whaling Museum, Cold Spring Harbor, Long Island, New York, 1977).

With the Whales, by James Darling and Flip Nicklin (NorthWord Press, 1990).

MAGAZINES AND JOURNALS

BBC Wildlife, BBC Magazines, United Kingdom

Defenders, Defenders of Wildlife, USA

Equinox, Canada

Marine Mammal Science, Society for Marine Mammalogy, USA

National Geographic Magazine, USA

Ocean Realm, Friends of the Sea, USA

Sonar, Whale and Dolphin Conservation Society, United Kingdom

The Whalewatcher, American Cetacean Society, USA

WEBSITES

American Cetacean Society.
http://www.acsonline.org/
The oldest whale conservation group in the world. A non-profit, volunteer organization devoted to education in the field of cetacean research.

Dept. of Vertebrate Zoology, National Museum of Natural History, Smithsonian Institution. http://nmnhwww.si.edu/departments/vert.html

Covers the issues surrounding the study of marine mammals as a part of the Marine Mammal Program.

Institute of Cetacean Research.
http://www.whalesci.org/

Ocean Link.
http://oceanlink.island.net/olink.html

Project Aware (Aquatic World Awareness, Responsibility, and Education).
http://www/padi.com/
Details of environmental and educational programs to help preserve and protect the underwater environment.

Society for Marine Mammalogy.
http://pegasus.cc.ucf.edu/~smm/

Whale and Dolphin Conservation Society.
http://www.wdcs.org/wdcs/index.htm
The leading voice for whales and dolphins worldwide; initiates and supports cetacean research and conservation.

WhaleNet.
http://whale.wheelock.edu/
An educational link focusing on whales and marine research.

WWF Global Network.
http://www.panda.org/
A comprehensive information source connected to the world's largest and most experienced independent conservation organization.

VIDEO CASSETTES AND CD-ROMS

The Free Willy Story, Keiko's Journey Home, (Discovery Communications, Inc., 1996). Discovery Channel Production, produced in association with ABC/Kane Productions. Genesis award winner, narrated by Rene Russo.

In the Company of Whales, (Discovery Communications, Inc., 1995). Discovery Channel CD-ROM for PC, Dr. Roger Payne, narrated by Patrick Stewart. Includes 45 minutes of video, more than 200 compelling photographs, hypertext glossary and much more.

In the Company of Whales: Gentle Giants of the Watery Realm, (Discovery Communications, Inc., 1992). Discovery Channel video produced in association with Channel Four Television, Television New Zealand. The scientific advisor and host of this video is Dr. Roger Payne, a world-renowned cetacean specialist, with narration by Jessica Tandy.

Marine Mammals of the World, CD-ROM, T. A. Jefferson,
S. Leatherwood, and M. A. Webber (Springer-Verlag, 1996).
Pacific Blue: Musical Soundscapes (I and II), (Holborne Distribution
Co. Ltd.).
Songs of the Whales and Dolphins, CD-ROM, (Marine Mammal
Fund/The Nature Company, 1993).
Whale Symphony, CD-ROM, (Ocean Studio).
Whales and Dolphins of the World, CD-ROM, (Webster
Publishing, 1996).
World of Whales, CD-ROM, (Teramedia, 1996).

MUSEUMS

USA
California Academy of Sciences, San Francisco, California
Cold Spring Harbor Whaling Museum, Cold Spring Harbor, Long
Island, New York
Museum of Comparative Zoology, Cambridge, Massachusetts
National Museum of Natural History, Smithsonian Institution,
Washington, DC
Natural History Museum of Los Angeles, Los Angeles, California
Scripps Institution of Oceanography, University of California, San
Diego, California

AUSTRALIA
Australian Museum, Sydney, New South Wales
Queensland Museum, Brisbane, Queensland
South Australian Museum, Adelaide, South Australia
Western Australian Museum, Perth, Western Australia

CANADA
BC Provincial Museum, Victoria, British Columbia
National Museum, Ottawa, Ontario
Newfoundland Museum, St John's, Newfoundland
Nova Scotia Museum, Halifax, Nova Scotia

JAPAN
National Science Museum Tokyo

THE NETHERLANDS
National Museum of Natural History, Leiden

SOUTH AFRICA
Port Elizabeth Museum, Humewood
South African Museum, Cape Town

SWITZERLAND
Zoologisches Museum der Universitat Zurich, Zurich

UNITED KINGDOM
Natural History Museum, London, England
Royal Museum of Scotland, Edinburgh, Scotland

INDEX

ACKNOWLEDGEMENTS
Illustrations are by Martin Camm: 26 (illustrations), 66, 104c, 106–107, 111, 116, 120, 132–133, 163; Ray Grinaway: 96, 104t; Gino Hasler: 14, 138, 139, 142, 145; David Kirshner: 24–25, 50, 59–59, 104b, 122; Frank Knight: 17; Kylie Mulquin: 26 (chart); Tony Pyrzakowski: 16, 18, 19t, 27–45, 74, 107b, 114, 117; Roger Swainston: 69, 71, 77, 118, 119; Rod Westblade: 19b.

Maps are by Kenn Backhaus: 210; Greg Campbell: 86, 90, 92; Chris Forsey: 97.